FRANK SIMOES' GOA

Frank Simoes was born in Mumbai on 7 March, at 7 a.m., on the seventh day of the week, in 1937. At the age of eighteen, he decamped from hearth and home for a 'working passage' on a cargo ship, a polite euphemism for six months' hard labour. Having splurged his wages on Bacchanalian revelry at various ports of call, he signed off in Genoa with two pounds fifty pence and all his worldly belongings in a backpack.

His experience in Europe over the next year: reluctant sailor, dharma bum, journeyman, writer, employee in pursuits as ecletic as dishwasher, porter, erratic typist and general dogsbody, provided a wining curriculum vitae for a career in advertising and a second career as a writer.

He was elected to the Hall of Fame of both the Communication Arts Guild and the Advertising Club, authored over 300 articles and two books, *Glad Seasons in Goa* (now reissued as *Frank Simoes' Goa*), and *Fare Forward Voyager*. A collection of his work was published posthumously in 2003 as *Frank Unedited*. He attributed much of his success to the lack of a formal education.

Frank Simoes passed away in 2002, in Mumbai, survived by his wife, daughter and countless friends and admirers around the world.

OTHER TITLES

Boman Desai	*A Woman Madly in Love*
Eric S. Margolis	*War at the Top of the World*
Frank Simoes	*Frank Unedited*
Jawid Laiq	*The Maverick Republic*
M.J. Akbar	*India: The Siege Within*
M.J. Akbar	*Kashmir: Behind the Vale*
M.J. Akbar	*Nehru: The Making of India*
M.J. Akbar	*Riot after Riot*
M.J. Akbar	*The Shade of Swords*
M.J. Akbar	*By Line*
Meghnad Desai	*Nehru's Hero Dilip Kumar: In the Life of India*
Maj. Gen. Ian Cardozo	*Param Vir: Our Heroes in Battle*
Mushirul Hasan	*India Partitioned. 2 Vols*
Mushirul Hasan	*John Company to the Republic*
Mushirul Hasan	*Knowledge Power and Politics*
Prafulla Roy, trans. John W. Hood	*In the Shadow of the Sun*
Rohan Gunaratna	*Inside Al Qaeda*
Rifaat Hussain, J.N. Dixit Julie Sirrs, Ajai Shukla Anand Giridharadas Rahimullah Yusufzai John Jennings	*Afghanistan and 9/11*
Rachel Dwyer	*Yash Chopra: Fifty Years of Indian Cinema*
Satish Jacob	*From Hotel Palestine Baghdad*
Sujata S. Sabnis	*A Twist in Destiny*
Veena Sharma	*Kailash Mansarovar: A Sacred Journey*
V.N. Rai	*Curfew in the City*

FORTHCOMING TITLES

C.P. Surendran	*An Iron Harvest*
Kalpana Swaminathan	*The Page Three Murders*

FRANK SIMOES'

GOA

Illustrations by Sanat Surti

LOTUS COLLECTION
ROLI BOOKS

Lotus Collection

© *Gita Simoes* 2004
All rights reserved. No part of this publication may be reproduced or transmitted, in any form or by any means, without the prior permission of the publisher.

First published as *Glad Seasons in Goa* in India
by Penguin Books India (P) Ltd., 1994

This edition published in 2004
The Lotus Collection
An imprint of
Roli Books Pvt. Ltd.
M-75, G.K. II Market, New Delhi 110 048
Phones: ++91 (011) 2921 2271, 2921 2782
2921 0886, Fax: ++91 (011) 2921 7185
E-mail: roli@vsnl.com; Website: rolibooks.com
Also at
Varanasi, Agra, Jaipur and the Netherlands

Cover design: Sanat Surti

ISBN: 81-7436-346-7
Rs 295

Typeset in Fairfield LH Medium by Roli Books Pvt. Ltd. and printed at Anubha Printers, Noida (UP)

To my mother

Maria Alba da Gama Rose Simoes

CONTENTS

A Cautious Introduction	ix
Prologue: Liberation	xv
Goa	1
Part I	**17**
ALL IN THE FAMILY	
Blue Genes	19
Radhika's Genealogy Class	41
Grandfather's Green Worms	51
Part-II	**61**
HEART AND HOME	
God's Chosen Acre	63
You Can Go Home Again	73
The Cobra That Nearly Never Was	101
Romancing the Rains	113

Part III 131
BOON COMPANIONS

A Few Wayward Goan Words 133
The Sea Wolves Take a Bath 161
Bernie Finklebaum Jr. Learns a New Word 171
Peace, War and True Grit 203
Three Thunder-Boxes and a Mandolin 249
Grandfather's Silver Rupee 259

Part IV 265
BOA FESTAS! FOOD, FENI AND FUN

Who's Afraid of a Little Cholesterol 267
Use Your Loaf 277
Everything You Ever Wanted to Know About
  Feni But Were too Drunk to Ask 281
Boa Festas! 291

Epilogue 301
ALBA AND SIMPLICIO

Alba and Simplicio 303

A Cautious Introduction

I was restrained by my publishers from attaching a sticker to the dust jacket of this book: Academic Purists Beware! Subversive, perhaps lethal, misconceptions and inaccuracies lurk in these pages. There is cause for the caveat. Every Goan assumes unimpeachable authority over everything Goan. To the keen observer, this comes as no surprise for Goa is eminently manageable, an extended and intimate neighbourhood, modest in area (3800 square kilometres) but, to the ceaseless delight of its one-and-a-half million inhabitants, extravagantly proportioned (green hills and lush valleys; highlands of burnt amber weathered by wind and sun; luxuriant rain forests alive with all manner of flora and fauna; palm-fringed crescents of golden sand at every other twist and turn of a beguiling coastline; unruffled rivers and exuberant waterfalls; an abundance of bird and wildlife sanctuaries; endless horizons of emerald paddy; groves of cultivated palm, mango, areca nut, bamboo and cashew; and blue skies nine months in the year).

Such a wealth of riches prompts strong proprietorial feelings. The humblest of fishermen will brook no argument over his inviolate knowledge of the vagaries of sea, tide and shoal, while nowhere does scholarship lie with such a stern and heavy hand as on the shoulders of our academics. As I

Frank Simoes' Goa

discovered to my cost many years ago. I had written an article on the pleasures of the Goan table for *Swagat*, the Indian Airlines in-flight magazine, and barely was the ink dry on the page, when two letters arrived in the mail from Goan intellectuals in high places. One, a feisty, well-informed bon vivant, a journalist with a national reputation and a protean talent, a man known to do public battle at the drop of a misplaced participle; the other as temperate, well-mannered and soft-spoken a Goan gentlemen of the old school as you were likely to find. They were highly regarded in Goa; they possessed the Knowledge and the Power.

Now, inexplicably, they had reversed roles. The bon vivant assumed a tone of charitable forgiveness, tut-tutting as one would to an idiot child. I quote:

I'm sure your characters Inocencio (not Innocence) Simplicio and Salvacao (not Salvacio), will share my immense respect for your literary style and my anxiety in ridding the text of any possible 'galicismos' (i.e. wrong usages/spellings and so on). You have 'Sopa de Catolina.' There is no such vocable in Portuguese as 'catolina.' You may had (sic) in mind 'Sopa a catala' which is a broth in the Catalonian style. Then, again, there is no such word as 'caldine.' It could be 'caldinho,' meaning that it is fish in a gravy of sorts. Likewise 'reacheade' is no word at all. Stuffing in Portuguese is 'recheio,' stuffed is 'recheado.'

... and so, chidingly, on. Never mind that classical rendering has over the careless years, given way to the seduction of phonetics and common usage. Riffle through a handful of Goan cookbooks and you will discover that there are as many variations in the spelling of sorpotel as there are

A Cautious Introduction

in its preparation. So I make no apologies. As the quantum physicists tell us, observer and observed create the world (and its spellings) in the precise act of engagement.

But this was trifling stuff compared with the reaction of the gentle antiquarian. He was in a towering rage. My article, he wrote, suffered from:

... self-aggrandizement (sic) and bumptiousness and inaccuracies. Your attempt to prove that you rate higher than all Goans by (sic) the strength of your being from Saligao and a Saraswat ... sheer bullshit! And he continued in this alarming vein for another five hundred words. How dare I hurl insult and calumny at Salcettans? How could I descend to such depths of depravity? I was promised a sound thrashing with chappals the next time I disembarked at Dabolim airport, whereafter, with a garland of the smellier footwear about my neck, I would be paraded in a public place before, presumably, being put out of my misery.

What had I done to cause such offence? A paragraph written in gentle self-mockery, no more, poking mild and affectionate fun at my own ancestors and their prejudices: ... being Goan was absolutely grand. While democracy in all things was encouraged, a nice sense of balance prevailed. I soon learned, by way of veiled reference, that there were Goans and Goans. Goans from Salcette – an unpromising lot – tended towards parsimony. Sanguem, that luckless district in the interior, was distinctly short on couth. Margao was all iron ore, ships, confusion and money. How could you expect culture to flourish in such poor soil? Bardez now was recognized by all fair-minded citizens (we came from Bardez) as supremely civilized, and it was common knowledge that the Gaud Saraswat Brahmin Roman Catholic Goan from Saligao in Bardez (us!) was clearly without peer.

Good clean fun at the expense of the Simoes clan, you would think; alas, the Goan sense of humour is not a strong point. I did the decent thing, wrote a letter of explanation and apology, while refraining, though sorely tempted, from mentioning that Genghis Khan too had lacked a sense of humour.

The virus still persists. As recently as a year ago, the editor of a local magazine (not a Goan but a new, zealous convert to the cause) waved an indignant flag from a fashionable bandwagon. In an editorial dripping with bile, he vented his spleen at the demeaning of the higher Goan values by – traitorous heresy! – quisling Goan columnists and cartoonists. Are Punjabis, he asked (having just returned, no doubt, from a jolly night out with the bad boys in the Terai, mowing down the locals with AK-47s) any less fun-loving than Goans? I was not surprised. The leader was the latest in a vanguard of angry Goan reaction (a highly vocal but insignificant minority) to any public celebration of the brighter side of life in the green and pleasant land of my birth.

One took the charitable view. Perhaps the angry editor had neglected to attend a village feast, a christening, a club ball, a wedding or spent an evening in his convivial local taverna in the previous month (tut, tut; abstinence so unGoan as to be utterly disgraceful). Given the blight that afflicts the human spirit wherever one turns, I would imagine that the ability to pursue the lighter side of life against grim odds would be cause for congratulation. I am

A Cautious Introduction

glad to report that the naysayers have no future. There is boundless resilience to Goa's blithe spirit; down the applauding centuries it has cocked a snook at the philistines, in rousing voice, with a guitar in one hand and a glass of vintage feni in the other, knowing full well that high spirits and high seriousness (will our dour Goan editor please take note) far from being mutually exclusive, are happily and irrevocably symbiotic. But I have been considerate to my meaner spirited critics. They will find in these pages all manner of fact, fiction, fable and flights of fantasy, rich grist for sullen pens. So, for the record, any merit this book may have owes all to the boundless generosity of the land of my ancestors; the flaws and follies are mine alone, protected, I may add, by the Constitution of India, the Civil Judiciary and a diminutive mongrel named Jimi a.k.a. The Dog Who Knows No Fear.

While facts have been assembled with as much accuracy as memory can bring to bear, purists should note that I have been expansive with their interpretation, for what good is experience if it cannot be recalled in the best and brightest light? Descriptions of events are enhanced by the magnitude of their potential for good or ill. Dialogue has been reconstructed to give proper due to character and intention. Humour and drama assume their rightful place, and good friends are celebrated in their virtues, as they should always be, with abiding affection and regard.

This book is a personal memoir, no more. It is an account of a lifetime's odyssey; in the discovery of my ancestral roots and heritage; in a burgeoning affinity with the people and the land, beginning with my search for the

Frank Simoes' Goa

perfect acre by the sea; it recalls the joys and tribulations of raising a roof over our heads; it tells of the friends we made, a mixed bag – fisherman, rock star, village pastor, industrialist, rural politician – each, in my experience, first among equals; there are humorous anecdotes and rousing festivals; a celebration of Goa's perennial joie de vivre, best expressed in the Goan greeting on days of communal merry-making, 'Boa Festas'; and, finally, a tribute, long overdue, to two remarkable Goans, Alba and Simplicio Simoes, my parents.

'Mea Casa, tua casa' is one of my favourite Portuguese phrases. You will hear it often in Goa, where hospitality begins with open doors and open hearts. A traditional greeting to a new guest, it means, 'My house is your house.'

Welcome to Goa.

Prologue
Liberation!

Liberation

When twilight descends on the villages of Goa, and the tavernas glow with lamplight and nostalgia, the villagers pass the feni around and recall, with not a little ribaldry, the events of the Great Liberation (when the Portuguese were driven ignominiously from the territory in a war which lasted all of forty-eight hours). Sooner or later, a favourite tall tale is retold. It concerns the defence of Goa's only airport, Dabolim.

An Indian squadron of Hunters flew in low from the west in attack formation, the sun at their backs, weaving and strafing. There was no response, no answering ground fire, only a deafening silence. The jets wheeled away and came in again. Now there was activity of sorts. From a window high in the red brick wall of the airport building, the handle of a broom poked cautiously out. Attached to its end and flapping forlornly in the wind was an undergarment of indeterminate colour and age. The Squadron Leader, holding his fire, observed this phenomenon with not a little awe. Minutes later two figures emerged, ignored the safety of the forest cover flanking the airport, and ran across the tarmac. Old men, of sunsoaked vintage, their progress was somewhat hampered by a wayward sense of direction and the amber bottle each man carried. Now and again, they would stop, take long and unsteady libations from the bottles, shake clenched fists at the Hunters and proceed urgently across the airfield.

The enemy clearly on the run, the Hunters departed, the Squadron Leader grappling with the daunting task of drafting his sortie report.

The gallant defence of Dabolim was over.

Goa

Goa

Regard a small miracle.

The land is evergreen and abundantly fecund. The rivers run blue and clear. The palms rise in their thousands through the mists of dawn, swaying before the breezes from the sea, challenging the rush of surf. The breaking light echoes to the songs of the fishermen as they guide their catamarans through the turbulent waves to the shore. In the bustling village squares the market day unfolds with crab and mussel, laughter and argument, woven baskets, squealing piglets, painted earthenware, and a baker's bounty of freshly-baked breads. Gossip drifts in the air like woodsmoke. The larger towns have gently but firmly rejected the urban crisis and sparkle, newly minted, in the fresh morning light. Church bells peal. The monks of Monte de Guirim look to their vineyards and cellars. Wherever you turn, small brown children share a subtle democracy with goats, pigs, chickens and dogs. The people smile easily. They are forever celebrating marriages or christening babies, making merry on feast-days or arguing with their saints. Goa wakes to another day, as it has each dawn for a thousand years and more. It is hard to believe that legions of foreign conquerors have passed this way, slaughtering, burning, pillaging, laying claim to all before them in the name of power, race, plunder and God.

Frank Simoes' Goa

There are no scars.

The world has turned a blood-riven decade since I made this entry in my diary, yet the truth of the land, I am glad to say, remains untarnished, and memories of Goa travel well. My parents left Goa for Bombay when I was ten years old; I returned after seventeen years. But Goa was a moveable feast and we took it with us wherever we went. My childhood echoes with Goan myth and memory. The whispering syllables, the lilt and languor of Portuguese; the lament of the fado raised at dusk; the bells of the Angelus and the murmur of shared prayer; the vibrancy of Konkani, a lusty, jocular, passionate tongue. One prayed in Latin or Portuguese, at a pinch in English, but could a mando be sung in any language other than Konkani?

Goa was our place of permanent and loving residence; Bombay was merely an occupation by necessity. Out on our balcony, high above the hurly-burly of the streets and the tenements, I watched the sun set beyond the tiled cornices of the Church of the Pentecostal Christ and marvelled at the ivory Madonna in my hand. A family heirloom for three hundred years, it occupied a place of high reverence on the altar in our hall. Time had gentled the pride in the bone; it was the colour of old parchment, delicately veined, glowing now in the afterlight of dusk. The palms were joined in prayer. The face, worn smooth by the touch of many hands, was serene and radiant beneath a filigreed gold crown. It was our most enduring symbol of Roman Catholicism; it was our raison d'etre.

God was all about me in my Goan childhood. He was neither biblical nor remote. At times he looked like my grandfather, Luis da Gama Rose, kind and gentle but never to be trifled with; at others, he was the arctic-eyed Spanish Jesuit principal of my school, St Mary's, who never spoiled a child by sparing the rod. Guile got you nowhere with him; dissemble as you would, just by looking at you, he knew all! I grew up with an easy familiarity with the saints, those benevolent intermediaries between God and myself. My favourites were St Anthony (who helped you find things and whom you could argue with and even scold), St Jude, (who granted favours but knew his authority and had to be approached with tact and circumspection), and St Francis, my patron saint, after whom I was named, but would never, alas, ever hope to emulate.

We prayed each evening as they do in the humblest and grandest of homes in Goa, saying the rosary, each of us telling a decade, kneeling dutifully before a splendid altar. It consisted of two enormous gilt-framed representations of Jesus and Mary, worked in silks and embroidery, encased in clear glass. So constructed that they always seemed to be looking directly at me, particularly when my attention wandered and I miscounted the beads, reciting one Hail Mary too many, earning a glance of the sternest disapproval from my mother; or when my head turned involuntarily in the direction of the good and glorious smells which wafted in from the kitchen.

If the Goan is passionately involved in an intimate and complex relationship with the Word of God, from birth to the hereafter, a lifelong absorption with food and drink is pursued next with relentless vigour. If my mother was not making mango jam, my father and I were prodding, inspecting, passing judgement upon and eventually buying immodest quantities of fish, flesh and fowl each morning at the local bazaar. Not a week would pass without one of my numerous aunts sending across a large dish of pork sorpotel, or my mother distributing, to carefully selected neighbours, generous portions of prawn balchao which 'had turned out well.' I grew up with apa da camarao and leitao, cabidal, xacuti and cafreal (wonderful Goan ways with prawn, pomfret, pork, beef and chicken). At the age of nine, there was no keener aficionado of the good things of the marketplace. I could tell the freshness of a lady's finger by snipping off a tip, the goodness of a mango by its colour and a single sniff, the provenance of a mullet by a swift inspection of eye, gill and texture. And I could winkle out a frozen lobster (dethawed; sacrilege!) at a glance from three feet.

I grew up with place names which had no meaning for me beyond my parents' nostalgia and the images I conjured up during long monsoon evenings. Saligao, the ordered, mannerly, gracious and exquisitely beautiful village (according to my mother) where her family led the vanguard of respected bhatkars, the major landowners; Colvale, an unruly perhaps dangerous place high in the brooding hills of the north where my father's family ruled the land with a grip of steel (my mother's version again). Years later, when I visited both villages I realized that the exaggerations held a kernel of truth. Panjim, the capital, jewel in the Goan crown, was recalled to vivid life from its magnificent centrepoint cathedral to the resoundingly Portuguese names of its avenues; from the grand palace on the heights of Dona Paula where a splendid governor held generous court to the friendly neighbourhood tavernas; a sun-splashed mélange of walks and promenades, mansions, churches and gardened squares, given over to intrigues and sophistry, in a setting Rousseau might have created: green hills unfolding into a valley and the scything, foaming thrust of the Mandovi as it met the ocean; a riot of bougainvillaea, raat ki rani and crimson gulmohar along the riverbank; across, girdling the high cliff of the promontory, the ancient Portuguese fort of Reis Magos guarding the estuary; older still, the scores of wooden catamaran, poised like delicate prehistoric birds of prey about to take wing, built and sailed by hand in a manner unchanged for thousands of years.

You had to be born to gracious living before Panjim would accept you. It had flair.

I grew up with the verity that there is no prejudice among Goans, liberal as we were, to the bone. We were all God's creatures but allowed to indulge, as I was to discover in time, in the smaller parochial vanities. These were flourished at discreet opportunities, the gloss, you might say, to my Goan upbringing. No sensible observer could deny that the Salcettans from the south tended towards parsimony. A certain lack of couth from Sanguem, deep in the interior, was but to be expected. Marmagoa was all iron ore, ships, confusion and the mindless pursuit of money for its own sake; could culture take root in such disheartening soil? The villages far, far to the north lay within hailing distance of the border of Maharashtra, and the less said about that, the better. Bardez now, was recognized by all discriminating citizens as being supremely civilized (my parents' villages were in Bardez), but even here, there were

Frank Simoes' Goa

villages and villages, families and families. At the end of the day, however, Goans were Goans, God be praised. As for the rest of the world, tread carefully my son and carry a big stick. Oh for a Rupert Brooke!

So much for wishful thinking and nostalgia. The family had fallen on hard times and Bombay's streets were rumoured to be paved with gold; and so we left Goa. I have only one memory of Goa which is truly my own, and remains today as vibrant as when it occurred. I remember a beach at sunrise. I made figures in the sand, running my foot from one crab hole to another, at random, cutting over and beyond the lines I had drawn until a pattern emerged. It resembled a many-pointed star with a single triangle shooting off at a vagrant angle. I ran a toe along its most distant point and was stopped short by a scarred, bare foot. I raised my eyes' level and gazed at a hard, knobbly knee. I looked up at a thigh, flat, firm and weathered as the trunk of a palm, a chest as broad and craggy as a cliff, a gold St Christopher's medal around the neck. In the near distance, the other fishermen, shoulder to shoulder, were straining against the surf, chanting in a single chorus, heaving the huge wooden catamaran onto the shore.

He gave me a mackerel. It was warm with blood just stilled, and heavy, and smelled of the sea. Two rough hands took me suddenly under the arms and swung me high in the air. I clung to my fish. Sand, sky and sea whirled all about me, making kaleidoscopic patterns with every rushing, breathless moment. Then he let me down, tousled my hair, and walked away whistling as he went, while my heart moved in my chest like a live thing.

We ate the fish at breakfast. My parents were happy for me. They only began warning me about strangers when we came to Bombay.

*

I returned many years later in a battered red Herald, with a journalist friend, Rahul Singh. History had cast a cold eye on the land yet again. There had been a liberation. Now an opinion poll was to determine Goa's future. I went with a single, light suitcase, the memories returning as we drove at twilight down the last, twisting mountain road across the Goan border. The memories still served. The myths had frayed a bit with time. What of the reality?

*

When you are conquered, what can you do? If you fight against a superior foe, you die. If you argue you are imprisoned. If you run away to another country you are unhappy. What, after all, can the conqueror take away from you? Your wealth lies in the riches of ocean and forest and good red soil, in an equable climate, in the beauty of river and valley, fruit and flower, in the rains from the west that bring the parched earth to life. Why then fight or argue or run away? Give all of yourself and bountifully of your land. God will provide a hundredfold.

An unsigned entry, translated from the Portuguese, from the ancestral diary of the Gama Rose, my mother's family. It is dated 1812 when, very briefly, the British invaded Goa.

*

Frank Simoes' Goa

They came with spear and bow, fire and sword, warship and cannon. They raged over tens of centuries, sacking and burning, conquering and conquered, in a confusing succession of dynasties; the Andrabhrityas, the Kadamas, the Chalukyas of Kalyani, the Yadavas of Devangiri the Bahamani kings and, last and most potently, the Portuguese, with sword and cross offering slaughter as the single alternative to Christian salvation.

They came from the lower Himalayas, the vast northern Indian plains, and, from the harsh landscapes of the Deccan plateau, the wiry, fierce warriors of the Maratha armies; they came across the Indian ocean from the Arab lands, and all the way from western Europe where men like Vasco da Gama, the great Portuguese explorer and General Affonso de Albuquerque, soldier of fortune, God and his King, pioneered the dangerous sea route around the Cape of Good Hope to the East. His enemies named him Albuquerque the Terrible, and the sobriquet was well-deserved. A brooding mountain of a man, fearless and unforgiving, given to the slaughter of entire townships in order to instil a proper sense of discipline among a newly conquered people. There is a statue of Albuquerque in the museum in Old Goa. It stands well over eight feet high. The lines of the mouth are firm and arrogant. The eyes are dark and set deep in the planes of a face which are broad, heavy and flat. An Old Testament face, acknowledging the superiority of no man, only the hegemony of a creator made in its own image and likeness.

With twelve hundred men and a handful of ships, under cover of darkness, led by a traitor to the Muslim cause, he sailed up the Mandovi and destroyed the last of the

Bahamani rulers in pitched battle. Albuquerque directed the battle from a point of high vantage in Old Goa which commanded a strategic view of the River Mandovi and its reaches. Victory assured, he ordered the slaughter of the Muslims and the razing of their mosques, then knelt, gave praise to God and ordered a chapel to be built on the very spot. It stands to this day.

For the next four centuries, Goa belonged to the Cross and the Portuguese. They were to change the land and the people forever.

*

To the casual observer, the Catholics may seem to dominate the Goan scene, but they are not the largest community. The palm goes to the Goan Hindu, and there is a strong Muslim presence. Though they worship at different shrines, Catholic, Hindu and Muslim live essentially the same lives, and speak the same language, in a harmony so seamless it is never noticed. Their lives are formed and tempered by the rhythms and cadences of a truly lovely land. A country of gentle hills and deep, rich valleys, blessed with an abundance of rivers and lakes, and a soil heavy with mineral wealth. Flowers, fruit (the peerless malcurada mango), paddy and sugar cane grow with a bare modicum of encouragement. The golden beaches are always happily at hand; they seem to flow, one into the other, briefly contained by soaring cliff and escarpment. Their names ring with the mellifluous tones of the bells of village chapels: Arambol, Colva, Betul, Vagator, Sinquerim, Candolim; mile upon mile of firm, white sand where, if you know where to go, yours are likely to be the only footprints. Schools of dolphin, unafraid and friendly, frolic a stone's throw beyond the shallows. They follow the fishing boats as they return with the night's catch, hoping to be thrown the occasional fish. The sound of the surf is always with you, changing voice with the seasons, a whispering murmur in winter and a foaming, roaring presence during the monsoon when it may be heard deep in the hinterland. The ocean sparkles and dances in the sunlight. It offers joy and sustenance. The daily catch is profuse: mackerel and pomfret, ladyfish and salmon, white and red prawns and fat, tasty mullet, baby shark, lobster and, in season, huge mounds of glittering sardines.

The villagers raise pigs, goats and chickens in an atmosphere of genial camaraderie. Original intentions are often blurred. I have known households where a favourite pigling, much loved and coddled, had the run of the house and slept in the kitchen. I have observed with awe a whole brood of pigs, a great grey matriarch followed in descending order of size by a large and unwieldy string of progeny, crossing the village square with the dignity and authority of the firmly established. They enjoyed unquestioned right of way. At one time, our house in Saligao supported a lively menagerie – two dogs, a mongoose, a lame cat, a squirrel, an African cockatoo with a small but risqué vocabulary and two love-birds – all pampered, well-fed and at peace.

Much charm and serenity await the traveller to Goa. Serendipitous backwaters. Precise crescents of virgin beach where the palm, seagull and sandpiper hold sway. Villages as unchanged as the generations of Goans they have sheltered. Tiny cottages built of amber laterite brick and Mangalore tile, each with a balcao where the family gathers at sunset to watch the world go by. Gardens are crowded over with papaya, guava, banana and mango trees. The houses cluster about a huge church (the shorter the distance between house and church, the greater the measure of piety); indeed one sees the church well before the village, dazzling white spires high above the palms, a beacon to the faithful and the true of heart who, in these unruly times, might well turn out to be blonde, bearded and beaded, Caucasian and broke.

In the early Sixties the flower children settled like clumps of weed on Goan beaches and they still come, but in numbers that are now subdued and uncertain. Calangute is the mandatory first stop. As the months pass, the hippies migrate north, beach-hopping as they go along – Baga, Anjuna, Vagator – then across the River Chapora to Arambol. Their progress accelerates in inverse proportion to a dwindling store of visible means of support, and at Arambol (where a fresh water lake and the sea are kept apart by a hair's-breadth of sand) they tend to live off the land, the indulgent locals and each other. But at points along this woeful pilgrimage they offer good value. The hippie ball on Anjuna beach by the light of the full moon has to be experienced to be believed. And at their weekly flea market (the location, for obscure reasons I have never been able to fathom, is made known only on the morning of the day) you are as likely to discover a first edition of Hermann Hesse as strike up a conversation with a slight blonde slip of a girl, with a dirty pigtail, badly in need of a bath, whose accent is pure, drawling Mayfair, who turns out to have schooled at Roedean, and whose Daddy chairs a bank back home and keeps racehorses as a hobby. The hippies may, on the rare occasion, turn out to be disastrous. They are never dull.

But the great hippie influx of the Sixties and Seventies has dwindled to a trickle. The quick fix is now more likely to be a bottle of the omnipresent Pepsi in a beach shack. Uppers and downers, brown sugar and coke (the sniffing kind) are no part of the vocabulary of the young, backpacking American Ph.D. seeking the quintessential Goan village experience, or of the Bavarian butcher off a Condor charter flight yearning to be toasted to a crisp over a fortnight of sun, sand and sea.

No matter. The Goan welcome, 'Mea casa, tua casa' is still theirs for the asking.

*

Rahul disappeared for most of the trip, interviewing people in high places and low. I kept a diary. Each day seemed more perfect than the last. From 7 March:

> ... the beach at Candolim, the sun nearly set, making old gold of the ruined ramparts of the Fort of Aguada, laying a sheet of cool, clean fire over a distant horizon of foam-flecked ocean and lowering cloud. Young Goans around a bonfire on the beach, the flames crackling in the wind, reaching out to light a face, a guitar, a bottle. Sunbursts of laughter. Voices raised in song. Small brown children, playful as puppies, feeding the flames with driftwood.
>
> The bells of the Angelus in Old Goa and a woman in black, fulfilling a vow, alone, tears in her eyes, moving on her knees down the long, wide aisle

of the empty cathedral towards the high altar. A christening at a font at the entrance to a chapel, where the baby, a reluctant convert, cried its heart out and two little girls watched and smiled behind their hands.

Panjim and dusk. The lamps along Campal lighting up like fireflies. The tavernas alive with good-natured banter and the musical clink of bottle on glass. Young couples promenading formally up and down the riverfront, at arm's length, moving closer as they go, to the gentle seduction of the touch of hand on hand, the willing assent of a glance, the innuendo of a phrase, the present forsaking the strictures of past and future, celebrating the glad brightness of the moment.

The fishermen at Betul, working canoes out of tree-trunks, harvesting clam and mussel in the shallows and black crab among the rocks; their womenfolk chatting and cooking over open wood fires, raising gossip to an art form. Villagers dressed in the aquamarines, lilacs and ambers of their land, walking a path between fields of emerald paddy towards a white church to attend High Mass on the feast of Our Lady of Joy.

A wedding party proceeding down a rustic cart track, with pomp and ceremony, in the sweltering heat of mid-summer; the men in dark, heavy suits; the bride and her entourage, were it not for their complexion, could well have stepped out of a church in Lisbon. The sound of the surf by the light of the full moon; ghostly wraiths of spray hurling patterns of lace at a luminous sky. The mystic stone face of Abbe Faria, hypnotist, healer, the most famous son of Colvale, my father's village ...

1

All in the Family

Gama Rose Simoes Family

Carmen & Marie Simoes.

Above
Alba Gama Rose Simoes, Frank Simoes, Dr. Gama Rose with Noella Simoes. Grandmother Gama Rose and Fred.

Blue Genes

My Uncle Vasco, now a dashing seventy, with a mane of silver hair and a profile that has caused heads and hearts to turn all his life, is the unofficial Keeper of the Gama Rose Chronicles. This is a family diary, going back three centuries and a bit, bound in red leather worn to a fine patina by the epistolary hands of many generations. Quill pens were used originally to record the lives and times of distant generations for the benefit of Gama Roses yet unborn. The Portuguese is written in fine calligraphic style. Pressure and pointillistic effects are perfectly rendered; flourishes and curlicues are executed with a swift, casual flair. The ink on the pages in the decades when the diary began has now faded. The paper has worn to the translucency of old parchment, and whole paragraphs are indecipherable. But the gist, even of the earliest diarists, may be garnered by patience and application. By and large, it is not a rewarding task, though the occasional nugget gleams among the dross.

The diary is given over to the minutae of sequestered lives. Time passed infinitely slowly in an idyllic, pastoral existence. My ancestors lived off the land and the labour of the mundkars, peasants who were housed on the estates, worked the fields and orchards for a portion of

All in the Family

the harvest, provided lifelong domestic service without cost, and were bonded to the landowners by mutual dependency, the inviolate traditions of centuries, and the loyalties and affections of family ties. This was the only way of life for landowner and landless alike. They knew no other.

The days and seasons passed to the measured rhythms of the vaddo or ward in which the ancestral mansion was the centrepiece, and the village at large, where our family and a handful of others controlled all of the affairs of the community. A trip to a neighbouring village was a laborious business while a journey to a town thirty miles away was an adventure, fraught with the unpredictable. It was planned weeks ahead of time. Roads were no better than cart-tracks; rivers were unbridged; wild animals were a hazard and, during the monsoon, vast sections of the way were impassable. One travelled by palanquins-on-wheels drawn by bullocks; rivers were crossed on frail wooden countrycraft held together by dried pitch and rope. It was an expedition, no less, thoughtfully organized and carefully provisioned, which took days. No journey of this nature was undertaken lightly; there had to be a good cause. A wedding in a distant branch of the family perhaps; better yet, a disaster calling for clan management (recounted with just the tiniest bit of relish) or a gilt-edged invitation to dinner at the Governor's palace in Panjim. Not as rare an occurrence as might be expected, for the family had brought forth eminent magistrates and colonial administrators, Monsignors of astounding religiosity, much honoured Members of the Bar in Lisbon, weightily decorated Men of Letters and – happily – the rare insurrectionist bad egg.

These grand events are recounted with fidelity, with a keen eye to nuance and subtlety, brightened from time to time, by the felicitous turn of phrase and the indulgence of a credible exaggeration. There is much of archival interest here, even when the diarists are occupied with the overwhelming monotony of similar lives. The landmarks of a single life are meticulously recorded: birth, christening, first communion, confirmation; then, a lengthy pause in all of this ecclesiastical activity; a decade later, a marriage is documented over ten pages down to the last detail of the wedding feast; a year to the day, there is yet another birth and the cycle ends sixty years later (the genes of longevity are everywhere in evidence) with a death, a funeral and a wake.

Names of people, places, times, dates, are never omitted. The repetition is mesmerizing and, after a while, the sense of novelty begins to wear thin. It is easy to become bored, to regret the rarity of the engaging observation, the riveting metaphor, the unusual or dramatic incident. But after a few days with the diary it dawned on me that there was purpose and method to the monotony. It had the resonance of integrity. The diarists were committed to an enterprise greater than the sum of their parts, to an abiding belief in tradition and family name. It is as if they are saying, we are Guardians of the Flame, and it must be passed on, no matter how dimly flickering, to the generations of the future. They were grains of pollen, my ancestors, each and every one of them, in the great fertility of the Gama Rose lineage.

All in the Family

So I persisted and was glad that I did so. Golden nuggets were there for the seeking, my great granduncle Leopold being a notable example, though I doubt he would have taken kindly to the description. But he would, I believe, have chuckled at 'insurrectionist bad egg', while applauding those family virtues discreetly glossed over in the diary. The Gama Roses, men and women, ate, drank and reproduced with prodigious stamina (as did the Simoeses). These virtues were clearly not inherited, but acquired from their Portuguese mentors who, along with cross and sword, introduced the hooped skirt, the stiff collar, a wonderfully varied cuisine, a laissez-faire attitude to life (religion strictly excepted) and all of the happier propensities of Iberia.

I suspect that this took time. It is unlikely that the two Brahmin priests who founded our clan (converting to Catholicism and taking Christian wives, a double-barrelled surname and a Coat of Arms to retain their power and huge landholdings) would have had any truck with the earthier Portuguese pleasures. Their assimilation would have had to wait a generation or two, but when they did, it was with unabashed fervour, embracing, with particular emphasis, those aspects of Iberian culture derived from the grand table, the grape and the Catholic connubial bed (where sex without the intention to sire was nothing less than a sin). They did so with an enthusiastic dedication unsullied by temperance.

By the time Leopold came along, the virtuosity of the Gama Rose liver was well established in family lore and legend. Biogenetics now tells us that an inclination for the hard stuff is inherited. Special receptors in the brain dance a little jig at the merest whiff of a double on the rocks, while the liver, if insufficiently lubricated, remains sullen and rebellious right through the day. Never were chemical nerve-endings exercised more diligently than by my bibulous ancestors. Leopold was a sterling example of this admirable genetic trait. In a long line of heroic drinkers his ability to knock it back was cause for awe. The Portuguese had thoughtfully provided the wherewithal. Unkind historians have suggested that one aspect of Portuguese subjugation was a sinister plot to keep the Goan masses in a mild state of permanent intoxication, thus foiling any coherent attempts at political organization. While one does not wish to do the memory of Portuguese rule an injustice as grave as this, there is no gainsaying the fact that every encouragement was offered to the drinker in search of his drink.

At last count before their precipitate departure, the Portuguese had seen to it that the Goan population of a few hundred thousand was serviced in its alcoholic needs by the output of 3,000 potstills. 31,000 acres of date trees, 161,000 acres of coconut palms and large tracts of cashew apple imported from Brazil were cultivated purely for this purpose. Well over 2,000 country bars and wine shops saw to it that the citizens' right to good cheer was never more than a brisk walk away. 'Besides this remarkable internal production,' says the historian disapprovingly, '44,582 gallons of wine, 5,546 gallons of foreign alcoholic drinks and spirits and 46,079 gallons of beer enter the country from Portugal each year for internal consumption.'

All in the Family

Too little too late, would have been Leopold's view, as he exercised his other talent by the light of an oil lamp well into the darkest hours of the night. He was inspired as much by his subject – Portuguese meddling in the affairs of the village communidade (common heritage) – as by the cut-glass decanter by the side of his writing pad. He was a journalist of distinction and his weekly column for the Portuguese daily, *O Heraldo*, was unfailingly and elegantly rude to the Portuguese, whom he despised. We are told that the quality of his prose improved as the night wore on, soaring to heights of excellence in inverse proportion to the rapidly dwindling level of pure caju feni in the Belgian decanter. He wrote in his cups and this, on occasion, gave rise to acute embarrassment. His copy invariably arrived at the press at the very last minute, was hurriedly composed, cast, and sent off for printing. One Sunday Goa woke up, perplexed and irritated, to one half of Leopold's column; the other half was lost to posterity, a blotch on the blotting pad on his desk. But genius is allowed its peccadillos and the matter was never spoken of. A flood of indignant letters to the editor was suppressed. He was not told of the lapse, let alone reprimanded, by his mentor and employer, the paper's major proprietor, Carvalho, Viscount of Bardez, who had all of Leopold's antipathy for the Portuguese, but lacked his eloquence.

If the family despaired of his journalism, they were at sixes and sevens over his refusal to take a wife. Leopold was a confirmed and adamant bachelor. Wedlock, he maintained, and his drinking and Portuguese baiting were mutually exclusive. While resentment against alien rule was spread far and wide, there was no organized insurrectionist movement. Trouble, when it did occur, was spontaneous, local and at the grass roots. It was dealt with ruthlessly by the Portuguese, who were most concerned that the powerful Goan upper class might rally to the cause. They kept a close ear to the ground, monitored gossip and rumours, encouraged quislings in town and far-flung village, dispensed privilege and power to consolidate their rule and kept a cold and vigilant eye on the press. The shenanigans of my great grand-uncle Leopold had come to their attention many years before, but, apart from polite and discreetly dispatched warnings to his father, they had held their hand. The Gama Roses were well connected beyond Goa's border, in the corridors of power in Lisbon. Theirs was a distinguished record of public service in Goa, Portugal and its colonies; indeed, a cousin sat in judgement at the very moment in the High Court in Lisbon. And the powerful Brahmin network (Catholicism notwithstanding) of which they were an influential part, would react with untold consequences at any punitive action against Leopold. But there were limits to the patience of the Portuguese, and an invisible red line that nobody could cross with impunity: the open call to insurrection.

Provocation came on a sweltering day in May. Under a blazing noonday sun, a young man was stripped to the waist and publicly flogged half to death for 'raising his hand' at a Portuguese official. On the following Sunday, Leopold's column was titled, 'A Call to Arms.' It was an impassioned plea for violent revolution. The same night four of the most powerful men in Goa met in the imposing

All in the Family

palace on the cliffs of Dona Paula: the Governor, the Public Prosecutor, the Chief of Constabulary and the Commander of the Panjim garrison. The Governor sought the legal view.

'Treason,' said the Public Prosecutor succinctly.

'If we let him get away with this,' the Chief Constable said, 'it will set a most dangerous precedent.'

The Governor sighed, 'That means an arrest and a trial, and as we are talking treason here, Gama Rose will have to be taken by the army.' He turned to the Commander of the Garrison, 'You know the village.'

'Yes, sir.'

'First thing tomorrow morning then. We shall have to wave the flag. Send in a troop of cavalry. There will be no violence, and,' he added with a flinty smile, 'tell the Captain to be polite. After all, the man's father is a judge.'

'Gama Rose is to be arrested tomorrow,' the Chief Constable told his wife at dinner that night, within earshot of Maria, the Goan cook. 'Mother of God,' Maria whispered, cleared the table, and rushed out into the night. A mundkar brought word to the house before first light, rather late in the day as it turned out, for the Troop of Cavalry had made an early start and was now, as dawn broke, at the Porvoreim plateau, a quarter of an hour's fast trot to the Gama Rose house. Leopold was in the deep, dreamless sleep of the good, the just and the hugely soused, when a patrician hand, richly bejewelled and with an authority that would brook no nonsense, woke him.

'Get up,' Carlottta Gama Rose said, 'as you are and

come to the porch. There's a warrant out for your arrest, my son, and we haven't much time.'

Leopold stood on the porch in his night shirt. Why, he wondered hazily, were the mundkars out in force so early in the morning? His mother followed him, her hooped, balloon skirt flouncing as she moved.

'Take your night clothes off.'

'Mother?'

'Off!'

The distant rumble of hooves became a dusty pounding. The troop charged in, scattering the mundkars, and was smartly called to a halt by the Captain. He took the porch steps two at a time, came to attention, bowed ever so slightly, said, 'Bom dia, Donna Carlotta.'

'Since when does a good morning begin with horses trampling my flower-beds?' There is no more fearsome spectacle than a Goan matriarch in full, angry cry. Donna Carlottta's bustle quivered with rage. Her voice could have felled an oak. 'Explain this intrusion at once.'

The Captain barked at his second-in-command. The troop dismounted at the gate, fixed bayonets, and marched to the house in a brisk, menacing formation.

Donna Carlotta was unfazed. 'Well?' she said.

'I have a warrant for the arrest of Leopold da Gama Rose,' the Captain replied formally, 'on a charge of high treason, with written permission from the Chief of Constables to search your house, Donna Carlotta.'

'My son,' Donna Carlotta said, lying with great conviction, 'left yesterday morning for a meeting in Margao.' Margao was a town sixty miles to the south. 'Get on with your search if you wish and tell those clumsy oafs to mind the china.'

Two troopers stood guard on the porch. The Captain and the rest of his men began to hunt for Leopold. They peered into cupboards, looked under beds and tables; they commandeered long ladders and went up into the cavernous loft, unsettling the bats; out on the grounds, they plunged into the tool shed; they took the bayonet to the piles of mangoes stacked floor to ceiling in the fruit barn; frustrated, they attacked the haystack with unnecessary violence; they even searched in the chapel, dipping fingers into the holy water font and genuflecting as they did so. There was no sign of Leopold. The Captain, seized with a thought, shouted, 'The Well!' It was a favourite hiding place for fugitives on the run. They rushed to the well, faces reflected palely in the still, dark surface, looking in vain for a tell-tale reed poking out of the water.

It took a good hour before the Captain made his weary way back to Leopold's mother.

'It appears ... ' he began.

'So it does,' Donna Carlotta said curtly. She had not moved from her position on the porch.

'Good day, Donna Carlotta,' the Captain said, mounted and led his troop out of the Gama Rose property, with, as Donna Carlotta observed later to her husband, the judge, 'noticeably less enthusiasm than when the brutes came in.'

Minutes later, a mundkar rushed in to announce that the troop had reached the foothills of Porvoreim. Donna Carlotta dismissed the mundkars, then did a rather strange thing. She giggled and bent forward from the waist, gathering up the hooped skirt as she did so. It billowed to reveal a derriere of engaging potential (which the modest cut of the prettily embroidered pink bloomers did little to conceal) and, great grand-uncle Leopold who was entwined about her ankles. 'You can come out now.' Carefully, joint by unravelling joint, Leopold emerged. His expression made it clear that he had begun, at long last, to appreciate the hazards of crusading journalism.

They made Leopold strip, smeared him from top to toe with coconut oil over which they rubbed in black kitchen soot. Unrecognizable, he was given a kashti to wear, the loincloth favoured by the fishermen, a blanket, a staff and a packet of food. There were tearful farewells; he could never return to Goa. Then, living off the land, he walked all the way to Bombay (safe haven in British India) four hundred miles to the north, there to become the popular General Manager of the very British Royal Yacht Club. It has, to this day, the best-stocked bar in the country.

The dramatic turning-point in Leopold's life is glossed over in the family diary in the briefest of summaries. But the diary was always enriched by an oral tradition and it was left to my grandfather, Dr Luiz da Gama Rose, to bring the incident to vivid, unforgettable life. He was a Goan raconteur in the classic tradition. His command of languages – English, Portuguese, Konkani, Swahili (he spent a good many years in Mombasa as Portuguese Consul General in British East Africa, the first Goan to hold the position), Italian and French (both self-taught) – was burnished by a knack for dialect and verbal mannerism, and a fine sense of the droll and the dramatic. If he embellished, as I am sure

All in the Family

he did, it was in order that I should never forget or forsake a family tree which flourished with such vigour and bore such wonderfully exotic fruit.

One afternoon I returned from school, bloody but unbowed, having defended the family honour against the class bully with bruising unsuccess. He asked me why I was in such a disgraceful state. I told him. 'That's nice,' he said cheerfully, 'blue blood to the breach again!' Blue blood. It was a way of life, a code never to be transgressed. It began with respect for one's elders, starting with older siblings and, in ascending order and importance, one's parents, grandparents and (more often than not) great-grandparents. It was taken very seriously indeed. One of my father's great-uncles had been banished from the family for life and exiled to Brazil for insolence to his mother at the dinner table. He was never allowed to return to Goa, but blood will tell, and he rose to become Chief Secretary to the Ministry for Health in Brazil, and a small town on the map bears his name to this day. Another Simoes had shot a tradesman in the leg with a hunting rifle for the man's temerity in calling in a long overdue bill, and adding insult to iniquity, by *delivering it in person to the house!* The authorities turned a blind eye to the deed. The community applauded.

There were the rare occasions when family honour and right action went by the board. One of my great-uncles, Auspicio Simoes, did not, alas, live up to the promise of his given name, though from all accounts, he did make an auspicious beginning. Everybody agreed that he was exceptionally brilliant but, as ever with young genius, he was not noticeably given to an appreciation of the ethics of mere ordinary mortals: there was talk of impropriety in the matter of examination papers and answers; he had a cavalier way with other people's money; his glad eye for the younger, more nubile temptations the village had on easy offer caused much heartburn among the elders. There was one incident too many and the family bundled him off to Lisbon where, with the greatest of ease, he passed the entrance examination to the Medical College. Four years later he graduated with the highest of Honours.

There are ten years of obscurity before we find him in Durban, married to the daughter of a Portuguese count, practising medicine, making a name for himself and eventually being raised to the highest of elevations – personal physician to the Earl of Salisbury. Doubtless the charms of his lavishly endowed wife and her noble lineage assisted his upward mobility. But her financial extravagances (Parisian shopping sprees; the best of European spas; racehorses which never lived up to their billing) proved his undoing. Fortune, in his case, did not follow closely on the heels of fame. The Salisbury connection was no more than an honorary distinction (it would never do to send a bill to an Earl), and the South Africans he ministered to were a healthy lot, robustly disinclined to fall seriously ill. But the ingenuity of the Simoeses in the subtle arts of keeping the wolf from the door had been honed for generations, and it wasn't long before Auspicio turned his commercial attention to the native population. He began to mass-produce an inspired version of a Magic Black Box filled with all manner of pills and potions, with the odd dried root thrown in for

All in the Family

good measure. It drew thriftily from the relatively expensive pharmacopoeia of allopathy, but generously and imaginatively from the dubious repertoire of the local witch doctors. Dr Auspicio Simoes' All-Purpose Panaceas offered the best of both worlds. They sold briskly throughout the territory and earned him a modest fortune which his wife spent as fast as he acquired it. They also brought him to the unfortunate attention of the Medical Council. There was an investigation. Auspicio was struck off the rolls and prohibited – under pain of imprisonment – from the practise of medicine.

The Earl of Salisbury promptly disowned him. He was abandoned by his wife who departed swiftly and haughtily for Lisbon with their children. He sank without trace there after, except as an object lesson to the young of subsequent generations on the dire consequences awaiting those of us who strayed from the straight and narrow!

Auspicio Simoes was an aberration. My ancestors, by and large, lived by a code of honour composed in equal parts of a high order of ethical behaviour, overweening pride, utter loyalty to the family diktat and all those in lesser places who were in fiat to it, and – in the most simple and elaborate of ways – the love of God, and His worship in the tenets and rituals of Roman Catholicism. But there was a darker side, a rigid conformity, no matter how terrible the consequences, to a set pattern of behaviour. It was most in evidence in the biological detritus of inter-marriage. The Saraswat Brahmin Roman Catholic community was close-knit, small, powerful out of all proportion to its size, and determined to keep its bloodlines pure. Marriages between first cousins, arranged by their parents, were commonplace. Insanity, alcoholism and hereditary degenerative diseases struck at will, kept company, it must be said, by robust longevity, brilliance, awesome application and the ceaseless honing of generational talents. Blue genes created whole clans of doctors, lawyers, clerics, alcoholics and eccentrics. But achievement and vicissitude alike were played down, when not completely ignored. 'Not quite herself' became a euphemism for mental illness, (if the afflicted drooled into the soup, no matter) as blandly dismissive as 'he's done well,' for a meteoric career. When my Uncle Alexander became the first Goan M.D. to perform major surgery in London after anaesthetizing a patient hypnotically, and wrote a paper – widely praised by the medical fraternity – for the British Journal of Medical Hypnosis in 1953, my grandfather chuckled and said, 'Abbe Faria from your father's village got there first in 1756.' And my Aunt Zelia's nervous breakdowns, as frequent as the common cold, were regarded as of even less consequence.

World War II and its aftermath brought cataclysmic change to four centuries of the Goan idyll. It saw the beginning of the great Goan diaspora. The peasants, no longer content to work the land for a pittance and patronage, now literate and sufficiently educated to hold their own at the lower commercial levels, emigrated in their thousands to British India and the Middle East. Neither were the families of the landed gentry spared seismic and permanent disruption. Their landholdings, with the growing paucity of labour, were no longer able to sustain the generous lifestyles and the large families, where a dozen or more offspring were

All in the Family

par for the course. Thousands left to seek their fortunes in Portugal and its overseas territories, in British India and East Africa, in Brazil, Canada and the United Kingdom.

Our families were scattered like so much chaff. The Simoeses abandoned the ancestral home in Colvale and emigrated en masse to Brazil and Portugal. My father spent many years in Bahrain, and lived the rest of his life in Bombay, never to return to Goa. But my paternal grandfather refused to leave Colvale, and died alone at the age of eighty-seven, cared for after a fashion by an enfeebled family retainer. Power of Attorney over the house and properties was given, carte blanche, to the village lawyer, notorious for his crookery. Before the year was out, he had appropriated the land. The house was left to fall to ruin.

When I first visited Colvale, I asked directions of the Parish Priest. He looked at me strangely, but not without sympathy, and said he would show me the way. We climbed halfway up a hill, then he stopped and pointed at the ground. There was no house, only a huge pit, with pieces of masonry strewn here and there. Not a stone upon a stone. The ghostly desolation of a long abandoned archaeological site. The ravages of time, weather and circumstance had wrought all to this dust. Where once there were floors covered in ornamental Italian tile, many-splendoured rooms with high vaulted ceilings and ornate carved furniture, a lifestyle given over to grand soiree, formal dinner, week-long family celebrations, the mansion echoing to the heady sounds of life, supreme and rampant, nature had now run heedless riot. I could not see the ruins for the dark-green, impenetrable foliage. Even the single, forlorn broken column at the far end was covered, base to crumbling tip, by thick jungle creeper.

I was glad to leave. We walked back to the church. An old peasant woman hobbled up the path, painfully bent, taking her weight on a walking-stick at every step. She looked up as we passed. The pale, vacant eyes blazed. She said the name Simoes and hissed at me in Konkani, a ripe and ancient curse. The priest touched my arm, urging me gently along. 'Her husband was your grandfather's mundkar,' he said, by way of explanation.

My mother's house in Saligao was spared the brutal fate of my father's, but brought equally low, in my view, by an act of tragic folly. To this day my mother claims that the family had no choice. She was the eldest of fourteen children. When the last of them arrived, Dr Luiz da Gama Rose, flaunting the sort of siegneural style that knows no tomorrow, adopted two more, a boy and a girl. Within two decades of my grandfather's triumphant return from Mombasa, with a large family and two African servants in tow, the family wealth had all but disappeared. The children, grown up and educated, fled, like so many birds of passage, to alien countries and strange destinies. Uncle Alexander joined the British Army Medical Corps and saw active service in the Second World War. Serving, with Montgomery's Eighth Army in North Africa, he won two medals for gallantry in the desert campaign against Rommel. At war's end, he went on to fame and fortune of a sort, married a Greek heiress, settled in Australia and died when the car he was driving went off a bridge into a river in flood one stormy night.

All in the Family

My Uncle Ruy, who shook the gladdest leg in Goa, couldn't tell one end of a gun from the other (and ardently desired never to do so). Despite strident parental objection, he took to western ballroom dancing in Bombay and did extraordinarily well at it. In a few short years, he had his own salon at the Taj, Bombay's toniest hotel. A few skeletons, no doubt, cartwheeled in the family vault in the Saligao cemetery when he dropped the 'Gama' from his name, and became the ritzy, alliterative Rui Rose. He obtained an exclusive franchise from the Arthur Murray School of Ballroom Dancing, the pre-eminent establishment of its kind in the West, and, in no time at all, was judging international competitions in London. His seventy-fifth birthday found him in Boston, married for the third time into the New England aristocracy, cheerfully unretired and managing – yes, indeed! – Arthur Murray's flagship institute with great aplomb and success.

Temperate climates provided sober havens for other members of the family, who met with moderate success and pursued eminently rational lives in Toronto, Lisbon, London, Nairobi and Rio. But it was the War which offered the most glamorous means of employment for the adventurously inclined. Because of his languages, my grandfather found himself Chief of Censors in Bombay, and I remember him bringing the naughtier bits home and, with deplorable but hilarious theatrical camp, reading them out to us while he sipped a large cognac after dinner. Throughout the War, he never spoke of his youngest son, my Uncle Victor. Strong-headed and impulsive, Victor had had an incendiary encounter with my grandfather in 1941. Then he ran away from home, lied about his age and enlisted in the Royal Air Force as an ordinary airman. His disappearance, an unsolved mystery despite my grandfather's best efforts, was never discussed. In 1945, a month after the Japanese surrender, the doorbell rang in our modest flat in Bombay. I ran to open it. There stood my Uncle Victor, filling the doorway, in the dark blue uniform of the RAF. He sported a chestful of ribbons, the rank of a non-commissioned officer and a daredevil moustache. 'Back home, are we?' said my grandfather, rising to embrace him, 'and just in time for dinner.'

After four hundred years in residence, the Gama Roses had left Saligao for good in the space of a single generation. The stately mansion with its medieval chapel, terrace gardens, orchards and servants' cottages, was left in the care of a loyal family retainer. She had neither the means, the youth, nor the energy to cope. The gardens were soon overgrown with weed, jungle grass and wild scrub. Bats, owls and pigeons made their homes in the loft. Monkeys vandalized at will. A pair of cobras took residence in the roots of the banyan tree. Thieves broke in and made away with the Belgian crystal and china, the sterling silver, the ivory-and-gold images from the chapel altar. News of all of this desecration drifted back to Bombay, by letter, by word of mouth, by malicious gossip within the community.

My grandfather, mercifully, was long dead. A maiden aunt, to whom all rights had been given owing to her spinsterhood, sold the house and grounds for a pittance, savage irony, to the son of one of my grandfather's mundkars, who had made a modest fortune in the Emirates. He painted the exterior a shocking pink with bright blue borders. The

All in the Family

fourteen rooms, perfectly complementary in size, architecture and purpose, were carelessly subdivided to accommodate brothers, cousins and their families. A violation no less shocking than the conversion of the garden to a vegetable patch (Donna Carlotta would have wept). But the house is undisturbed; the oval granite stone sunk into the soil at the garden's exact centre remains unscathed. It commemorates, in Roman script and numeral, the conversion of my Brahmin priest ancestors to the Portuguese fold four centuries earlier, and bears their name, a Coat of Arms and a motto which has now faded into oblivion.

Gita and I salvaged what we could before the house was sold. The carved wooden altar in the chapel was broken open and flung, all fourteen feet of solid Burma teak, onto the flagstones of the floor. In every room white ants had taken their toll of furniture and panelling. Sideboards and easy chairs crumbled to the touch. We brought bits and pieces back to Bombay and spent a year restoring what we could. The altar, a statue of the Virgin Mary which stands as tall as I do, an intricately carved dining table with matching chairs, and a love-seat. Resurrected with care, and as much accuracy as we could muster, they adorn our drawing-room in Bombay as I write. Only the four-poster remained intact. I shall never know why. My grandmother had given birth to fourteen children on that bed. Polished to a deep shine, strong as the day it was carved by the craftsmen of Cuncholim, it now graces the master bedroom in 'Rockheart,' our house in Goa.

All else has gone, lost on the ebbing tide of a brief but proud piece of history. Only myth and uncertain memory remain. I would have to build again, a house of my own on an acre by the sea, unsullied by the hand of man, chosen by a personal God concerned still with small matters, blessed by the ebullient, cavorting spirits of my ancestors. It took ten years and an odyssey into the past, but the luck of the Simoes and the Gama Rose held good. On a stormy, twilight evening in September, I discovered God's chosen acre ...

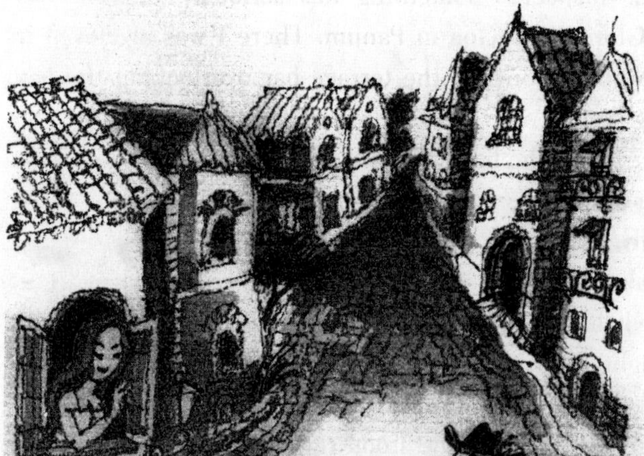

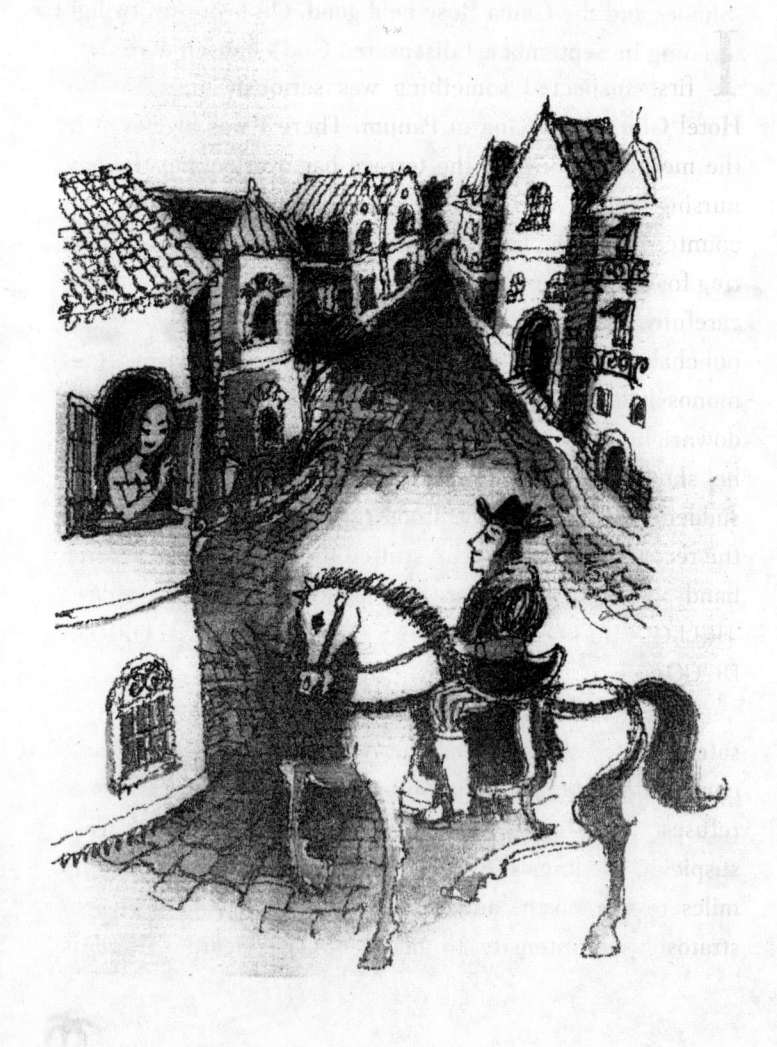

Radhika's Genealogy Class

I first suspected something was seriously amiss at the Hotel Gloriosa de Goa in Panjim. There I was at eleven in the morning, alone on the terrace bar overlooking the bay, nursing a feni in the rain, when the phone on the bar counter rang. The bartender threw it a look of disgust, let it ring for a minute or two, finished polishing a glass, placed it carefully on a rack behind him and with a world-weary nonchalance, picked up the receiver and said, 'Yes?' – a curt monosyllable clearly meant to convey exasperation, if not downright annoyance at this disturbance of the peace. Then he shouted, 'BOMBAY!' and galvanized as though bitten suddenly in the rump, he stood rigidly to attention, pressed the receiver to his right ear, stuffed the forefinger of his free hand into the other ear, and bellowed into the phone, 'HELLO, HELLO, HELLO, YES THIS IS THE GLORIOSA DE GOA.'

The Panjim telephone exchange boasts the latest in satellite microwave technology. A trunk call is as clear as a conversation across a sitting-room, but the local Goan refuses to be fooled; he views high technology with dark suspicion. He knows that Bombay lies four hundred and fifty miles to the north, and that it requires decibel levels of stratospheric intensity to make himself heard. There is another pressing concern; he must avoid misunderstanding at any cost. In the interests of unambiguity, he repeats everything that is said to him, slowly and clearly, at the top of his voice. The bartender's conversation ran true to form.

'You want to speak to Room 104? I will connect you.'

'Sorry, madam. You were connected and the party is out.'

'Have you paged the lounge?'

'You have paged the lounge.'

'Have you paged the public areas?'

'You have paged the public areas.'

'He is not in the lounge or the public areas.'

'He did not leave a message at Reception, and they said to try the bar.'

'Yes, this is the bar.'

'I understand, madam. He likes a drink at this time of day. What did you say his good name was?'

'Yes, that's a Goan name. But there is no Goan in the bar. Only one Italian gentleman with grey hair and black eyebrows.'

'Is he drinking? Yes he is drinking, madam. This is the bar.'

'What is he drinking? Feni. Caju feni.'

'Did you say how many, madam?'

'His third.'

'That sounds like your husband, madam?'

Ho hum.

I stand six feet and an inch in my socks. The bathroom scales hover between 178 and 182 pounds and stray a couple of pounds higher when I return from a fortnight in Goa. My hair falls thick, straight and white (a legacy from my father's side of the family) and I was once asked by a lady in her cups, did I dye my eyebrows? Only, I said, when I'm in Goa. When I travel in Europe I become an instant casualty to mistaken identity. Once, outside the Cathedral in Cologne, I was embraced warmly by a bearded stranger who greeted me in Basque. The Monmarte street artist, François, who did a charcoal sketch of me in the summer of '92, said that my profile (perhaps, mon ami, not the nose) was unmistakably Sicilian and clearly of noble origin. In Italy they are certain I am Andalusian. In the caves above Granada one night, a gypsy flamenco dancer said I was the first Moroccan she had ever entertained. If I can help it, I shall let the next random encounter in Tangiers pass me by.

My grandfather would have said that, given my boisterous genes, it couldn't be helped; I was, however, entirely responsible for my nose. When I was an infant and found myself in disagreement with my parents over some trifle or the other, I would express disapproval by rubbing my nose violently, with adhesive determination, against the nearest hard surface until peeled off. My mother maintains to this day that I was born with a nose as uncompromisingly aquiline as my elder brother's. If so, it was the only physical resemblance we shared. He stands five feet six inches in his socks, weighs in at a trim and athletic 135 pounds; his hair used to be black and curly but has, alas, over the uncaring years, abandoned the high ground for a wavy rearguard action at the back and sides. If my three sisters had lived separate lives in Rio de Janeiro, New York and Genoa they would be considered true-born natives.

All in the Family

We are (there I go again!) a typical Saraswat Brahmin Roman Catholic Goan family.

If you follow the advice of the poet in Goa and 'prepare a face to meet the faces that you meet' you will end up awfully confused and with a permanent tic. Goa is a genetic melting pot bubbling over irrepressibly with the inspired and creative infusions of the centuries. Begin, if you will, with the Hindu caste system. If you think that having met one Brahmin, you've met them all, pause and think again. Which variety of Brahmin did you meet? A Gaud Saraswat, perchance, whose ancestors emigrated from faraway Kashmir by way of the Punjab (where, in a famine, they learned to eat fish), Bengal, Gaud and the Konkan and settled in Goa? Or was the fellow a Chitpavan (with the fair skin and light eyes of a distant Armenian ancestry) whose forefathers, shipwrecked millennia earlier along the Konkan coast, were brought into the Hindu fold? And where and how did the warrior Kshatriyas and the industrious Sudras become untangled from the Hindu genesis? And when the bloodlines mingle – as they did to such splendid effect all over the place – what do you get? Never mind. If you really wish to compound confusion, you must take into account the Goan Muslims who have made their presence felt to such salutary effect: take your pick from descendants of Arab Sheikhs, Hindu converts, the Afghan Khans or the Khoja Shias of Persian origin. The Portuguese did their bit for flag and country by introducing a rich vein of 'mesticos' and 'descendants' (as the Eurasians are called) into the motherlode. And what do the original inhabitants, the Dravidian Kunbis who, for the main part, have kept culture

Radhika's Genealogy Class

and bloodlines pure, have to say about this seething cauldron? They aren't telling.

My own blue genes are joyfully precocious, emerging from the mists of a distant Brahmin past; going their wilful way down the mischievous centuries; making merry in lively and fertile genetic pastures; establishing the kink in the hair and the curl of an African lip here, a haughty Arabian nose there, now and again an Aryan flush, anon (if rarely) a dazzle of Dravidian brilliance; encouraged, these past four hundred years, by the irrepressible exuberance of Iberia, a cheerful propensity for the pleasures of the flesh and an abiding antipathy to the thought of hard labour. But hidden mines lie in wait for the unwary in these genetic fields of cloth of gold. On one occasion, prior to the National Elections, when the politicians were playing fast and loose with caste and community, putting violent passions to flame for despicable ends, I decided to send up the whole sorry mess in a column I contributed at the time to the Sunday *Times of India*. Titled 'An Agenda for Hearth and Home' the spoof began, 'It is not easy for a Roman Catholic Saraswat Brahmin Goan to manage a constituency in these trying times ... '

Pure satire. Laughter is the best revenge. Up the clowns! Etc. Fool! There I was at the China Garden in Bombay, taking a breath between the spicy seafood soup and the pomfret in black bean sauce, when a large man with unfriendly eyes approached and shook my hand.

'Frank Simoes?'

'Perhaps,' I replied neutrally.

He tightened his grip, thwarting any attempt at flight.

'In the normal course,' he boomed, 'I enjoy your

All in the Family

columns in the *Times*.' Nobody paid the slightest attention. Then he lowered his voice and in a penetrating whisper, which set the noodles quivering and brought a sudden hush to corner tables, he said, 'Why must you flaunt your Brahmin ancestry before the rest of us?' and dressed me down vehemently for the next ten minutes while my pomfret congealed in its black bean sauce. I apologized, of course, cowardly Brahmin that I am, reflecting that it wasn't the first time – and would certainly not be the last – when caste made the fur fly.

Now, if I'd only had the good fortune to be an OBC, that magical new genie in the bonfires of the electorate, feted by an uncritical press, courted by self-serving politicians, whom everybody wished to lead by the hand into the promised land, Radhika would have been blessed with a sunrise future. Not that it seemed to matter in the least bit to that morning's issue of *O Heraldo*. We were in Goa for the Diwali fortnight and, in order to avoid the Bombay mob, we had settled into a cottage on a beach near the Tiracol Fort, as far north as one could comfortably get and still claim to be in Goa. *O Heraldo's* front page confirmed that all was well in the land. The Black Destroyer and the Brown Bomber were to join in battle, in a fight to the finish, in the Sancolda ring. Respective weights, pedigrees, wins and losses, were neatly listed below their pictures. I had never seen a meaner pair of bulls in my life. There would be blood in the sand that evening! Not the bulls (just a bit of rough and tumble, horns locked, fearsome snorts) but the fans who, once roused, could make a stadium full of soccer hooligans seem like a Sunday school class. I turned to Page Two. Who, I wondered, was Caetano Jose Pereira, and why was he wishing himself a happy fiftieth birthday in so public a place? There was a self-congratulatory air on Page Three as well. Alzira Pimenta Dias gave herself a pat on the back for a well-deserved First in her M.A. Finals, and if she wished to celebrate all she had to do was contact Auntie Eliza's Bakery for the finest bebinca in Goa, 'highly commended by the HIGHEST in the land!' or raise glad voice at the mando contest in Margao for 'a supercalifragilisticexpialidocious first prize.' I was intrigued; what could that be?

'Antonio Da Silva proceeds to Harvard on scholarship,' I read aloud, bemused. 'This is news?'

'You're homesick for Bombay,' Gita said from the kitchen.

And indeed I was. Where were the stirring daily events which made life so wonderfully stimulating in my city of residence? Thugs shot dead in police encounters; the burning of an undowried bride or two; dozens laid low by poisoned hooch; crores worth of scams dismissed in a paragraph; bomb blasts, rapes, bloody accidents ...

'And not an OBC in sight,' I said.

'Daddy,' Radhika said, 'what's an Obeecee?'

'Organized Bloody Chaos.'

'Be serious, Doods.'

The filial respect of seven-year-olds may never be ignored. 'If you must know, Other Backward Castes.'

'Are we Obeecees?'

'We may belong to an equally neglected minority.' Suppressed mirth from the kitchen. 'But the Simoes bloodline,' I continued with dignity, 'is nothing if not distinguished. Gather around and be quiet. Once upon a time in faraway Saligao, or do I mean faraway Colvale, never mind, there lived two Opulent Brahmin Citizens ... '

'How long ago is once upon a time?'

'Four hundred years to be exact. Please stop nit-picking. Where was I? Ah yes, Opulent Brahmin Citizens. OBCs in short, but you'd never believe it. They were dazzlingly Aryan, irresistibly Saraswat, awesomely holy. Revered for their wisdom, benevolence, sanctity and, above all, for their landholdings, hectare upon hectare of the finest paddy and coconut, mango and cashew and bamboo, acquired for the most part by sly and illegal misappropriation.

'Into this Eden, in the fateful year 1510, there came a terrible firangi ... '

'What's a firangee, Doods?'

'Look it up, Radhika, and don't interrupt. It unsettles the creative flow. As I was saying, into this Paradise in the year of Our Lord 1510 there came a terrible ... '

'You said terrible before.'

'Very well then, mad and terrible firangi, a Portuguese general with a fleet of warships, state-of-the-art cannon, a predilection of prelates, and the unpronounceable name, Affonso de Albuquerque. Democratic to a fault he slaughtered Hindu and Muslim alike, taking every care to avoid discrimination and pausing now and again in this demolition (he was a fair-minded man, remember, and a good Christian) to offer potential slaughterees a choice – convert, or burn and forfeit your lands.'

'Wow!'

'Death held no fear for my brave pandit ancestors, but the thought of all that lovely property falling into greedy alien hands brought out the best in them. They made the ultimate sacrifice for generations yet unborn, converted with indecent haste, and took Christian wives. The wives were a novel experience, as were their new names. The Portuguese who had a healthy respect for property and the institution of marriage – second only to their extraordinary religious fervour – rewarded my pandit ancestors with a triple-barrelled surname and a Coat of Arms, crossed pennants, a falcon on a fist and the motto, "Never Enough!" Ten generations later, the result sits before you, a tall, fair and – ahem – brilliantly successful Saraswat Brahmin Roman Catholic Goan.'

Radhika giggled. 'How come you're tall and fair, Dad? Look at Uncle Joe ... '

Out of the mouth of babes ... oh well. 'Blame it on a recessive gene or, to put it plainly, on a dashing Portuguese cavalry officer on a white charger who happened to chance upon a lady of our house singing a fado on the balcao. He cast a lustful eye in her direction (he turned out later to be a fado fancier as well), sensed a corresponding enthusiasm, reined in, tumbled out of the saddle, leaped onto the balcao, bowed deeply, and made an indecent proposition. The rest, as they say, is history.'

'But wasn't she married, Dad?'

'To somebody else, a petty inconvenience.'

'Did they have children?'

'You bet. No Portuguese cavalry officer took his duties lightly.'

All in the Family

'Then you can't be a Saraswat Brahmin whatever it is. And look at Uncle Joe. He's short, dark and his hair is frizzy.'

'Another set of naughty genes, I'm afraid. Goa's full of them – Portuguese, Arab, Dravidian, Aryan, Maratha – in this particular instance, full-blooded African. They don't come any tougher. A great, great, grand-uncle, done with adventuring abroad, returned to Goa with a very plump Swahili lady, who turned out to be extravagantly pregnant. Made an honest woman of her, I'm told.'

'Gosh. Now I'm really muddled, Doods. If I'm not a Saraswat or an Obeecee, what am I?'

'An Original Basket Case, Radhika. If you don't believe me, ask your mother.'

And I called out to my half Bhaibhand, half Amil Sindhi, pure caste Khatri and resolutely Hindu wife, 'Gita,' I said, 'Radhika wants a word ...'

Grandfather's Green Worms

The mists of memory swirl into a single golden day, a day which touched my life with enchantment and the first brush stroke of wisdom. In my grandfather's long and illustrious career in diplomacy and medicine, this was, to my nine-year-old mind, his finest hour. He was in his seventy-second year at the time, though you would never believe it. The sparkle in his eye and the spring in his stride belonged to a man ten years younger. He had made and lost several fortunes, seen twelve of his children leave Saligao for good, buried two others, adopted two more, and borne witness to the decline and fall of the house of his ancestors, yet he looked upon the world with an equanimity unmarred by triumph and disaster. He had accepted life's contract with good grace and come to terms with the small print. Now busily retired, he was devoted to two lost causes; a medical practice dispensed free to his beloved villagers, and the care and wise tutelage of his grandson, a lad lovable enough, but given to an outlandish sense of fun (Colvale!) which took some watching.

That morning his step was lighter, more insouciant than usual. The cane swung a trifle more jauntily, a tribute to high spirits rather than a concession to age. The sola topi had a rakish tilt to it, and the face it shielded – the strong bones and profile of a Portuguese grandee, the steady grey

All in the Family

eyes, the resplendent moustache and French goatee trimmed to a nicety – was now alight with mischievous purpose. I knew that look. There would be joy this day. My grandfather was up to no good again! Now he looked up at the sky, dark and heavy with the monsoon clouds of July, chuckled and said, 'It's a fine day for worms.'

'Worms, Grandpa?'

'Earthworms,' said my grandfather, 'You will now run off, my boy, and find me six of the fattest earthworms in Saligao.'

'Earthworms?'

'E-a-r-t-h-w-o-r-m-s. Plump. Bursting with vim and vitality. To the number of six. Do I make myself clear?'

'Why earthworms, Grandpa?'

'A profound experience awaits them, my boy. Once you collect your worms, and I have no doubt that you will do so with your usual efficiency in such matters, take the bus to Panjim, to Deolikar's shop, and give him this note. He will give you a bottle. At seven this evening, bring the bottle and the worms to my consulting rooms.'

'A bottle?'

'Green dye,' said my grandfather triumphantly, 'and I want the worms alive and wriggling. Off with you now.'

Earthworms and green dye ... a trip to Panjim with demon driver 'Caju' Khaitan at the wheel, a man who never drove unless he drank ... life was full of intrigue and danger. What a day it would be!

At seven that evening I was at my grandfather's consulting rooms. He wore a long white smock, the sleeves pushed back to the elbows. His manner was absorbed, thoughtful, a professional about his business. I looked on, fascinated, as he poured a little of the thick green dye into a saucer. He opened the box of worms, examined them critically, and chuckled, 'Just what the doctor ordered.' He was about to tip the worms into the dye when he paused, turned to me and said, 'Drowning earthworms in green dye at the age of seventy-two is no way to prepare to meet your maker. Get me some water.'

He chuckled again, and a monstrous thought unfolded musty wings in my mind. Was there a hint of a cackle in the chuckle? A wild gleam in his eye? And why was he humming a gay little Portuguese music hall ditty while laying out a scalpel, clean towels, a wicked stainless steel probe, tweezers and a solution of antiseptic, looking for all the world like a mad scientist about to destroy the universe? Would there be blood? 'Water,' he roared, and I fled to the tiny dispensary.

It was a magical place. The compounder, a young pharmacist, made prematurely solemn by his responsibilities ('Lives are in your hands,' my grandfather reminded him regularly) mixed potions with an air of anguished calm. He worked feverishly with pestle and mortar, beaker and shaker. Sharp ammoniacal smells added piquancy to the air and the powders, mixed, shaped and cut with a knife and folded into little paper packets (or diluted with evil-smelling liquids) made me want to sneeze. I confess I lingered, for I feared for my grandfather. But when, reluctantly, I returned with the water, I knew at once that all was well.

My grandfather winked; he was in high good humour. 'What took you so long? Knocking back the methylated spirits again, eh?' He diluted the dye liberally with water, stirred the mixture with a spoon, tested it with a fingertip for consistency and colour, and announced, 'Your worms will survive, wiser for the experience no doubt.' He tipped the worms into the dye. 'One tampers with nature,' my grandfather observed, watching dark brown worms turn a bright green, 'at one's own risk. Perhaps the good Lord will decide this once that the means, though unworthy, will justify a truly noble end. Mmmm ... just right I think. Six green worms to order.' He covered the saucer, put it on the surgical trolley which he drew up carefully to one side of the examination table. He placed two chairs a bare arm's length apart, settled into one and crossed his legs. He seemed vastly pleased with himself. 'Right, off you go, my son.'

'But, Grandpa ... ' I protested (bring on the wild horses!).

'Very well, you may stay. Nip into the dispensary, there's a good lad, and leave the door ajar. But not a sound, do you hear, not so much as a whisper. Breathe lightly and God help you if you sneeze.'

I crouched behind the dispensary door and peered cautiously through the crack. There was a timid knock, a quavering voice, 'Dottore.' My grandfather's welcome rang out, confident, reassuring, 'Come in, my dear lady, come in.'

The old crone who entered was ancient beyond imagining, bent at the waist, hobbling on a stick, and as mad as a March hare. I recognized her at once. The Witch in the Water we called her, for she bathed thrice a day with all her clothes on in the natural spring at the top of the hill. She was retired, pensioned off, and living alone after a lifetime of servitude to the Gonsalves family in Asagao. She belonged to what I had heard called 'the servant class,' a term of reference which made my grandfather livid. ('Judge a man by his merits,' was one of his favourite aphorisms.) Not only had he spent a whole valuable day preparing for her visit, but here he was, displaying his most impeccable bedside manner, treating her as an equal.

'Come sit by me.' My grandfather waved to the chair by his side and the old lady settled into it, only to start as though pinched. A spasm of pain passed across her face. She wailed and covered her ears.

'One of them moved, Dottore.'

'Which side of the head?' my grandfather enquired gravely.

She tapped at her right temple.

'Hmmm ... I thought as much. Was it a quick or a slow movement?'

'It wiggled, the wicked thing wiggled. There was a green stain on my pillow this morning, and would you believe it, Dottore,' – she muffled a sob – 'slime!'

My grandfather sighed heavily. 'The first time I met you, I admit I had doubts. But I am afraid,' – he threw her a level, steady glance – 'you are right. It is not your imagination. I am inclined to believe that Dr Drego's diagnosis was wrong. A good man, mind you, but ours is by no means a perfect profession and, on occasion, we err. Let's see now ... .' He picked up a heavy, leather-bound book and leafed through the pages. 'It has happened before. Here we are ...

'South America. A small town in Chile in the year 1880, a woman of means, oddly enough, the wife of a doctor. Your symptoms exactly. Blinding headaches, a constant buzzing in the ears, a faint but distinct wiggling sensation in the head, wet green stains on the pillow in the morning. It's all here ...' He tapped the book's cover with an elegant forefinger.

'I'm not mad then, Dottore?'

'For heaven's sake, certainly not! You are afflicted with green worms in your inner ear,' my grandfather said, with serene conviction, as though reciting Holy Writ. 'I suspect that the spores, waterborne as they are, settled in while you were bathing in the fountain, lodged deep in the ear, a warm and fertile spot what with all that sticky wax, and bred into worms. There is now a colony, a small colony, in residence.'

'Mother of God!'

'Fortunately, they have not yet punctured the eardrum and eaten their way into the brain. I imagine at night they stray in the wrong direction, descend on the pillow and make for the nearest drain. There is absolutely no cause for alarm. I shall perform a tiny operation. It may hurt a bit, but we can't let those worms stay where they are, now can we? That may cause ... serious complications.'

Guiding the old woman gently by the elbow, he led her to the examination table and helped her up. 'Lie down and face the wall.' He placed a pillow under her head. 'There. Is that comfortable? Good. Now close your eyes. You'll feel a slight prick, no more, as I go in.' He swabbed her ear carefully with cotton wool dipped in antiseptic, picked up the scalpel and nicked the earlobe ever so gently, swabbed again and held the swab in place for a moment.

'Be very still now,' he cautioned. With a quick movement, he picked up one of my green worms with a pair of tweezers, brushed a squirming end against the woman's cheek and exclaimed, 'Got it! Did you feel that?' The grey head nodded vigorously. 'It shouldn't take long now,' – enthusiasm was writ large in every syllable; it was not feigned; my grandfather was enjoying his work – 'they are much closer to the outer ear than I thought.'

Worm followed green worm till all six were wriggling in alarm on a large white plate. 'That's the lot I think, but let me have a closer look.' He shone a flashlight into her ear, pulling the lobe gently this way and that. 'Not a sliver of a worm in there. You can get up now.' He led her back to the chair and showed her the worms, turning the plate to the light and peering intently down at them. 'Look, Dottore, they're green. I knew it all along. You've saved my life.' Pure, idolatrous worship shone in the rheumy old eyes. She kissed the back of my grandfather's free hand; he winced, recovered swiftly, put on an amiable smile. 'Think nothing of it, dear lady,' he said briskly, 'and how is the headache?'

'Gone. It's a miracle.'

'You'll be fine in a couple of days. Take this,' – he pressed a small bottle containing a clear liquid into her hand – 'three heated drops in each ear, morning and evening.'

'Will they come again, Dottore?'

'Not a chance. Take a few simple precautions. Do not bathe in the fountain, worm spores all over the place! Eat well and use the drops regularly. In all of the annals of pathology,' said my grandfather, lying like a Trojan, 'there has never been a recurrence of green worms.' He helped her to the door. 'Goodnight and mind the step.'

In a trice I was at my grandfather's side, awed at the enormity of what we had accomplished. I, Jose Francisco

Simoes, co-creator of the world's first green worm, perpetrator-in-arms of the grandest sleight-of-hand in the history of medicine. My grandfather said, 'You may now proceed to traumatize the worm population of Saligao. Distribute those things,' – he pointed to the plate – 'judiciously about the neighbourhood.'

'Why mustn't she bathe in the fountain, Grandpa?' My grandfather sighed, 'Old wives and their tales. She believes the spring water cures arthritis and she's well over eighty. We don't want her catching pneumonia now, do we? Besides,' – my grandfather laughed out loud for the first time that evening – 'I have it on very good authority that water in the ear does nothing for the health and well-being of green worms.'

There was a sudden lump in my throat. I could find no words to say what I wished. I was overwhelmed with joy and pride and love for my grandfather. He was wise, kind and good. Massed choirs of cherubim would sing his praises in immortal, glorious Hosannahs. Forever cherished, he would sit by the right hand of God, blessed for the rousing epiphany of his life, ever ministering to his own ...

2

Heart and Home

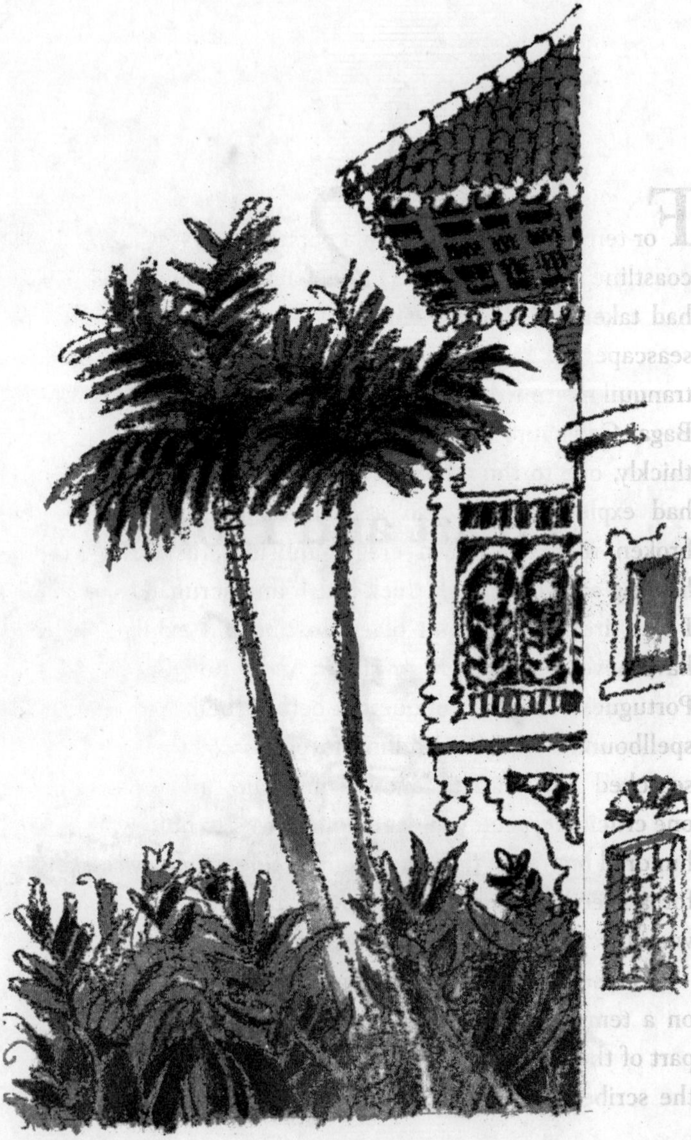

God's Chosen Acre

For ten years I had been on a personal odyssey along Goa's coastline searching for the perfect acre by the sea. My quest had taken me beach combing, from the lonely, windswept seascapes of Arambol and Tiracol in the far north, to the tranquil riverine deltas of Betul and Sal in the deep south, to Baga, Calangute and Sinquerim, where the villages cluster thickly, one to the other, and run down to the sea's edge. I had explored cliff, cove and headland, clambering over broken rock and down craggy hillsides, as often as not beating a path through thick brush and scrub. At day's end, I was tired to the point of exhaustion but exhilarated as I have never been before or since. And I now knew why the Portuguese and the conquerors before them had been held spellbound by the bewitching loveliness of the land. But I searched in vain. The law was inviolate, and rightly so, in one crucial respect: you were not allowed to build within two hundred metres of the year's highest tide mark. I was looking for a piece of land with a house, or the remains of one, which I could restore as I wished.

I discovered my piece of the good earth quite by chance, on a tempestuous September afternoon, while exploring a part of the village of Candolim called Scrivaddo, the ward of the scribes (an omen?). My grandfather did not believe in

Heart and Home

coincidences ('God's way, my son.') Like Carl Jung, whom he admired immensely and whose books occupied half a shelf in his library, he was firmly convinced that happenstance was merely a perceived instance of an alien and profoundly important dimension of being, concealed from us, the reasons for which would forever remain beyond our understanding. The Gama Rose house had not stood and flourished four hundred years by chance, but by grand design. He loved the ancestral house with a fierce sense of possession. One's home, he maintained, was the place where the heart claimed first residence and for him, without question, it was the vaddo in Saligao where the Gama Rose mansion embodied the very best of the Goan sense of saudades and alegria, the Portuguese words for nostalgia and joy. 'A strong house,' my grandfather had once said, 'and a good family are greater than the sum of their parts.'

What would he have made of the cosmic arabesque which brought together an office colleague, Rukmini Abreu, a lame mongrel puppy, an inspired architect, Sanju Walawalkar, the Goddess Shanta Durga, a distant cousin twice-removed whom I had never met, a seventy-year-old water diviner convalescing from a by-pass, and this sublime acre of Goan beach? It was a perfectly formed natural rectangle set between two dunes covered with thick mangrove grown to the height of a man. The dunes levelled down to soft white sand, an ancient stone cross with a protected niche for the offering of blessed candles, a thatched fisherman's hut and, just beyond, to a five mile crescent of palm-fringed beach. At the far end of the acre there was a large house with half a roof – deserted?

occupied? – of a vintage so rare and delicate I felt it would crumble to the touch. A grove of coconut palms planted with parade-order precision stood serenely between the houses and the sea; at the rear, a drumstick tree, heavy with autumnal abundance, a flowering cashew and a venerable banyan made unlikely neighbours. The air was lit with twilight and scented with raat ki rani. Swallows swooped and soared among the wild bougainvillaea. Formations of gulls explored the lower sky flying straight as arrows to urgent and mysterious destinations. Squirrels appeared among the bushes, vanished, appeared again as if by sleight of hand, then rushed into hiding as a pair of owls flew in low looking to supper. God's own acre. Here, the troubled heart could learn to be still.

But not, as it soon transpired, without some heartburn. None of the villagers in the fishing hamlet had a clue about the owners. I enquired with the sarpanch, the priest of the parish, old landed gentry, to no avail. Disheartened and with time running out, I returned to Bombay. There the kindly hand of congruence dealt me an ace. Rukmini Abreu, a colleague at office, was leaving on holiday for Goa, and I made her promise to visit the Land Survey Office in Panjim. 'All I want is a name,' I said, 'and an address.' She returned a fortnight later, burst into my office and announced with a beatific smile, 'My uncle owns your piece of beach and is quite happy to sell it to you.' Was that my grandfather chuckling in the wings?

Gita and I took the next flight to Goa. We acquired a solicitor, bought the land for a price which made me smile, only to discover that we had acquired a tenant as well, a lame female mongrel pup which we came upon abandoned and left to die on the main village road. She would never win a beauty contest, but she had a mind of her own. Yelping with joy (we had fed and fondled her), she followed us to the property, trotted behind us around the boundary, marking it as her own in the only way dogs know, and made it clear that she had arrived to stay. In deference to her total lack of canine presence, we named her Aunt Jemima.

At Bobb's Inn & Bar that evening we discussed plans for the house, architects, landscaping, a garden, and soon came to a rueful conclusion. Given our firm, highly individual – and often heatedly divergent – views on what a beach house in Goa should be like, made even more complicated by the monolithic obduracy of the prima donna architects we knew in Bombay and Delhi, the cause seemed not so much lost as irretrievably entangled. 'Oh well ... ' Gita said, when, brooding over our second large fenis, we heard a chuckle. A young slip of a girl, with a winning smile and pigtails stood at our table. 'Sorry to interrupt,' she said, holding out her hand, 'but I couldn't help eavesdropping. Sanju Walawalkar. I designed the Taj Holiday Village.'

Not only did the chemistry between us prove an alchemist's dream, Sanju was the perfect catalyst. Gita wanted a beautiful house; I wanted a Goan house; both of us wanted a house for our collection of my family's heirloom furniture and Gita's paintings and antiques, and my venerable red Underwood typewriter, and Gita's Portuguese lithographs, and my books; above all, we wanted a house which would make happy and timeless conversation with us and the elements. Sanju would have none of this waffling.

God's Chosen Acre

Never did an architect go about designing a house more obliquely. She disappeared with Gita for hours on end on mysterious forays – on catamarans to distant islands, to the government's archives, to waterfalls and rain forests and bird sanctuaries, to crumbling monasteries and plant nurseries, to old, distinguished Goan homes and the huts of fisherfolk with hard cow-dung floors, to the tilemakers at Verem and the potters of Bicholim. They returned with stars in their eyes and samples of stone and tile, flowering plant and wood panelling, clay pottery, stained glass and exotic fish recipes. I couldn't get a word in edgeways. Sanju was clearly unimpressed by my architectural opinions, but she insisted on reading every word I had ever written about Goa and my family. She spent long evenings plying me with large fenis, while I told her how I felt about Goa and why. Once, in a moment of rare introspection, she said, 'A house should be built with the belief that it will last forever. It should be the way you are, the way you feel about life, and each other.'

One morning, she announced briskly that she was off to Bombay and would see us in a month with drawings and a site plan. Thirty days later we had both, the plans of a house and a friend, for life. Now we had to appoint a contractor, and what should have been an easy task proved a strangely difficult proposition. They came; they saw; they quoted and then, inexplicably, at the eleventh hour, they would say no, apologize and depart with undue haste, never to be heard from again. There was nothing for it but to call in Devendra Nayak. Very pricey (he had built a fine beach resort) but honest, quick and good at his work. We agreed terms and timescales; a contract was drawn up; then it happened again.

Nayak, immensely unhappy at having to let us down, did so. But he had the good grace to tell us why: 'Shanta Durga will not allow me to build your house. A female spirit lives in your cashew tree. She must be appeased by shedding the blood of a cock on the land.'

At the far north of Candolim, where the village gives over to fields of emerald paddy, in a glade shaded by mango, banyan and bamboo, stands a temple many hundreds of years old, dedicated to the Goddess Shanta Durga. No contractor will build so much as a buffalo-shed in the village without performing a special puja seeking the blessings of the Goddess. Exquisitely wrought in brass, four feet and a bit, she has behind her a penumbra of brass leaves, ten at each side, set in a perfect circle, like a peacock's fan. The pandit performs the puja, then soaks a bunch of tulsi leaves in a vessel of holy water and, very carefully, places a green leaf on each of the brass ones; they adhere. When a question is put to the Goddess, she responds: a leaf falls to the ground. If the leaf falls from the left, the answer is yes; from the right, no; the leaves do not fall in sequence, from top to bottom, but at random, and this, again, holds special significance. All of our earlier contractors, to a man, had asked a single question.

'May I build a house for Gita and Frank Simoes at Scrivaddo?'

'No.'

Devendra Nayak, with much trepidation, had gone further.

'Will you let me build the house if I give you an offering?'

'Yes.'
'Flowers and fruit?'
'No.'
'Rice, coconut and mithai?'
'No.'

Dread shaking his heart: 'Does a spirit preside over the land?'

A leaf fell.

In these matters, Nayak explained to us that evening, there has to be fresh blood spilled on the sand. A young cock, he added, would do nicely.

Gita was appalled. She is staunchly vegetarian and sensitive about animals to a fault. Had we discovered the perfect acre only to find that we could never have a roof over our heads? The next morning, Sanju and Gita went to the temple to plead with the Goddess in person. Subdued, they sat silently while the pandit went about the ritual. The tulsi leaves were put in place and Gita said, 'I am a Hindu and have a deep reverence for living things. I believe that all life is sacred and that the spilling of blood will bring abiding unhappiness and ill luck to the house, the land and my family. Won't you please accept another offering?' For long moments, not a leaf stirred, then three leaves on the left of the circle detached together and fell to the floor. The pandit was amazed. 'Three leaves at once,' he said, well pleased, 'we must give thanks.' That evening, just before sunset, the pandit performed a puja that lasted for an hour, with a havan and five kinds of fruit – bananas, apples, mangoes, chickoos and oranges. These, together with agarbatti set alight, kum kum, a small mirror, holy oil and a ribbon were placed at the

Heart and Home

foot of the cashew tree. 'The female spirit is now appeased,' the pandit said.

The next morning the offerings were gone.

The long arm of coincidence had not done with us yet. Nothing – not Shanta Durga's blessings, not the promise of a fat advance, not all of Sanju's powers of persuasion – could make Nayak change his mind. He would not build our house. As a last resort, a friend in Mapusa suggested we approach the city's biggest contractor. 'Slim chance, he's a tough customer, but you lose nothing by trying.'

The contractor gave Gita polite, but short shrift. 'I'll think about it,' he said, 'but it's very unlikely. If I'm not at the site tomorrow morning, take it that I'm not interested.'

Gita left her visiting card and returned, near tears. At first light the following morning, a jeep bounced across the dunes. A tall, lean figure leaped athletically out, embraced me warmly, and exclaimed, 'Francisco!' I hadn't been called Francisco since I was a child. He turned to Gita and said, 'Why didn't you tell me that you were married to Frank Simoes. He doesn't know it, but I'm his second cousin from my mother's side.'

But no builder, no matter how closely related, can build without water, and the engineer from the Public Works Department was not encouraging. 'The watershed has been mapped along this entire beach,' he said, 'dig if you will, but you won't get a drop of fresh water.' Was Jung chortling offstage? I had made a beachcombing friend, an ancient party who shuffled at the water's edge with a cane every evening, startling the sandpipers. He lived in Bombay and was convalescing from a bypass. When, feeling like Job on a bad day, I told him of our water problem, he chuckled and said, 'Let me have a go.' He was a water diviner, among other things, and had inherited the gift from his father and grandfather. There he was the next morning, ambling all over our property, with a crescent of thick copper wire held before him, twitching merrily as he went along. Once in a while, he would be seized by what appeared to me – looking on in alarm – to be a terminal convulsion. The copper twisted into knots. His forehead filmed over with sweat. He paused to rest, marked the spot with a wooden stick, and started all over again with a fresh strand of copper wire. After half an hour of this, he turned, beamed at us and said, 'Dig here.' Three weeks later we did and, lo and behold, an abundance of clear, fresh water burst forth from a perennial spring.

Everything went swimmingly after that. The foundation of the original plinth was redug, and our obliging pandit performed an elaborate puja on the site, while the parish priest blessed the stones. Two laterite bricks took centrepiece in the ceremony. A cross had been carved on one and a small gold cross laid within it. A swastika was inscribed on the other brick and inlaid with the five precious jewels of the zodiac – pearl, coral, sapphire, emerald and ruby. Evil spirits would do well to stay away. And when I climbed down into the foundation, sprinkled holy water on the bricks, and broke a coconut, a collective 'Ah ... ' went up, for the coconut had split cleanly, at the exact centre, into two perfectly symmetrical halves, and I could have sworn I heard a distant voice whisper, 'Blue blood to the breach once again.'

At dusk, a loving congruence gave us one last, immortal blessing. Radhika, two and toddling, was playing in the sand.

Heart and Home

I heard the carpenter's boy take a sharp breath and drop his chisel. Six feet away from her a black cobra lay coiled, head raised, hood spread, absolutely still. Aunt Jemima, taut as a bow string, stood between my daughter and death. Her hackles were up, the upper lip drawn back over her fangs. She growled deep in her throat. For an unbearable moment, the dreadful tableau was frozen in time and space, then the cobra retracted its hood and slid with astonishing speed across the sand and into the mangroves.

That night, I stood on the land and looked out over the dunes as the surf came roaring in on a moonspun tide. I reflected on happenstance, pride and possession, and gave silent thanks to the powers that guide our destiny. My grandfather had said that no one owns the good earth. I was a guest, no more. As a bee is given a flower and the nightingale its song, I had been granted happy residence for the rest of my mortal time on one of God's chosen acres.

You Can Go Home Again

The phone rang at first light, six thirty on a rank Bombay winter's morning. The smog lay thick and murky in the air, a disfiguring haze over the manicured lawns, the rows of disciplined flower-beds, the ornamental trees and, small mercy, the towering grey skyscrapers beyond. As the day progressed the smog would crystallize into a fine dust covering every surface in the house. The floors were swept and mopped twice a day; every article of furniture cleaned; inevitably a lost cause – within the hour you could feel the dust gathering underfoot again. In Goa at this time of the year, the late November mist from the sea settles gently over palm, casuarina and mangrove. As the sun rises behind Rockheart, the mist clears in a series of measured, unfolding revelations: the disembodied tips of the casuarinas appear first, graceful, ephemeral in the wind, suspended in cloud between earth and sky. It is an enchanting metamorphosis. The mist diffuses even as you regard it, palely drifting, parting in reluctant tendrils and swirls. A golden Goan morning takes wing: cresting breaker, whispering palm fronds bejewelled with the gathered dew, hovering kingfisher, cloudbursts of butterflies settling like giant confetti on the honeysuckle beds. Through the curtain of mist, the neighbour's cock appears on the tiled cornice of the

Heart and Home

guest cottage, an unruly apparition, puffing and fluffing and crowing endlessly with the arrogance of the unassailable, driving Jemima and Scruffy to frenzies of despairing frustration (while O Cat throws him a glance of the deepest contempt and decides to let the fowl live!). Darker shadows take shape and substance at the base of the jambol tree as the vaddo's pigs and goats forage among the leaves and fallen fruit for their breakfast. The sand, made smooth and firm by the night's tide, disappears seamlessly beneath the breaking, frothing waves as the catamarans, returning with the catch, challenge the surf. The fishermen leap over the sides, up to their shoulders in the heaving swell, and haul the cumbersome wooden boats in on tree-trunk rollers until they are well above the highest tide mark, while the disenfranchised (the very old and the very young) who pretend to help in the hauling are rewarded with a fish apiece.

The phone continued to ring with a persistence that told me at once that this was no Bombay caller. Patience at such an ungodly hour is not one of Bombay's virtues. I was right. A familiar voice rang out. Cheerful. Top-of-the-morning. All's right with the world. 'Frank sah!'

'Joaquim!'

'How you, sah? Madam? Radhika? My family sends loves, sah. We have new baby boy. When you come see?'

Joaquim and his wife, like millions of other rural Indians, are the despair of the nation's family planners. The new baby is their sixth in eight years.

'Congratulations, Joaquim. Where are you phoning from?'

'Bobb's Inn, sah. We kill thousand big white prawns. I send you two hundred by Manvin courier.'

Heart and Home

Two hundred big white prawns would fetch Joaquim's wife a thousand rupees in the Mapusa fish market. A rare windfall which would go a long way. I could not accept his gift; I could not refuse his gift. I sought refuge in guile.

'The prawns will spoil, Joaquim.'

Pray God my friend, Jerry Manvin, never hears of the slur.

'No problem, sah. I go now Manvin. Pack in dry ice. You get prawns this afternoon. Cook for dinner, sah.'

A flash of heaven-sent inspiration. 'We don't have a cook, Joaquim. She took off yesterday for a week's chhutti. Who will cook the prawns?'

Never underestimate the perseverance of a Goan fisherman when he comes bearing prawns. 'No problem, sah. My cousin brother's wife lives Bombay. Bandra, sah. Top class prawn cook. I phone ask her to come your house, sah.'

'But Joaquim,' – Solomon in all his wisdom – 'I can't eat two hundred prawns all by myself. Besides, Gita and Radhika are vegetarian.'

I should have known better than to try conclusions with Joaquim. A long, pregnant silence. A triumphant guffaw. I would not go prawnless this day. 'I make balchao, sah. Four jars. Send tomorrow. Also two kilos fat drumsticks from our tree, sah. For madam and Radhika.'

To the back of the class Solomon.

'Make a good day, sah.'

'Have a good day, Joaquim.'

'Yes, sah. Sorry, sah. Make a good day, sah.'

I was not about to look a gift horse. No man in his right senses would refuse four (four!) jars of Goa's celebrated prawn pickle. Three months' supply; no, make that two; the maid and cook, by the dark of the moon, were no mean purveyors of prawn balchao.

'Thank you, Joaquim. Goodbye. Kiss the baby for me.'

Friends like Joaquim had come into our lives in Goa as naturally and effortlessly as ripe mangoes in May, and with the honest goodness that lasts a lifetime. When the priest of the parish, Father Victor, appeared in an immaculate white soutane to bless the laying of the foundation stone of Rockheart, who could have foretold that, three years to the day, our friendship would lead to the creation of another residence, the Arc of Hope, rising like some impossibly compelling mirage out of barren ground to bring shelter and refuge to the oldest, most destitute women of the village. And if our sarpanch, Tomazinho Cardoso, had not extended the hand of friendship, would I have been privy, a decade later, to the high drama, low intrigue and celebrated victory of the War of the Vaddos?

Some of the friends we made we employed.

I shall never forget the evening Sawant presented himself. A small knobbly man, swarthy and eagle-eyed, with a military moustache of fierce disposition, he stood ramrod straight in the uniform of a sergeant in the Indian Army (a rank he had once held in the distant past, the very distant past if his uniform was any indication.) It had seen better days. The khaki had faded in blotches into a pale, stonewashed yellow, patched here and there with rough-and-ready approximations of the original thing. The ancient rifle he held at the ready was cause for real alarm. If it ever went off, bits and pieces of rusty barrel and worm-eaten wooden stock would cause considerable harm to the immediate neighbourhood and permanent damage to Sawant's future prospects. My fears were set to rest. The weapon, Sawant said, was twenty years old and unable to fire. Once a day, he paraded it around the vaddo, under his right arm, shotgun style. It served as a splendid deterrent to potential evil-doers, and God knew – with a swift glance over his shoulder – there were plenty of those around. He showed me a letter of recommendation from a retired colonel of the regiment he had served in, now resident in Candolim. Experience? He could turn his hand efficiently to anything: handyman/ watchman/gardener/general factotum/occasional cook (strictly occasional with, I must understand, a limited but tasty repertoire).

Just then Aunt Jemima trotted up, applied her shoe-test to Sawant's polished boots, and went delirious with joy. Sawant beamed. It was love at first sniff.

'Kutta ka naam kya hai, sahib?'

'Aunt Jemima,' I said.

Sawant grappled with this, brow knitted, lips moving, for a moment or two, then came to a brisk military decision.

'Jimi,' he barked, clipping off the last vowel with parade-ground panache. To my ever-lasting shame, Aunt Jemima made small, happy noises, grinned foolishly, rolled over on her back and pawed the air.

From that day on, Aunt Jemima became Jimi and Sawant became part of the family. But, as I was soon made to realize, it just wouldn't do (besides being highly illogical) to have a gardener without a gardener's boy. There was the fetching and carrying to be done, the fixing and unfixing of hosepipes, the opening and closing of tool sheds (not to mention front and rear gates), the shushing of crows after the dogs' food, the collection of the mail from the postman twice a day, the pressing of buttons to start the pumps ... small tasks to be sure but, if neglected, with the potential to do irreparable damage to the health and well-being of the garden. And what, pray, would Sawant be doing while his boy hewed wood and drew water? Sawant would apply his mind to Senior Horticultural Management, that's what, pruning and pampering, mixing and applying judicious quantities of fertilizer and pesticide, meeting lengthily with our consultant, Mr Mendonca, travelling expensively to nurseries in faraway places there to take brow-furrowing and weighty decisions, at enormous cost, for the greater glory of the garden. But good, honest gardener's boys were thin on the ground (observe the unremitting petty larceny going on in Ashok Deshpande's garden down the road) and it was indeed fortunate that Sawant's son was not merely honest as a new rupee but free at the moment and might be open to the right sort of offer. Just the lad for the job – and lucky us! – ready to come to work at a day's notice.

So Anil joined the rank-and-file. He had a tendency, when he thought no one was looking, to droop languidly over a flower-bed, immobile, for several minutes on end, but I put that down to the lack of his father's military training. I should have known that, sooner rather than later, Sawant's stressful senior management responsibilities would not allow for short-order forays into the kitchen. And so it came to pass. How on earth did word get around so quickly? Scant minutes after Sawant announced his defection from the pots and pans, Bernadine was at the back door with a sheaf of glowing testimonials: the high point, Asst. Cook for an evening, at a banquet at the Governor's mansion. 'Don't look a gift horse,' Gita said. I had no intention of doing so. Bernadine, a grandmother twice over, took over the kitchen with the bouncing efficiency of a seventeen-year-old. A week later, Gita said, 'Enough is sufficient! Have you ever tried managing a husband with nothing to do, a six-year-old daughter, a handyman, a handyman's handyboy, and a cook through a twelve-hour working day?' Before I could invoke Parkinson's Law, Esperanca and Asha, housekeeper and maid respectively appeared like genies, joined the fold, and were beavering away all over the place.

Most of the time I regarded them amiably and, indeed, thought of them as a sort of extended family (help in Goa, by inexplicable osmosis, soon become blood relatives), but I must confess to dark moments when they became – albatross-like – the MOB.

One winter's morning five years later, the Mariner's Bell at the gate leading to the beach rang with an imperious authority. Once, twice, impatiently, thrice. Sunday, the day off, finds the house deserted. I ran to open it. A figure, wreathed in mist, bearing a huge kingfish, stepped onto the flagstoned path without so much as a by-your-leave and marched briskly to the kitchen door. I was, to put it mildly, taken aback. I had seen nothing like him before: a mane of unruly black hair, wet from the sea, glinting here and there with the occasional fish scale, tumbled down to his shoulders. The three-day stubble of beard gave a risque emphasis to high cheek-bones, a great hooked nose, a strong lantern jaw and deep, dark, hooded eyes. A swashbuckling, give-'em-hell face. He wore the traditional fisherman's loincloth, a langote, and nothing else. He stood, feet apart, the kingfish on his forearms, all wiry, rippling muscle and easy grace. There was a bouncing confidence about him. His manner made it clear that he was on a social visit.

From the moment I first set eyes on him at the gate, I had been struck by a sense of déjà vu, and now the penny dropped. Here was the spitting reincarnation of a younger, wilder Sammy Davis Jr. He held the kingfish up by its tail, gave it a gentle shake and an admiring look, moved it to his other hand, held it high for my inspection, shifted his weight from foot to foot. He seemed just moments away from a soft shoe shuffle.

Had he come to sell me the fish?

'How much?' I asked.

'Him gift, sah. We kill ten big kingfish tonight. This one for you, sah. No money. Gift.'

'Well, that's very kind of you, but ... '

'Joaquim Antonio Silveira,' he rolled the syllables around with great relish, stuck out a hand, withdrew it quickly, wiped the palm on the back of his langote, stuck it out again and smiled, a grin of huge, spreading happiness and goodwill. Buccaneer to boon companion in the space of a smile. 'Everybody call me Jackie.'

It is quite impossible to be ungracious to a fresh kingfish. I led the way into the kitchen. From the back of the langote, Joaquim drew out a knife, six inches of wicked, gleaming steel. His eyes narrowed; he looked at the fish for a second, a professional about his business, then held it up at an angle by the tail and with swift, carefully measured strokes, descaled both sides. A silvery shower descended on the kitchen sink and floor. Bernadine would be livid. Then he gutted the fish, blade moving in a blur this way and that, sighed with deep satisfaction and turned to me with two large, perfectly formed roes in his cupped hands. The kingfish had been a lady well in the family way. Should he slice the fish or fillet it? No, I said, Bernadine would never forgive such an indignity. I gave him a clean towel and pointed to the guest washroom. Joaquim would have none of it. He cleaned at the well, using the handpump and the rubber hose with great exhilaration and towelled himself off vigorously. I invited him in for a drink and he sank into a sofa in the sitting-room, hugely pleased with the morning's work.

I knew enough about fishermen returning from a night's hard labour to dispense with the niceties. I poured him a Parsi peg of Director's Special, my favourite tipple, three fingers into his glass and a smidgen into my own. I knew better than to offer him soda or water or (grave slight) to let him drink alone. He took a polite sip and I suppressed a smile. With his fishermen friends in their thatched beach hut which served variously as club house, retreat, conference room, repair shop and twenty-four hour bar, it was usually mud-in-your-eye, bottom's up and pass the bottle. This morning he was clearly on his best behaviour. He made small talk. Yes, he and a crew of four men and a boy went fishing every night and returned at daybreak. It was very hard graft. The wooden catamaran was worked by oar and sail. It took many hours to reach the shoals of fish and then, more often than not, they had to make do with the meagre leavings of the five-ton mechanized trawlers, illegal marauders, with nets the size of football fields. But with God's grace they managed to eke out a living. Now, if only he could afford a Yamaha outboard motor ...

Déjà vu again; now where had I heard that mournful phrase before, 'If only I could afford ...'

But to his credit, he did not dissemble; he came straight to the point. 'Will Sah lend me thirty thousand rupees for Yamaha? I own house, sah. I sign paper for house your name for secure loan. I no pay, you take house. Worth fifty, sixty,' – a speculative look from the dark eyes; what would the market bear? – 'maybe hun'red thousand. I return every paisa. With Yamaha I go far, very far, kill hundred fish. Pay back soon, sah. Promise on my son's head,' – a pause; had he missed out something; he had! – 'interest too, sah!'

I hadn't the heart to refuse him outright. I gave him a second drink (an extra finger this time, a Goan peg, to cheer him on his way) and said I would give the matter serious thought. That winning smile again; much later I would discover that every day was God's good day for Joaquim. He knocked the drink back like a true and thirsty ramponkar and there was a lilt to his stride when he left.

I must confess to a few misgivings. Rueful experience had taught me that there was no such thing as a noble son of the soil. There were degrees of honesty and/or the lack of it. Local yokel skullduggery was every bit as crafty and artful as Bombay's at its most dazzling, as I had learned to my cost. There was the small matter of 'pure white sand' for the raised flower-beds in the front garden. No other sand, I was told, would marry successfully with soil, manure and seed. It could only be had with much labour and expensive truck haulage from a dry riverbed at an estuary ten miles north. Bemused by such expertise, I agreed, and soon found myself poorer by sixty thousand rupees, while a huge and mysterious hole had appeared overnight in the beach just beyond the mangroves. And why did the price of coconuts fall by twenty per cent only when our crop was harvested? A conundrum, till I discovered that a Goan landowner counted each coconut as it was felled from the tree, counted again, hawk-eyed, as they were packed in gunny sacks, and negotiated the sale to the wholesalers at Mapusa personally. And how come the cost of anything I wished to acquire – a boat, a mango grove, an antique Madonna – assumed an astonishing bouyancy no sooner it became known that I was involved?

I had not, however, reached the point of irreversible paranoia, and I did not wish to do an injustice to as fine a fellow as Joaquim seemed to be: I had, after all, promised to give the matter serious thought. So I sought the counsel of the two wisest men in the village, Tomazinho Cardozo and Father Victor. Between them, the well-being of Candolim's five thousand villagers was in very good hands; they balanced judgement with action; the secular and sacred were in fine, fruitful harmony. They were very wise men indeed; if a leaf fell out of season, a chicken found itself in the wrong pot, a boundary stone was surreptitiously moved, a pigling was purloined, they were the first to know. Their knowledge of the village, the villagers, and all that went on, was positively Proustian. They were Founder-Members of the Village Trust: Tomazinho Cardozo, Sarpanch of the Panchayat, third-term elected president of the village governing council; Father Victor, our indefatigable parish priest; as a junior member of the Trust, I comandeered the rear, so to say, and to this day I can't understand how I came to be scrounging for funds in Bombay and other hostile points of the compass beyond Goa, prising the charitable rupee from the coffers of reluctant Captains of Industry.

I put Joaquim's case to them in the Church Refectory.

'I know him,' Father Victor said, 'a good man by all accounts, honest and reliable.'

'The trust can't help,' Tomazinho pointed out, 'he lives just beyond Candolim's jurisdiction, and under the terms of our charter we aren't allowed to disburse funds outside the village.'

'Of course,' Father Victor added, reasonable as ever, 'that wouldn't come in the way of a personal loan, if,' – a keen, sidelong glance – 'he could find a generous benefactor.'

'He wants thirty thousand rupees,' I said, 'for the Yamaha.'

'Inflation,' Father Victor observed sadly.

'Do you know how much a kingfish costs these days?' Tomazinho said.

Too close to the bone for comfort, that.

'Oh well ... ' I began.

'Don't do anything rash', Father Victor cautioned, 'you must take every care.'

'I couldn't agree more', Tomazinho said 'I shall have him checked out for you.'

'But ... '

'An Agreement of Hypothecation will have to be drawn up,' Tomazinho said, now in his Senior Sarpanch mode, 'I know just the lawyer. Deepak Sardesai in Panjim. Good man.'

'Experienced. Reasonable charges ... '

'Wait a minute ... '

'Right then,' Father Victor said briskly, 'must rush. Lots to attend to in the parish this morning.'

And off they went. So did I, reflecting ruefully that the devil hadn't a prayer in Candolim with Father Victor about, and without the shadow of a doubt, Tomazinho would be elected to a triumphant fourth five-year term. The competition hadn't a ghost of a chance.

*

It took all the will I could muster to look Joaquim in the eye. The Agreement of Hypothecation lay on the table between us like an Immovable Object. Joaquim leaned forward in his chair, quivering on his heels, an Irresistible Force. A reluctant party to this primordial confrontation, I felt about as sanguine of the outcome as the quarter bottle of Director's Special which now languished – with no bets on its future – between us.

The Agreement had been drawn up in the usual obfuscating jargon on five hundred rupees worth of impressively stamped Government Bond. I interpreted it for Joaquim. First, the good news; the loan was friendly and free of interest.

Then the bondage:
1. We were now joint owners of the good boat Avelina.
2. The loan had to be paid in monthly instalments over two years.
3. The two-year repayment period was inviolate. Under no circumstances would it be extended.

4. Insurance, repair, running costs, depreciation and incidental expenses were to be borne by Joaquim.
5. Joaquim could not take out a second lien on the boat.
6. If a single monthly payment went in default, I could have the Court's bailiffs seize the boat, sell it lock, stock, barrel, nets and Yamaha motor, and recover the loan.
7. All fees, duties and taxes applicable to a motorized vehicle (as opposed to Avelina's earlier tax-free status as a country craft) would be borne by Joaquim.
8. Monthly instalments of repayment would be deposited in a joint bank account (in Joaquim's name and mine) at the Saraswat Co-operative Bank in Calangute. I would have exclusive Power of Attorney over the account.

I explained each clause to Joaquim in the greatest possible detail, but I began to falter as I went along, guilt and apology rising in my voice in inverse proportion to each fresh excess of legalese. Joaquim, however, seemed quite unfazed, the smile cheerful as ever, the Yes Sahs, OK Sahs, No Problem Sahs, brightly optimistic. It was only when I came to the matter of the plaque that his face fell.

9. The borrower shall affix a plaque in a prominent place on the exterior stating that the vessel has been hypothecated in favour of the lender.

'No, sah,' Joaquim said firmly.
'Why not? You have a problem with that?'
'Yes, sah. Big problem, sah.'
'What's your problem, Joaquim?'

'I lost my face with other fisherfolk.'

'No problem, Joaquim,' – how easily one fell into the habit! – 'the plaque goes.' And I scored out the offending clause and initialled the margin with a satisfying flourish.

We signed the document with the due solemnity. Gita and Bernadine signed as witnesses. I could tell by the warm smile of sympathy Gita bestowed on Joaquim and the tight-lipped look of searing disapproval I received, that I would have to tread carefully over the next few days. A fresh, sealed bottle of Director's Special was ceremoniously produced by a beaming Bernadine with a brace of my finest cut-glass Belgian tumblers. Four-finger Goan pegs, no less, for each of us. I couldn't say for Joaquim but I was in dire need of good cheer. Let the guilt begone!

Joaquim did not touch his drink. He was having trouble with his trousers. He had arrived, much to my surprise, dressed for a legal occasion. The Mickey Mouse T-shirt and military jeans with pockets all over the place, shiny brass zips, buckles and studs, were gifts, as I learned later, from a grateful American he had retrieved from wild seas off the Baga estuary. Both T-shirt and jeans were several sizes too large and had been literally cut down to size by the simple expedient of shearing off the sleeves and the bottoms of the jeans with, if the results were any indication, the lethal weapon used so efficiently to eviscerate the kingfish.

Joaquim was now struggling with a thick sheaf of folded paper which he had tucked away into a long, narrow pocket extending from hip to knee. An unequal struggle which went on in utter silence for a couple of minutes. Eventually, with a mighty tug and what sounded suspiciously like a violent

Konkani oath, he managed to get the document out in one piece, wiped the sweat off his brow, smiled wanly, opened, flattened it and laid it on the table.

'Sorry, sah, I forget.'

Another legal document, no less, impressive and intimidating, stamped with many more rupees than my own, typed, generously initialled, neatly punched and intricately bound with red velvet ribbon tied in a bow and sealed with wax. Wow!

'What on earth's that, Joaquim?' I asked.

'Deed for house, sah,' – there was just the touch of the forlorn in his voice – 'I promise sign over to your good name, sah. I go lawyer in Mapusa. He make paper. You read, sah. See is good.'

Get thee behind me Shylock!

'That won't be necessary, Joaquim.' I raised my glass. 'Up the trawlers. May they come to a swift and sticky end!'

'Let engines fail in high sea, sah!'

'Well said, Joaquim.'

Thus did Joaquim and I toast the good ship Avelina and her crew in their brave new avatar.

The Director's Special worked its splendid magic The morning glowed with the promise of bright new beginnings. We were at ease, relaxed and unforced, and when Joaquim reached for the bottle and poured himself a second jumbo drink well before I had done with my first, I knew that we had become friends. He talked of his love for boats and the lure of the sea; of a hard apprenticeship at the age of twelve and a rite of passage where danger and the cold hand of sudden death lay ever in wait for the foolish and the foolhardy; the rip tide, a line of foaming water concealing, just below its surface, a swift and treacherous current which could overturn a boat and sweep the crew under in the time it took to shout a warning; the deadly seasnakes entangled in the nets and the huge jellyfish, poison sacs swollen, lurking in the shallows, half-buried in the sand, whose sting could lay a man on his back for a week and had been known to kill. But there was joy in equal measure. He told me of the ways of dolphins with their young ('Just like people, sah!'); of the hours' long love play of the great sting rays; of the mysteries of Grand Island, out of bounds to all but the most intrepid, where at night, under cover of jutting cliff, among jagged rock formations, they hunted the big, bad rock fish, long as a man's arm, fat as a young pig, the Ugliest, Most Delicious Fish In All The World. No rod, line or net here. Flippers, mask and spear, water-proof flashlight. Strong lungs and a good right arm which drove straight, hard and true. Strange things happened when the moon was full. On deserted, bone-white beaches the voice of the turtle could be heard in the land. They crawled like shadows out of the waves and into the mangroves, there to lay hundreds of eggs before returning, with the same slow, stealthy discretion, to the sea. The highly prized black crabs, driven as well by moonspun madness, emerged from the rocks and the heaving tide, came ashore in dark, scuttling masses, and wandered every which way, a free and moveable feast for the men and boys in the coastal villages. Huge shoals of tiger prawn collected in a feeding frenzy where the tide-driven breakers, whipping about hidden rock formations brought thick fogs of algae to the surface. Dangerous, beckoning clouds of foam and mist, sharply etched by the moonlight, reward beyond reckoning for the sturdy of limb and stout of heart. He would take me one night by the light of the moon to what was surely a wonder of the world – Arambol, a mile-long crescent of pure white sand which shimmered like a river of molten silver between the ocean and a lake of fresh water. Few men knew of Arambol. No track or path led to it. No footprint other than your own could be found on its sands. Shielded by thick jungle, hidden by curving escarpment and soaring cliff, only a long night's journey by catamaran, guided by the moon and stars, could take you there.

The sun was high and hot above the palms. The bottle of Director's Special would never see another day. With shy pride Joaquim spoke of his wife and children. God had been good. They loved one another. Then, with an affectionate sense of paterfamilias, he told me about his crew, relatives all by blood or marriage, except for the boy, David, who was an orphan. 'They good men, sah.' Finally, an invitation, 'Come tomorrow morning, sah. Have breakfast. I show you boat. Meet my family, sah, and my friends.' It dawned on me then that this was a charmed moment, not a conclusion but a felicitous beginning. Magic casements had opened on a place I had sought all of my life, a place of much serendipity and joy, a place long known, long lost, elusive as a will-o'-the-wisp, always near, ever beyond reach, a place which, with luck, I could now make my own.

*

I was in no condition for a hike across a mile of soft sand the following morning, but the next week I wandered down the beach to have a look at the Avelina, now transformed by the

Yamaha into a swift and vengeful machine. Up the trawlers! You could tell where one seaside vaddo merged with another by the white-washed crosses – the traditional demarcation, rising a man's height above the mangroves and the dunes – and the heart of each vaddo by the cluster of fishing boats drawn up on the beach in neat rows of a dozen or so. The prows, port and starboard, were made colourfully over to elaborate painted images, intricately wrought, with names that gave rousing testimony to the deeply held faith of their owners. The Infant Jesus and Mother Mary, in various incarnations, led the vanguard, followed closely by a veritable litany of saints, with Christopher and Francis, clear favourites, ahead by several haloes.

I heard Joaquim well before I saw him. 'Sah! We here, sah.' He stood some way down the beach, slightly in front of what was unmistakably a reception committee in its Sunday best – long-sleeved, trousered, gleamingly shod. I shook hands formally with five Silveiras (Vincent, Joseph, Avilino, Francis and Johnny), three D'Souzas (Banny, Diego and Simon), one brave iconoclast, Alex Mascarenhas, the boy David who emerged shyly and reluctantly from behind a boat, and a young slip of a girl Joaquim brought forward by the hand. 'Anna, sah.'

'Your eldest daughter, Joaquim?'

Roars of laughter.

'This my wife, sah.'

Six children in eight years and a figure that would have sent Jane Fonda into terminal depression. As if at a signal, a frolic of children appeared at the crest of the dune and came gambolling down the beach. Joaquim's lively brood. I shook a round of hands once more and kissed the baby. Then I was ceremoniously led, like a prized Presidential candidate, to inspect the good ship Avelina and pass judgement on my investment. I was astonished at her size. She was made of seasoned mango-wood planks each thick as a man's fist, twenty feet from prow to rudder, six feet high, another five across. Two slender logs of planed hardwood balanced the boat. One was lashed to the prow, the other to the stern. They extended at right angles, eight feet or more, slanting to run parallel with the boat's waterline and lashed again at the far ends to a foot-wide surfboard, flat, smooth and tapered. Thus balanced the boat skimmed over the surface of the water. The Yamaha was mounted at the stern on a pivot with two locking positions: one, up and in, when Joaquim and his crew heaved the vessel over log rollers through the unruly surf into calmer waters; then, out and down, with the propeller in a precise position beneath the waves to drive the boat with smooth, sustained power well beyond the horizon where the huge shoals of mackerel, kingfish and sardine gathered to feed.

But technology had introduced a new and dangerous element, a quite unexpected hazard. 'Tricky to balance with motor, sah,' Joaquim said, 'we move very slow, very careful.' The boat had not been built for speed; it had been designed for oarsmen and sail and the Yamaha outboard brought mixed blessings. The boat could now venture far and fast and stood a fair chance against the trawlers, but it was a precarious journey. The higher the speed, the more tentative the balance. Joaquim and the fishermen who went out with him, and shared the catch in proportion to their experience and tenure, handled the boat with an agile instinct, honed and tempered by many seasons in rough seas. When they moved, it was never more than two at a time, to a graceful minuet, keeping a certain distance between each other, never straying from the exact line of the hull. It was now second nature, a ballet of grace and precision as they unravelled and cast the nets, a man to port, another to starboard. Eight hours later, when they hauled the nets, it was an even more exacting operation and it took all of their skill, the nets now heavy with the night's catch, until the boat settled low in the water with the weight of the fish, and came at last to some measure of stability.

And all these years I had harboured the illusion that advertising was the toughest business known to man! How I would have loved to take one or two of my nastier clients out on a moonless night and bounce them over the side. Rally around, ye jelly fish! Do your thing, O sea snake! Where are you, dear rip tide, when we need you most? Joaquim's offer of breakfast brought me out of this delightful reverie. Retribution would have to wait. I was famished. Anna led the way to a tiled cottage, to a dining-room, to a groaning board which could have put a dozen large ploughmen to their severest test. There were six bottles of caju feni arranged in a hexagonal centrepiece, a bunch of Moira bananas, each a foot long, a wicker basket piled to overflowing with golden malcurada mangoes, a caramel custard, Anna's recipe for which must surely have begun, 'Take forty country eggs ... ,' a fruit cake with almond icing, two bolos (the sweet country bread baked with toddy and molasses) the size of small boulders, enormous serving dishes with the savouries: Goa sausages, fried prawns, broiled sardines, marinated and grilled pork crackling, chicken winglets cafreal and a baker's rhapsody of hot, fragrant breads.

Joaquim, the five Silveiras, the three D'Souzas and Alex, the lone Mascarenhas who dared to be different, were rolling up their sleeves purposefully. The children held plates and forks at the ready. Anna was rushing about distributing bottles and glasses. The family dogs sniffed hopefully at the periphery. Even David's solemn face had broken into a smile. Joaquim raised his glass. I raised mine. Half a tumbler of the finest caju. We would feast this day.

'We make good party, sah!'

And so we did.

*

The letter arrived at our flat in Bombay a year later in the week before Christmas. It bore the unmistakable signature, the unforgettable flourishes and curlicues of high finance, of the Manager of the Saraswat Bank in Calangute and had been composed in the desiccated style bankers employ when dealing with triumph or vicissitude. The fisherman, Joaquim Antonio Silveira, second and unempowered signatory to the Agreement of Hypothecation, had paid back the entire loan a year ahead of schedule. The full amount, with accrued interest, was now in credit. Could he have instructions as to its disposal. He would recommend a fixed deposit over ninety days at eleven per cent interest when, he had been given to understand, I planned to return to Goa and the disposition of the sum could be discussed and agreed between us.

I handed the letter over to Gita. She chuckled and said, 'Let me write to Joaquim.' The note she gave me to sign that evening was a model of brevity.

Heart and Home

> Dear Joaquim,
>
> The Manager of the Saraswat Bank in Calangute tells me that you have Rs. 32,000/- to your credit in our joint bank account. A cheque for this amount is enclosed. How will you spend the money?
>
> May the fish always bite!
>
> Yours,

I signed the cheque and the letter with a warm glow (thus must Scrooge have felt when he saw the light) and added a postscript.

> PS. Make *a very happy Christmas!*

*

But life is often harsh to happy endings. We returned to Goa in April and no sooner we reached Rockheart, I went up to the terraced veranda on the first floor to look out at the sea. I was appalled. A fleet of trawlers was spread, like a lethal and ugly infection, from one end of the horizon to the other. I counted fifty. They were scattered as if in battle formation, some within hailing distance of the beach, others mid-distance, a few thinning out towards the horizon. Ten miles of the sea, from Sinquerim to the Anjuna headland, had been drawn and quartered and was now being eviscerated. Flocks of scavenging gulls fluttered about the stern of each boat where the huge trawling nets were cast from mechanized winches. All the natural sounds of the sea were lost in the obscene throb of idling diesels, old, ill-serviced engines which leaked dark, oily patches onto the waves. There wasn't a catamaran in sight. I should have known that the confrontation was a tragically unequal one from the moment the battle lines were drawn. Power, corruption and greed had won the day.

No Yamaha could compete with the rapacity of the morally dispossessed. The laws governing trawler ownership had been drawn up with a cynicism worthy of Machiavelli. A new trawler cost a million rupees. With much public fanfare, subsidy schemes were announced and banks appointed to provide loans at negative rates of interest, so that the disenfranchised ramponkars could form co-operatives and acquire trawlers. No elected representative – Minister, Member of the Legislature or Sarpanch – would be allowed to own a trawler. On the face of it, altruism writ large; the con was hidden in the small print. As a first step, a licence had to be obtained and here, unless a huge black money premium was illegally paid (a sum well beyond the resources of the ramponkars) the fishermen found themselves entangled in a morass of red tape worthy of Kafka: lengthy assessments of a fisherman's net worth had to be established and notarized only to be rejected on one technicality or another, guarantors had to be found; applications were never in order. Weeks and months passed. Not a single fisherman owned a trawler, yet they began to appear, an evil menace, in coastal waters, bought by politicians through middlemen several careful removes from the centres of power. They reaped rich, untaxed rewards.

The depredations of the trawlers went well beyond the day's catch. Though they were officially banned from fishing at five fathoms or less, they broke the law with impunity, raiding the traditional preserves of the ramponkars, trawling with weighted nets at the bottom of the shallows, in a dragging process which denuded the waters, destroyed fish and prawn hatcheries, and drove mature shoals, with the noise of the diesels, to seek ever more distant feeding grounds. Not every fisherman could afford a Yamaha and even those who could had to fish farther afield for catches which shrank visibly from week to week. A way of life was being torn apart, a cultural milieu generations in the making would be destroyed in a matter of years.

Joaquim was more fortunate than most. His skills were acknowledged by friend and foe all along the coastline. He fished where no other ramponkar would venture. He knew every metre of coast over a stretch of thirty miles, every quirk of tide and weather. In the dangerous months before the monsoon, when the swells often rose to four and five feet, he would guide the Avelina to the rough waters of the estuaries where mullet, ladyfish and tiger prawn bred and no trawler would dare follow. Even so, it was hard going. He was forced to reduce the crew to three men and David could no longer be employed.

Like most of the fishermen with Yamahas, Joaquim began to supplement his income with imaginative and risky forays into the tourist trade. They took boats, overloaded with large, unwieldly Germans and drunk Finns off the charter flights on hazardous excursions to Arambol and Grand Island. Some turned entrepreneurs, set up thatched shacks on the sand stocked with all manner of dubious merchandise, and quickly learned to fleece the foreigners. Many who could not afford outboard motors made distress

You Can Go Home Again

sales of their catamarans to fishing villages in the far north, too distant from their home bases to attract the trawler fleets. With weary resilience they began renting out rooms, bed and rough board to foreign back-packers. First one small room, then another, soon the entire house, while the fisherman and his family moved into a make-shift lean-to in the backyard, and served as cheap labour to their guests.

But some kept the faith.

One morning I rowed young David in a choppy sea across the Baga estuary to St Anthony's Bar for a lunch of stuffed crab. He deserved the treat. The previous evening he had cycled twenty miles to a fishing hamlet to the north for work. He was in luck. A boy was needed. They laboured for ten hours for three buckets of fish worth five hundred rupees. David's share was forty rupees and three mackerel. There were angry red welts on the back of his hands where the net cords, held taut against the swell for hours on end, had bruised and torn the skin. His eyes were rimmed with salt spray and bloodshot with exhaustion. They held no resentment, only bewilderment and a certain regret.

'When you grow up, David,' I asked, 'what would you like to be?'

He was silent for long moments. Then he said, 'A good man.'

And it dawned on me that no matter how long and hard and despairing the journey, if the heart holds steadfast and true, you can go home again ...

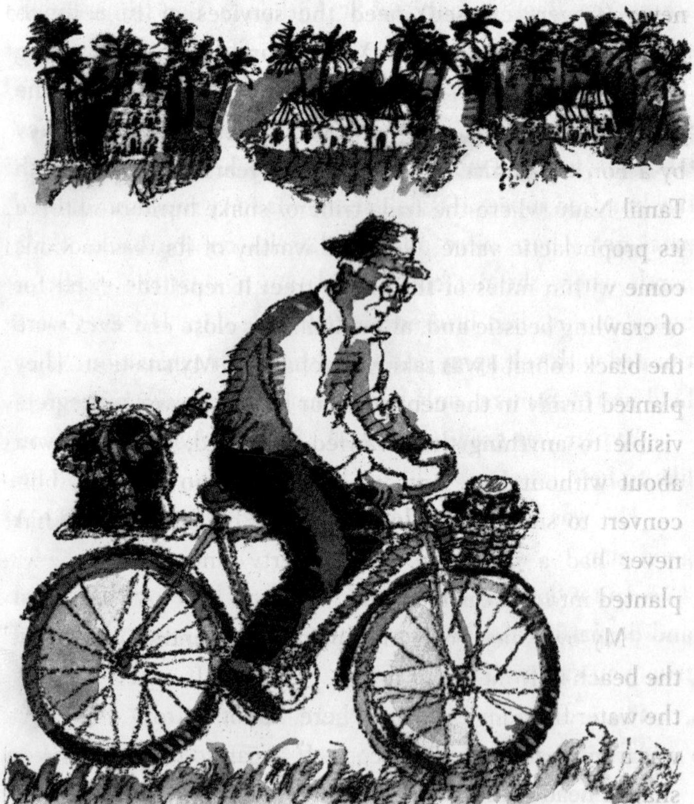

The Cobra That Nearly Never Was

Now that we have a snake stick in the house, I shall never (fingers crossed) need the services of Eurico's old friend from Mapusa, Felix Xavier Furtado, with his coil of coir rope, bag of rice, marigold flowers, agarbatti, and jumbo-sized tin of Nescafe. The snake stick was given to me by a Forestry Officer who had spent years in the jungles of Tamil Nadu where the Irula tribe of snake hunters swore by its prophylactic value. No viper worthy of its venom would come within miles of the snake tree. It repelled all manner of crawling beastie and, after Radhika's close encounter with the black cobra, I was taking no chances. My snake stick was planted firmly in the centre of our largest flower-bed, clearly visible to anything that crawled, slithered, hissed or went about without legs. And while I am by no means a blind convert to snake mythology, it has to be said that we have never had a snake on our property since the stick was planted into the earth.

My own close call took place two hundred metres off the beach in front of our house. I came up from a dive, shook the water from my eyes, and there, a foot in front of my face, was a small and erect periscope. It began to undulate, spade-shaped head held forward, tongue flickering. For a second or

Heart and Home

two we stared at each other in utter horror. Then, as one, we flipped over backwards never to meet again. I learned later that the venom of the sea snake is tenfold more poisonous than the cobra's. It feeds on small fish. A lightning-swift bite. Within moments, the fish has no future and the snake has lunch. But it is timid, avoids human contact and, in living memory, has never been known to strike at a person. There is a moral to be discovered in this; when swimming off a Goan beach the morning after the night before, even if you feel like a dog's breakfast, it's best to pretend you're a person.

Snakes abound in Goa. 'Part of the ecology,' my Forestry Officer friend had said cheerfully, 'We need them more than they need us. Poor devils, ever since Eve they've had a bad press. My son keeps a young boa as a pet, friendly little fellow.' Give me a cocker spaniel, thank you very much, but the point was well taken. Visitors to Goa need not pack the antivenom with the sun block. I suspect there is more snake lore about than snakes, and in twenty-five years I couldn't have set eyes on more than half-a-dozen. There are, however, a few things that the budding herpetologist should know about Goan snakes. They come in two varieties: harmless and lethal. Alas, hundreds of the former are mistakenly slaughtered for the latter. These are four in number, distinct in appearance and, for all practical purposes, invisible: the cobra, the Russell's viper, the krait and the saw-scaled viper. The first three are large nocturnal hunters, acutely sensitive to ground vibrations, and flee silently at the most distant sound of a human footstep. The saw-scaled viper is bad news. A foot in length, no thicker than a thumb, sand-coloured and stupid, it is difficult to detect underfoot and

The Cobra That Nearly Never Was

strikes in a fast blur at the slightest provocation. The good news: it is rarely found where lots of people live.

Snakes figure prominently in the Goan Tall Tale. As the feni goes down, inspiration takes wing. You will hear of cobras seeking vengeance after weeks or months at some real or imagined slight; snakes with two heads; rat snakes the size of young pythons breaking legs and arms with careless abandon and the swish of a tail; mating vipers disturbed in their dalliance, forsaking pleasure for hot pursuit; and so on. The truth of the matter is, happily, far less dramatic. There is nothing snakes abhor more than a fang to face confrontation with a person. They are shy and self-effacing though, on the rare occasion, as we shall see, they can be foolish. They pay dearly for the lapse. When a poisonous snake is cornered, it is set upon with savage cries and heavy sticks by strong men bent on murderous annihilation. Rat snakes are put down without thought or care (though, at six feet, thick as a man's upper arm, swift, agile and generously fanged, one would think that discretion would be the better part of valour). The Russell's viper is dispatched ignominiously. Kraits are beaten over the head and incinerated. But the cobra is sacrosanct. It is worshipped as a living deity and never harmed. What then does one do with a cornered cobra? The Cobra That Nearly Never Was, my own true snake story, offers one possible solution.

A pleasant way to spend a crisp winter morning in Goa is to visit my cousin Eurico Ribiero's antique shop situated on one of the most charming lanes in the village. Lined on either side by flowering gulmohar trees, it ambles up a

Heart and Home

hillside to the Fort Aguada Beach Resort, dropping sheer on the right to the ruins of a moat, and cresting gently hundreds of feet on the left to the ramparts of the fort, the old Portuguese lighthouse, and the plateau which boasts two distinctive features; a fabulous view of bay and beach; and a fertile breeding ground for snakes of all kinds, sizes and proclivities. These, at times, pay unannounced and unwelcome visits to the traditional Goan cottages which follow the lane, gardens overrun with bougainvillaea, mango and chickoo trees, coconut palms and ornamental hedges. They are built in an age-old fashion with amber laterite brick, dressed by hand and open-faced, and Mangalore tiles for the roofs which are supported on interlaced lattices of exposed wooden beams. The places between the tiles and the beams contain innumerable nooks, crannies and dark, concealed corners impossible to get at, where pigeons nest, lizards, rats and bats make homes, and the odd rat snake may be glimpsed at night trying to organize a warm supper.

Eurico had converted one such cottage into his shop, going to elaborate lengths to maintain its original architecture and character, right down to the easy chairs on the wide veranda, the carved side tables, the pewter beer mugs from Macao and the chilled Arlem lager, frosting even now in an ancient icebox, a bottle or two of which we proposed to consume on this fine December morning. Nothing ever disturbs the tranquillity of Eurico's approach to life, not even a Californian tourist brandishing a thousand-dollar traveller's cheque. He greets customers horizontally, feet crossed on one arm of the easy chair, offers a mug of the finest, a languid hand, and a smile that says, pleasure, my

The Cobra That Nearly Never Was

dear fellow, before any talk of business. It is an amiable philosophy and has served him well.

We were at the cottage gate when a piercing cry shattered the pastoral calm. I heard the crash of a table overturned, the sound of glass shattering on tile ('Oh dear,' I thought, 'not the Macao mug'). A figure came hurtling down the veranda steps, shirt tails flapping behind it, a long-handled broom clutched aloft, covered in cobwebs and old dust. Eurico. Pale beneath the tan. Violently agitated. 'There's a cobra in my roof!' he shouted, 'a cobra! a cobra!' for all the world to hear. The announcement took immediate effect. In minutes, out of airy nothingness, a truly rural crowd of villagers materialized. The word 'sanp' passed in a horrified whisper from lip to lip. 'Cobra.' There is no more chilling noun in the reptile lexicon in Goa, but these were stout-hearted sons of the soil, and it just wouldn't do for a fellow Goan to have a cobra about the house. A solution must be found. The crowd broke up into small animated groups. Earnest conclave ensued, heated discussion, nervous wit. Opinion was sharply divided. 'Smoke it out,' suggested a young firebrand. His friends, instantly enthused, chorused, 'Yes, yes.' 'No, no,' Eurico was now as close to wringing his hands as I have ever seen him. 'No smoke without fire, eh?' said an old wag, and the crowd, jolly and feisty at the prospect of an entertaining morning's work, guffawed noisily. Eurico was not amused. I took him aside. He had the look of a man who has plumbed the very depths. Would he ever be the same again? 'Firecrackers!' a voice bellowed, 'that's what we need, firecrackers!' Eurico twitched. I sat him down under the shade of a gulmohar. 'Tell me all about it,' I said soothingly.

Heart and Home

The morning had held out the promise of a truly lovely day even for December. A cool breeze brought the scent of marigolds wafting into the veranda. Pigeons cooed in the eaves. Fluffy white clouds chased each other in a clear blue sky. Puppies played with their shadows on the lawn. God was out on a Goan ramble this day, well pleased with His work. Eurico poured the perfect head of beer into the Macao mug, raised it to his lips, and was about to give silent thanks for small blessings when, out of the corner of his eye, he thought he saw a shadow move on a beam above his head where the tiles rested on the rafters. It moved again, sinuously. A rat snake, Eurico thought, and rushed fearlessly to the store room for a long broom and a torch. He shone the one and prodded vigorously with the other, bringing a shower of cobwebs and ancient dust down on his head. The snake refused to budge. Then a thought struck Eurico. He turned the broom upside down and banged on the rafter with the hard end, hard enough to rattle the tiles. He heard an angry hiss, saw the spectacled, spreading hood, yelled, and ran for his life. The cobra moved swiftly up and away, disappeared into a cranny, and there it hid, reflecting no doubt on the injustices of life.

'I cannot have a cobra in the rafters,' Eurico said wanly, 'suppose he falls on the head of an American tourist?' I had to admit that it was not an encouraging prospect. Then a village elder laid his hand on Eurico's shoulder and said, 'You will have to send for Felix Xavier Furtado.'

'Felix,' Eurico repeated, eyes alight with remembrance and hope. 'Yes, we will have to send for Felix at once.' A motor cycle taxi was summoned. A young man, in a crimson

The Cobra That Nearly Never Was

vest and a bikini arrived astride a racing Enfield, grinning from ear to ear, flexing his biceps and scattering the crowd. Given instructions and payment in advance, he shot off, revving his engine as though at the start of a 500 cc Grand Prix. The crowd ducked for cover. The village elder said, 'It will be a good hour before Felix gets here. He will travel on nothing except his Raleigh bicycle.'

'Who,' I asked unwisely, 'is Felix Xavier Furtado?'

The village elder gave me an icy look.

'He has a way with cobras,' he said, appalled at my ignorance.

It proved to be an eventful hour. A few of the braver young spirits decided to enter the house. A brown bottle had appeared mysteriously among them. It was passed from hand to hand. Generous swigs were taken. Fortified, armed with long bamboo poles and flashlights, they charged up the veranda steps. Eurico and I followed cautiously behind. From room to room they went, banging on walls and floors and rafters. The beams of their torchlights criss-crossed the ceiling. They shouted; they drummed on empty kerosene tins with coconut ladles; they careened into each other around blind corners to muffled curses. The youngest of the lot, inflamed with Dutch courage, climbed onto the shoulders of the tallest, leaped for the nearest rafter, missed, fell to the floor in a crumpled heap and dusted himself off sheepishly. The din should have brought the house down, let alone a cobra. Now, terrified out of its wits, the snake had probably decided to hibernate for the rest of the winter.

Undeterred by their lack of success, the young villagers rushed out of the house. We followed gladly. One of them went off and returned with a long wooden ladder, a bamboo pole, and – Eurico gasped and clutched at my arm – a string of firecrackers. They brushed off his protests (the second bottle was making the rounds with much greater urgency than the first). Eager hands tied the string of firecrackers to the end of the pole. The ladder was propped up against the roof. The young lad who had challenged the rafter with such unsuccess now redeemed himself. He scampered to the top, set the crackers alight, and waved the pole above the tiles. The noise was deafening. Showers of sparks descended on Eurico's roof. A great cheer went up from the crowd. All the cocks in the neighbourhood began to crow. But not a hint of a speckled scale, not a slither, not the faintest suggestion of a hiss.

The bedlam died down. A disappointed silence took its place only to be replaced moments later by growling suspicion. A voice was raised, 'Had there ever been a cobra?' Another, rudely, 'Does my aunt have balls?' A third, 'Probably drunk and imagined it all.' ... 'A waste of good time.' ... 'Does he think we have nothing better to do?'

'It was a cobra,' Eurico said in a small voice lacking in conviction. The tinkling of a bell intervened bringing a sudden hush to the crowd. A brass bell, the kind one found on the handlebars of bicycles fifty years ago, with a small metal thingumajig sticking out at the side which one pushed rapidly this way and that with a thumb. The bell was attached to a Raleigh pedal-pusher of magnificent vintage, clearly a family heirloom, lovingly handed down from father to son; the thumb belonged to a weathered old party who wore broken horn-rims tied with string and a pork-pie hat.

The Cobra That Nearly Never Was

He pedalled furiously towards us. The crowd made way respectfully. The old man came to a racing stop and leaped lithely off the saddle. Eurico embraced him with a grateful cry, 'Felix!'

It has been ten years to the day, but what happened next remains as vivid for me as this morning's news. Felix Xavier Furtado wasted few words. With an equal economy of movement, he untied a large tin of Nescafe from the carrier of the Raleigh, a jute bag and a coil of thick, rough coir rope. These he took to a coconut tree nearest to the roof of Eurico's shop. He tied one end of the rope to the trunk of the tree, a foot and a half from the base, uncoiling the rest as he walked to the house and climbed up the ladder to the roof. There, negotiating the tiles with nimble ease, he tied the other end of the rope tightly to the cornice. The rope now stretched taut and firm from the top of the roof down to the tree trunk.

He clambered down the ladder, returned to the coconut palm and took the lotus position, legs crossed, squatting before the trunk. He placed a clean white handkerchief on the ground before him. From the jute bag he removed a handful of marigold flowers, three sticks of agarbatti and a small brown paper bag of raw rice. He arranged the flowers and a handful of rice on the handkerchief, stuck the agarbatti upright into the soil and lit them. The pungent incense spiralled around the tree, made a wreath about his head and settled on the rope passing a foot above the porkpie hat. Then Felix Xavier Furtado did a very strange thing. He extended his arms, palms open, facing towards the earth, and began chanting a mantra in a low, pure, lilting cadence. The mantra rose and fell, rose and fell, a mesmerizing chant. It travelled barely a quarter of an octave. It had no beginning and no end, each phrase dissolved into the next, yet it seemed informed with a distant and mystical yearning.

Suddenly, there was a quick, collective drawing of breath. Heads turned towards the roof. A black cobra, in full grown prime, was making its leisurely way along the tiles towards the cornice. There it paused, lifted its head, and aligned its body with the angle of the rope. Then it began a gingerly descent. I held my breath. Surely it would lose its balance and fall right into the crowd, angry, writhing, striking. But, if anything, it moved more quickly as it descended finding secure purchase on the rough coir strands, passed over Felix's head, slid down the tree and coiled before him. The ribcage expanded; the hood spread to its full terrible oval, the tongue flickered inches from Felix's eyes which were now open and wonderfully calm. The mantra rose to a warmer pitch, then fell, softer, softer yet to a whisper. Felix lowered his palms above the cobra's hood, and as his hands and the mantra fell, the hood slowly retracted. The cobra lowered its upper body and lay its head between Felix's knees while the mantra faded into the magic of the day.

Felix opened the Nescafe tin, stuffed the docile cobra in like so much soft plasticine, put the lid back, thumped it down, and dusted his hands off. He smiled. It had been a good morning's work. He accepted no payment and was not offered any. He gave Eurico a hug and off he went on the ancient Raleigh, rope, bag and Nescafe tin securely fastened

The Cobra That Nearly Never Was

to the carrier. The cobra would be released later in the day in the rain forest of Valpoi.

Commit the name to memory as I have: Felix Xavier Furtado from Mapusa. On those awkward occasions when a cobra drops in for a chat and a quick bite, he is a good man to know!

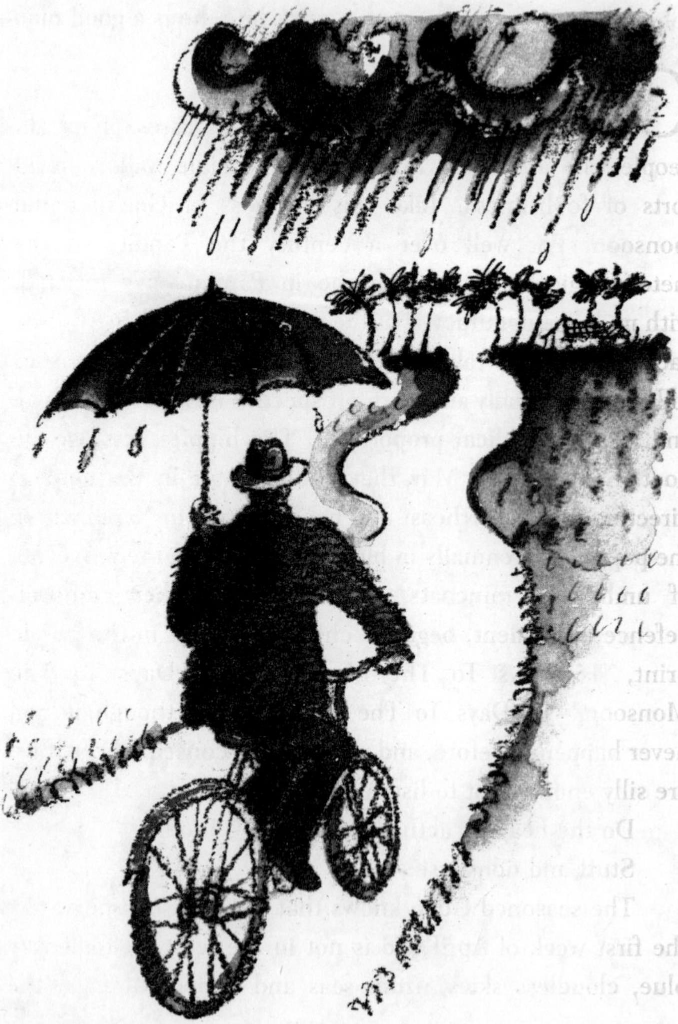

Romancing the Rains

Our capacity for self-delusion makes asses of us all. People who are otherwise sane and sensible wallow in all sorts of foolishness. Take this business of Goa's annual monsoon. For well over a century the Pandits of the meteorological office in Alrinho in Panjim have insisted, with mulelike obduracy, that the monsoon breaks on 10 June each year, give or take a week or two. The travel brochures follow suit slavishly and warn prospective travellers of deluge and flood of biblical proportions. The hippies don't give a hoot. Sometime in May they sniff the air in the general direction of the northeast and book passage to Nepal where the poppy is perennially in bloom. On 25 May, the purveyors of umbrellas, raincoats, gumboots and other monsoon defence equipment, begin to chant in unison in the public print, '15 Days To The Monsoon,' '14 Days To The Monsoon,' '13 Days To The Monsoon,' as though it had never happened before, and warn of dire consequences if we are silly enough not to listen.

Do the heavens actually open on 10 June?

Stuff and nonsense.

The seasoned Goan knows that the monsoon begins in the first week of April and is not in the least bit fooled by blue, cloudless skies, azure seas and temperatures in the nineties. On 1 April, in our first year in residence at Rockheart, Joaquim and Johnny came bearing gifts. These were contained in tour bulging gunny bags slung over their shoulders which they deposited in the veranda. Then they began taking the goodies out in slow motion as if afflicted by sudden arthritis, smiling conspiratorially, pausing for effect as each parcel was laid on the floor, and adding unnecessary footnotes.

'Dried bangra,' Joaquim said holding up a bundle of what looked alarmingly like mummified mackerel preserved in green fungus.

'Para,' Johnny said proudly, brandishing a glass jar filled with a thick red mush with an oil slick floating on top.

'Prawn balchao,' Joaquim said, 'my wife make, sah.'

Johnny began unravelling a long string of Goa sausages which had managed to tie itself into knots. This took the better part of ten minutes. 'Best in Bardez,' he announced, 'maybe best in Goa. My cousin's mother makes in December. Smokes six months over kitchen fire. Mouth withering, sah, ask Joaquim.'

But Joaquim pretended he hadn't heard. He was busy dusting off four bottles corked and roughly sealed with wax. The contents were too murky to be feni. Was I meant to gargle with it? Drink the stuff? Or rub it in when I ached?

'Sugarcane vinegar,' he explained, 'put in sorpotel. Mmmm ...'

Johnny was not about to be upstaged.

'Mangada,' he said, opening a large plastic jar and holding it under my nose. Mango cheese. Soft and moist and irresistible. I went to the kitchen, returned with a serving spoon and scooped out three large chunks. We munched in appreciative silence.

'Mouth withering,' I said.

Two more jars of thick red paste were deposited on the floor of the veranda.

'Recheado masala,' Joaquim said, 'fry in fish.'

'What,' I asked, 'is all this in aid of?'

They exchanged smiles. Then Johnny said, slowly, clearly and kindly, as though talking to a retarded child, 'Stock up ladder for monsoon, sah. So heavy rain, you trap in house many days.'

'Four ... six ... ten days!' Joaquim said, holding up the appropriate number of fingers.

Behind me I heard Bernadine giggle and offer a swift sally in Konkani. Joaquim and Johnny laughed. 'You foreigner, Frank!' Gita added her tuppeny's worth quite, I thought, unnecessarily. I looked up at the sky. A perfect blue to set the heart strumming. Where was the monsoon? It lay in glorious disarray on the veranda floor.

That evening Father Victor and Tomazinho Cardozo dropped in unexpectedly. Everybody in Goa drops in unexpectedly, greets you like a long lost relative discovered after decades of anguished separation and stays without the slightest fuss for breakfast, a drink or two, lunch, tea, a drink or three, dinner, and a happy and extended reunion. Not only had I learned to find these sudden visitations fun, but had begun to sally forth in similar fashion myself whenever the whim took me. 'Let's see now, Gita. We are in Campal. Angelo Pereira lives just round the corner. Why don't we ... ' to be greeted, it must be said, with genuine welcome and the sort of Goan hospitality which begrudges nothing.

But my parish priest and sarpanch were not on a social visit.

Father Victor regarded me with concern and said, chidingly, 'You have not begun your monsoon preparations. I expected as much. Before you know it, the rains will have arrived.'

'The monsoon is six weeks away, Father. I can have the chicks up in a day.'

'Your fancy plastic chicks,' Tomazinho said, 'will blow apart in the first storm.'

'Have you had the wells cleaned?' Father Victor asked.

I confessed I hadn't.

'Best to have it done now, when the water levels are at their lowest. I know just the man for the job.' He turned to Tomazinho, 'Caetano from Simer.'

'Well,' Tomazinho said, 'personally ... '

'Caetano,' Father Victor said firmly.

'Caetano it is, Father!'

'And what about provisions?' Tomazinho said. 'Has Bernadine stocked up?'

'It is customary,' Father Victor added, 'to harvest the coconuts before the end of May.'

'Tell Bernadine,' Tomazinho advised, 'that the smoked kingfish keeps its flavour and cooks much better than the salt mackerel. Difficult to get enough of it, though. If she has any problems, she should let me know.'

'I will have a word with Joaquim,' I said.

'It's best poached,' Father Victor said, 'in white wine for

an hour or so, tightly sealed to keep the flavour in, and eaten with garlic mayonnaise.'

'The next best thing,' Tomazinho said, 'is dried Bombay Duck. Thoroughly cleaned, soaked overnight, beaten very thin and fried in recheado masala.'

'Quite delicious,' Father Victor said, 'with boiled rice and plain sorac.'

'Avoid the pork if you can.'

'The chicken's safer.'

'Don't forget to stock up on garlic,' Tomazinho said.

'And red Kashmiri chillies,' said Father Victor, 'they simply disappear from the markets during the rain.'

'Ah yes,' Tomazinho said, 'pickles. As many different kinds as Bernadine can manage. Irene will be sending across some of her mother's water pickles. Raw mango and carrot.'

'You make it sound,' I said, 'like a siege.'

'Well,' Father Victor said, 'it does rain you know.'

'It can pour for days on end,' Tomazinho said.

'Everything gets very wet.'

'Sopping. Water logged. There are days when you can't stir out of the house.'

'When it really rains,' Father Victor said, in his gravelly God-bless-you-my-son ministerial voice, absolving me of all responsibility for the monsoon, 'it's wiser to stay home.'

They refused a drink. A portentous sign. Tomazinho usually had a glass of chilled water flavoured with a quarter peg of Director's Special. Father Victor could hold his liquor like a prelate. But no, drink was out of the question. Now I was mildly concerned. The rains were obviously a serious matter. They left with parting advice on provisions, retrieval recipes for dried fish and a miscellany of odds and ends which would ensure our survival during the monsoon. I walked them to the front gate. Scruffy and O Cat followed, noticeably subdued. Did they know something I didn't?

'Take care,' Tomazinho said.

'Look after yourself,' Father Victor added.

Was Bernadine's dinner a harbinger of things to come? Boiled rice, boiled Goa sausage, deep fried salted bangra and prawn balchao? Or was she merely getting some practise in? After dinner, I sat up on the balcony with a caju liqueur. The stars denied all existence of any such thing as the monsoon. Then the phone in the master bedroom rang with magisterial authority. Shivanand Salgaocar calling from Vasco da Gama, reluctant heir to an industrial empire and boon companion these past ten years, taking time out from managing a clutch of iron ore mines, a score of companies, a fleet of ocean-going bulk carriers and the fortunes of two thousand employees to offer advice and support in this most woeful of seasons.

Captains of Industry don't beat about the bush.

'Those flimsy plastic blinds you bought in Bombay are a waste of time, Frank. I'm sending one of our construction people across to measure your upper and lower verandas for heavy duty canvas awnings. Metal swivels and steel bolts. Just the ticket for the monsoon.'

Shivanand said, with a touch of asperity – not a single drop shed and the monsoon had begun to get me down – 'those flimsy plastic blinds are triple-thick Venetians which let in the light at the touch of a finger and keep out the rain when you want it kept out. Designed by the Swiss for tropical hurricanes. Not just high technology. Olympian. The same pioneering human genius which put men on the moon, invented by-pass surgery, created computer networks and satellite communications and is now exploring the brave new frontiers of genetic engineering.'

'Child's play,' Shivanand said chuckling, 'compared with the Goan monsoon.'

'I am not afraid of a little rain.'

'Heavy duty canvas,' Shivanand said, 'and don't you forget it. Must run. Love to Gita and Radhika. And buy yourself a good pair of gumboots!'

I was not a complete neophyte. No Goan, no matter how many years or distant an expatriate, is wholly uninformed of the meaning of the monsoon. It is as much a social event as a grand climatic tour deforce and begins, quite properly, early in April. In the towns and villages of the interior, the heat descends in a shimmering haze, temperature and humidity soar, and the great exodus to the beaches begins. Here, the balmy pre-monsoon breezes blow in from the sea all day and all night, cooled by the moisture heavy in the air. Swimming as the tide comes in – and only as the tide comes in! – is as invigorating as a whirlpool bath. Seafood is never better. The precipitation far out in the Indian Ocean increases the content of salt in the water and the fish are fatter and tastier for it. All along the Goan coastline, the salt pans are dug broader and deeper, to four feet and more, to form breeding ponds. These are flooded at high tide by sea water swarming with an abundance of baby fish. They feed on algae and in three months' time, when the monsoon settles in, are ready for the table. Fish with names as exotic as their flavour:

Heart and Home

choncul and candoeur, cocoro, shetuk and veleu. Crab, mussel, clam and oyster come into their own. Pineapple and jackfruit appear in the marketplace and in May, the peerless malcurada mango is ripe on the branch. The garafaos of feni, laid down six months earlier, are guaranteed to keep the chill from the bones and the blues away in the long, lean, rainy months.

In every rural household a ritual unfolds. Sea salt is bought in kilos and stored in bamboo baskets lined with dried cow-dung to absorb moisture and keep the salt dry. Roofs are repaired and loose and broken tiles replaced. Firewood is chopped and stocked, floor to ceiling, in mud-walled outhouses. Dried sheaves of palm leaves, arranged in layers of interwoven latticework and lashed to bamboo frames, are used as rain shields. Vast quantities of sun-dried and salted fish are packed away in earthenware containers. All manner of pickles and preserves are prepared. Small bamboo mats are laid down on every patio with chillies and other condiments spread thickly over to catch the last of the summer sunshine. But the greatest care of all is reserved for the garafaos of feni, copiously sampled to test for taste, strength and maturity and then stored for swift and easy access in those moments of monsoon crisis which occur with such happy regularity twice a day, every day.

One would imagine that, barricaded with such severity, the average Goan would mope his way through the monsoon. Nothing could be further from the truth. Ask any Goan, resident or expatriate, when he loves Goa best and he will tell you, 'When it rains.' If you live in any of the great metropolitan centres in India's monsoon belt, this may seem strange, if not inexplicable. I live and work in Bombay and while I know that the monsoon will bring some relief from the oppressive heat, if asked to be honest about it, I would say that there is no more dismal season in the year. There is no joy to be found in the light, passing shower, no natural theatre in the angry violence of a heavy monsoon cloudburst, no awe at the torrential downpours of July. The rain arrives in Bombay only to collide with the very worst of urban realities: concrete and steel, stripped of all humanness, tower greyly above the miseries of the streets, obscure the grandeur of massed, black, low-slung cloud and the dazzling antics of forked lightning, muffle the cannon-rolls of thunder to muted, distant abstractions. And when the rain finally comes to ground, it is not embraced by good clean earth; there is no rejuvenating symbiosis, and the seasonal fecundity of green and growing things is given the vile urban lie: muck, steaming garbage on street corners, drains choked beyond hope of retrieval; and floods of waist-deep stagnant water, when the city simply closes down.

That's when I remember my first Goan thunderstorm which was, without question, arranged for the greater good of my education on the upper balcony of Rockheart on the beach at Candolim. It was the end of May and when Sawant suggested that we batten down the canvas awnings (Shivanand had had his way!), I scoffed.

'The monsoon,' I said, not quite able to keep the impatience out of my voice, 'is a good three weeks away. There is absolutely no need to panic, Sawant. I refuse to be cooped up without a view. We shall put the awnings down in the first week of June.'

'You can never tell about the rains, sahib,' Sawant cautioned gently, 'the fishermen expect an early monsoon.'

I shooed him off and was just as firm with Joaquim a few days later when he dropped in at the house one morning with a brace of lobsters.

'Big rain come early, sah,' he warned, 'I tell from sea and fish shoals. Fast current, even at low tide. Bad waves. Fish afraid, sah. They deep, very deep in water. You put canvas up soon, sah.'

'Even if it does rain early, Joaquim,' I said, 'we can put the canvas up in an hour. Where's the rush?'

'Monsoon break with bad storm, sah.'

But I shooed him off as well.

On 3 June, I stood in the garden with Sawant and waved at blue cloudless skies and a sparkling ocean as if it were all my own doing. 'See what I mean, Sawant. We'll fix the canvas on the fifth or sixth.'

Sawant looked distinctly troubled.

That evening I sat on the balcony with a drink to watch the sunset. There was no breeze. Not a leaf stirred. The pariah kites which began their gliding, swooping, plummeting hunt for supper at this time of day were nowhere in sight. The fruit bats, with their febrile, twittering arabesques, were strangely absent; usually, no sooner the light began to fade, they were out in hundreds. There was a swollen, ominous calm to the sea. Then a thick black line appeared where sea met sky, as though drawn with a felt tip marker with exact precision from one end of the horizon to the other. At first I thought it was a trick of the light. The sun had just set in a perfectly clear sky. The evening star shone brilliantly in the gathering dusk. The afterglow of twilight was held captive in the rising and falling breakers; their whitecaps were washed with a pale, rose phosphorescence while the sea glowed still with the prismatic colours of sunset.

But I had not been deceived. The thick black line was now a deep, dark grey wash moving towards me across the lower sky with a furious, roiling turbulence, driven by a strong wind from the southwest. The palms began to sway and bend. The sea changed colour swiftly even as I looked, from a light blue flecked with rose, to a restless blue-green, then a heaving, frothing metallic grey. The waves rose with the wind, cresting ever more swiftly, breaking with fury on to the shore at the highest line of the tide. Rolling thunderclaps exploded one into the other. Forked lightning whiplashed across the black, thundering clouds. A thick fog of rain hurtled across the beach. The storm hit Rockheart with a tearing, rending suddenness which caught me wholly unprepared. The gale crashed into the roof, dislodging and hurling loose tiles high over the palms. I heard Sawant's faint, muffled shout from below, 'Sahib, jaldi andar ajao!' I rushed into the master bedroom and took shelter behind a wall. The wind howled through the house. It tore the mosquito net off the four-poster and paintings off the walls. I heard a loud crack then a violent crash. One of the teak doors of the main wardrobe which had been left slightly ajar, had been torn off its hinges and hurled to the floor.

The next ten minutes were utter chaos. Six inches of water covered the verandas and bedroom floors. It took all of our strength before Sawant, Anil and I got the canvas awnings down and lashed. It couldn't have been worse if we were battening down in high seas in a gale. But minutes after we were done, the storm blew over as swiftly as it began. One moment, mindless savagery; the next, an eerie calm. Nature had put on a display worthy of Wagner in full cry. The storm was fully spent. I could not see the sky for the stars and the earth smelled of life newly and richly risen; for me, then and forever, divine revelation in a minor chord. Only the debris remained to tell of the storm's passage. Two of the oldest palms had fallen. Some of the raised flower-beds had been scythed down to mush. Dead birds and bats lay broken on the sand. Well over a dozen tiles had been blown off the roof. And the cupboard door was submerged under water on the bedroom floor, mute testimony to the ignorance of its owner. We set about cleaning up. I had got my comeuppance in spades, but to his eternal credit, not by word or look did Sawant say, 'I told you so.'

In the weeks that followed, I learned like all Goans do, to love the rains. To live in Goa during the monsoon is to observe, with awe and gratitude, nature at its reincarnating best. In villages many miles inland, the sound of the breakers may be heard, as wave after fifteen-foot wave hurtles onto the shore with a spine-tingling, tumultuous roar. As far as you can see, every shade of green imaginable greets the eye. The valley floors are covered with young paddy fields, rippling lakes of emerald, flirting with the wind, anticipating the harvest months ahead. And nature throws in a bonus: no matter how hard it rains, there is natural drainage; in moments the soil absorbs the water and is firm and springy underfoot; for every two days of rain there is a day of sunshine when all of Goa's splendours are, virtually, at your feet.

I walk a great deal in Goa in the monsoon. The land is green and fragrant. The views are spectacular and if you are lucky (as I was one August evening when I walked for an hour from Rockheart, through the village, along the winding road up the Sinquerim hill to the lighthouse at the Fort of Aguada) there, across the estuary of the River Mandovi, the lights of Panjim at dusk glittered like a thousand fireflies, blessed, high above, with the arcing benediction of a perfect rainbow.

Our house is built on an acre of sand, a natural rectangle, within hailing distance of the sea. To reach it, one has to walk well over a hundred and fifty metres from the end of the tarred road which services the vaddo, across the sand, towards the sea. To our left, a sand-dune covered by scrub and inhabited, variously, by mongooses, jackals, kingfishers, wild pheasants and the occasional snake, descends to a deep gully which separates the house and its surroundings from the road. In summer, we take the short cut down the gully, skirting a venerable banyan tree, but in the rains the gully is transformed into a miniature creek, where the tide, swollen by rain, foaming and frothing across the dune, brings hundreds of fish. A family of herons takes residence in the banyan tree and feeds elegantly on the fish.

In May, the sand is hot enough to sear the feet through canvas espadrilles (and quarter boil an egg buried in it for ten minutes). Three weeks of rain and all is forgiven. A soft carpet of thick green moss covers and firms the sand. Tortoises appear overnight; where, one wonders, do they disappear to the rest of the year? An effulgence of frogs give voice in irrepressible chorus at sunset. Thousands of fireflies flicker in the trees like fairy lights. And the gulmohars are set aflame with crimson blossom.

When I was a child, the months of April, May and the first fortnight of June were set aside for a celebration of the nascent monsoon. We moved, en masse, from the ancestral home in the village of Saligao to a large, rambling house on the beach in Calangute. There the family (fifteen strong: grandparents, parents, assorted aunts and uncles, siblings, two dogs, a cat named Susegade, a cousin priest who said mass for our flock each morning at the dining table and a bachelor uncle with a roving eye) spent the summer and saw in the first week or two of the monsoon. Every few days my bachelor uncle would dress to the nines (jacket and tie and jaunty fedora), fasten his trousers back at the ankles with bicycle clips, unfurl an umbrella, mount an ancient bicycle and cycle off into the mist and drizzle, whistling the latest Portuguese music hall ditty. Nothing overt was said of these forays, but reading between the lines I gathered they had to do with affairs of the heart. Straight as an arrow he went and I awaited his return eagerly, sitting with patience and not a little discomfort on the hard bench on the balcao of our house. It was well worth the trouble, for the speed and rock-steadiness of his departure was not anywhere as impressive as the waywardness of his return after romancing in the rain. He weaved between the palm trees, collar askew, tie out of place, hair tousled, guiltily rumpled, tinkling the bicycle bell furiously at real or imagined transgressors to his right to the road. The whistle was replaced by a joyful tenor giving full voice to a romantic mando and luscious memories (which never failed to frighten the pigs). God's grace and a little luck saw him safely home, always in high good spirits, and always ready for a meal of awesome variety and proportion.

It says a great deal for my grandfather's sense of balance that the family took all of this in its stride. Indeed, I do not recall a word of censure directed at my uncle; nor do I remember him ever being late beyond a half hour of his appointed time, or cheerful beyond a certain degree of high spiritedness. Many years later I learned to appreciate the other reason for my uncle's glowing well-being. Feni in the rain. It transforms the monsoon to a thing of beauty and a joy forever. Boredom and monotony are put to flight. One learns to appreciate nuance and subtlety. It is one of the truest of Goan rituals. An easy chair is set upon a high balcony or some other position of vantage. A side table is drawn up at half an arm's length. Bottle and glass are set on table. Four fingers splashed in. Take your first long sip. On cue, an impressive cloudburst does a theatrical turn: rolling thunderclaps, forked lightning and a brief but torrential downpour are orchestrated for your pleasure alone. The hot boiled gram with chilli and lime, and the marinated baby prawns grilled over charcoal make perfect foils to your second and third fenis, and when, on your fourth (and last but you make no promises) you decide to conjure up another of nature's displays – and succeed! – you begin to understand, as all of us have learned to do, that anything is possible in Goa in the rains.

But the feni must be true of heart. I drink from my private monsoon stock (loftily proofed), unbranded, distilled by a genius with a name I shall never reveal, who practises

Heart and Home

his art in a village which must forever remain secret and unattainable as the Grail. Yet, if you drop in at Rockheart in September, I shall share some of my feni with you and a memorable dinner as well. Perhaps a few kindred spirits will join us, with a guitar or two, and sing mandos for their supper. We shall talk of all manner of inconsequential things of great importance, and take a walk on the beach in a light but comfortable drizzle, with the moonspun magic of the monsoon all about us.

The end of my first monsoon in Goa found me light-headed and lyrical and in no mood to put pen to anything as mundane as prose. So I composed a few lines of unworthy verse:

> Born of summer flame
> and marauding gale
> Answerable to no man
> or God the rains descend
>
> All is mist, refracted image
> Palms yearn for flight
> The earth
> risen newly
> with languor and desire
> remembers
>
> Seed slakes thirst
> The bud returning
> refuses to consider its exile
> Emerald takes residence again
> in the reverential eye

Saint Anthony
stern, yielding
coy as any nun
Patron of the Rains
presides (amid much grumbling)
over the illusion
of a brief retreat

A windblown windfall time
What better reason for
the sacramental prawn
dried and deified
the pot-pourri of spices
mackerel in brine
necklaces of onions
taradiddles of trotters
vinegared young mangoes
a veritable merriment
of sausages hung from the
kitchen ceiling
to dry?

An apothecary's blessings
for the well-being of the inner man
in this most woesome time
of glorious siege

Until the sandbar across the river
wonders if the sea is safe again
for fishing

Heart and Home

and urged by holy water
and a proper ceremony
agrees to go away.

In the turning of two moons
the harvest will sing.

3

Boon Companions

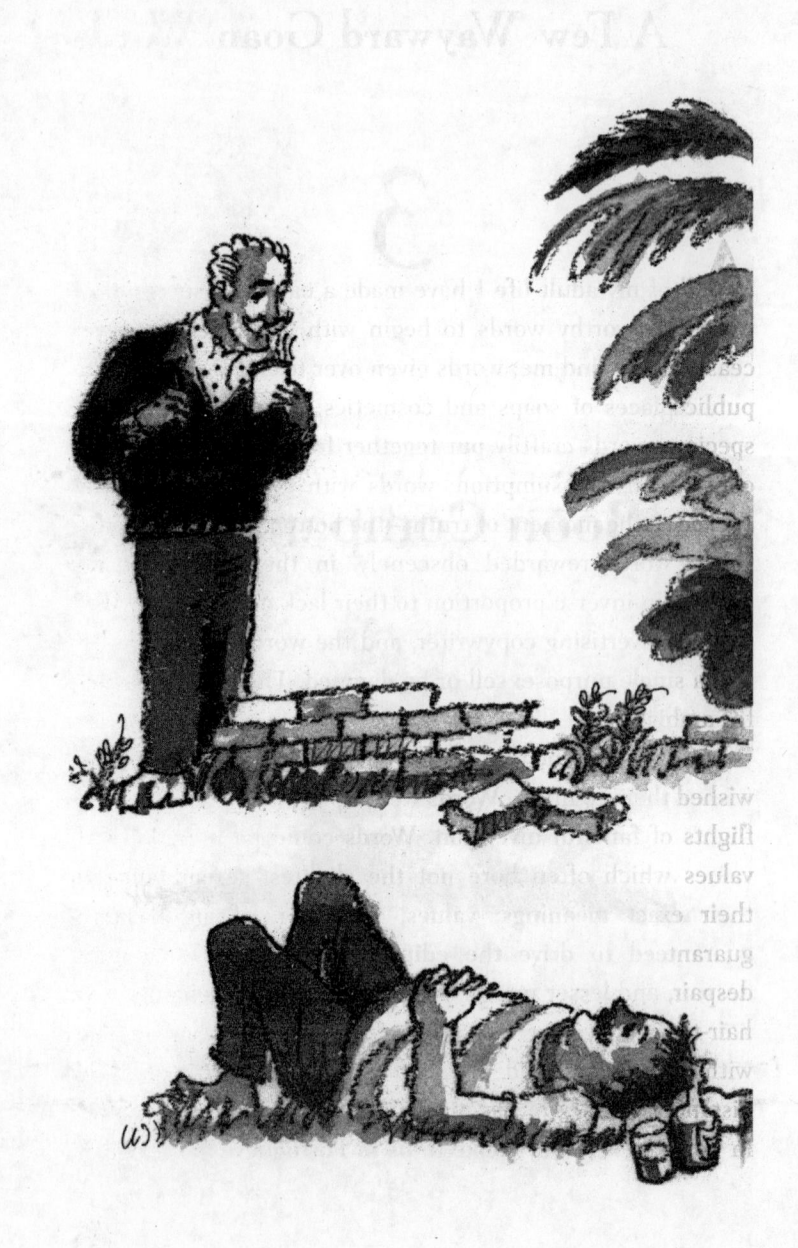

A Few Wayward Goan Words

All of my adult life I have made a career of sorts out of words. Unworthy words to begin with, as my peers never ceased to remind me; words given over to indecent praise in public places of soaps and cosmetics, baby food and beer; specious words craftily put together for the greater glory of conspicuous consumption; words with a weather eye ever cocked to the moment of truth – the bottom line of a balance sheet; words rewarded obscenely, in the opinion of my betters, in inverse proportion to their lack of honest worth. I was an advertising copywriter, and the words I put together had a single purpose: sell or be damned. There was no room for ambiguity.

Goa taught me that words mean just about anything you wished them to mean. Words were ripe with the potential for flights of fanciful invention. Words could be invested with values which often bore not the slightest resemblance to their exact meanings; values, moreover, of an elasticity guaranteed to drive the editors of the O.E.D. to quiet despair, and lesser mortals such as Bernie Finklebaum Jr. to hair-tearing, teeth-gnashing frenzies. I grew up in Bombay with Portuguese and Konkani vocabularies truncated by distance and lack of usage. My parents talked to each other in Portuguese. They spoke to us in Portuguese and English, often using both languages in a single sentence, while we replied in English, the language we used in school. They instructed the servants in Konkani; we coped with Bombay at large in broken Marathi and pidgin Hindi. In this bewildering polylingual chatter, Goan words soon lost their multifaceted personalities; were gradually shorn of drama, scope, character, muscularity; became the brief and precise descriptions so dear to the soulless world view of lexicographers and tourist phrase books. Thus, that splendid universe of a word, susegade, came to mean 'lazy'; phale from the Konkani was 'tomorrow'; saudade was vaguely equivalent to 'looking back'; alegria to an ill-defined form of 'well-being'; malcreado, that scathing assemblage of consonant and vowel, to a mere 'ne'er-do-well'; simpatica, to cloudy, emasculated 'fellow-feeling.'

As we left Goa when I was ten years old, my primary education in the creative harnessing of the wayward Goan word only began seventeen years later when I returned with Rahul Singh, an editor with the *Times of India*, (a journey I've mentioned briefly in this book). Rahul was to report on – and I to observe – a public opinion poll which would decide Goa's future. The issue in balance was critical; would Goa retain its unique historical and cultural identity and remain independent within the Republic of India under a benign Centre, or would it be made to merge without trace with Maharashtra, the enormous, hugely successful political entity to the north, generally acknowledged to be the first state in the Indian Union. I was vigorously partisan: Goa for the Goans! Rahul, keenly neutral, as all good journalists should be and rarely are, reserved editorial judgement.

We drove down in my flame-red Standard Herald, an ancient machine just short of antiquity, recently painted to camouflage a creaky provenance. With the Herald there was joy in the journey, but you were never quite certain you'd get there; the Maserati red and the black racing stripe was the perfect example of the triumph of hope over experience. But on this day all went splendidly. She sprinted along straights, caromed down hillsides, negotiated hairpin curves and dizzy gradients with a sprightly and youthful brio. In eight short hours we were at the foothills of the Ghats, where the mountain range which flanks the length of Western India descends to the Goan plateau, river and valley, rain forest and sea. We were an hour from the border town of Ponda and as twilight settled on the land, I felt a sudden and wonderful déjà vu, unlike anything I had ever known, a sense of revival, of previous belonging, of returning at long last to an original and beloved place, and to first and best purposes.

The freak storm broke near Ponda. One moment there were bright early stars in a pale sky; the next, a fierce hurricane, whipping the tree tops into a dark green blur; low, black, rolling cloud; thunder claps like cannon fire; brilliant forks of blue lightning. Then the rain, a few, slow, heavy drops like gunshots on the windscreen, turning, in seconds, to a lashing, blinding torrent. Visibility dropped to a few yards. The gale drove the rain at the car in horizontal sheets. The potholes in the road filled with mud and slush. When we ploughed over one, a wave of thick brown muck hit the car. The wipers only served to spread the misery. We crawled along, stopping ever more frequently to rush out, clear the windscreen and rear window and rush in again, wet to the skin. An hour of this and we were ready to give it all up, lie down, and perish.

Then, in the near distance, I saw the flicker of an oil lamp under a spreading banyan tree. Hearth and Home. Frabjous sight! I turned the Herald hard over and skidded to a halt under the banyan bare inches from the entrance of a hut made of mud bricks and thatch, with hard cow-dung floors. A gang of mundkars, just in from the fields, huddled about a roaring wood fire. An Angel of Mercy dispensed instant salvation into small earthenware bowls from a large garafao balanced on a sturdy hip – strong, potent caju feni, neat, to the quivering brimful, sipped at once so as not to waste a single, precious drop. A rough-and-ready peasant sorpotel, with an aroma to reduce strong men to tears, simmered and bubbled in an enamel pot suspended over the fire. A straw basket was piled to overflowing with steaming hot sanas.

We ordered two bowls of feni. Down the hatch. The promising glow in the region of my belly button called for encouragement. Two more. Goa shall forever remain free! Another round, dear lady. Despite your advanced years, there is a beckoning lilt to curve and sway, to thrust of hip, to cozening eye. Bless you. Storm? Ho hum … One more for the road? Why not? A light supper of sorpotel and sanas. A ribald sally or two with these noble sons of the soil. Wonderful chaps. This round's on us, and the next but last, and away we went. Who's afraid of a little rain? Heel on accelerator, toe on brake, clutch in first, I revved the engine and shot off into a racing, skidding start. Straighten her up. Foot down hard. Out of my way Mansell! Eat my dust Alain Frost! Goa, here we come. Laid back and laughing. Never in my life had I felt such swift and glorious rejuvenation, such a sublime sense of psychic replenishment. Was this what they meant by the word susegade?

We arrived at the Tourist Hotel in Calangute at midnight. Our rooms overlooked the courtyard where the Herald, now in the saddest hour of a gallant career, languished. The racing red was a murky maroon; the front bumper hung askew; the left rear tyre was fast giving up the ghost; the engine had leaked dangerous puddles; the windscreen was an entomologist's joy, covered from edge to edge with a rich assortment of squashed insect life. Despite the caju feni I felt a trifle squashed myself. I would have to pamper the Herald the next morning. The desk clerk was obliging if a bit too well-humoured for the occasion. Much as I loved the green and pleasant land of my ancestors, comic relief at midnight puts affection for the auld sod to a severe test.

'Been in the wars then?' he said, chuckling.

'You should see the other fellow,' I said wearily.

'You want a boy to clean the car?'

'If it's not too much trouble.'

'I know two reliable lads ... ' – again that chuckle.

'One will do.'

'Brothers,' he said, grinning broadly, 'they work as a team.'

'All right then.' I was too tired to argue. I was ready to hire a family and a dog if I could get to bed in the next five minutes.

'Very cheap,' he said, eyes alight with mischief and merriment, 'two for the price of one.'

'Could you send them up at eight in the morning?'

'Certainly, sir.'

At eight on the dot, the team announced their arrival with a series of thunderous knocks on the door. Two dishevelled, unkempt figures, bloodshot and bleary-eyed, stood in the doorway swaying on their heels. They were short and plump. They wore identical boxer shorts, clenched-fist T-shirts and expressions of scowling resentment. There was a potstill and roast pig smell about them. Tweedledum and Tweedledee. Drunk as lords.

Tweedledum stuck out a grimy hand.

'Bartholomew,' he said, taking his time about it, syllable by careful syllable.

Tweedledee gave him an affectionate, bone-crunching slap on the back.

'This my brodder,' he said, 'Nickname Barty. I am known to all of vaddo as Bostao ... Bostao,' he said again, 'Bostao,' repeating the name several times as if to make certain he had it right, first giving full play to the consonants, slurring the vowels, then dramatically changing form and pitch, the hard sounds got short shrift, the vowels a loving roll. 'You know how say now, Bostao!'

A response seemed called for.

'Bostao,' I said, experimentally, rendering the second syllable as in 'miaow.' It seemed to serve the purpose. Bostao looked pleased. Bartholomew scowled and dug him in the ribs; the conventions were yet to be concluded. Bartholomew hitched up his trousers in a crisp, businesslike fashion.

'Your good name, sah?'

'Frank,' I said warily.

'Franco!' Bartholomew exclaimed. A free and easy interpretation not, I had to admit, without a certain Gothic merit.

'Francisco,' said Bostao, getting into the spirit of the occasion.

'You want we clean your car, Franco?'

'We charge five rupees.'

Bartholomew dug Bostao in the ribs, or was it the other way around? I was beginning to get confused. Bostao said, 'My brodder and me go talk now. You wait.'

They retreated down the corridor, out of earshot, and plunged into heated confabulation in loud whispers which, as the minutes wore on, became more vigorous, loudly recriminatory with much throwing about of arms and finger-waving under noses, threatening, with a push here, a shove there, to erupt into violence. The desk clerk shouted up the stairwell, 'Stop that racket, you clowns!' He was clearly a figure of authority. An immediate silence descended on the landing. The brodders shuffled back to the door.

'How many days you want we wash car?' Bostao asked.

'Ten days,' I said, 'not later than eight in the morning. My friend and I make an early start.'

'What you pay?'

'Five rupees for each wash.'

Scornful laughter.

'Franco make joke,' Bostao said.

'Francisco good sensayuma,' Bartholomew said.

'Very well, how much do you want?'

'For ten days, two hundred rupees him,' Bostao said cocking a thumb at his brother.

'Same two hundred rupees him,' Bartholomew added, with a nod of the head towards his sibling.

There was no room for misunderstanding, but I was beginning to enjoy this. The unGodly would be laid low. Ancient reflexes began doing little jigs. If I had worn long sleeves, I would have rolled them up, first one, then the other, fist clenched, arm out-thrust, the enemy transfixed with a hard look. I had learned to bargain in the cut-and-thrust of Goan village fish markets. No holds barred. The weakest to the wall. To the strong the kingfish. Slit-eyed and ready for battle, I said, 'Five rupees, not a paise more.'

'Fifteen,' Bostao said.

'Five.'

'Twelve,' Bartholomew suggested, testing the water again.

'Five.'

'Ten?' Bostao offered, but his voice held no conviction.

'Five.'

'Nine,' Bartholomew said in a sad, little whisper, 'a man must eat.'

'And drink,' I said, relenting a bit, 'seven each and fish curry for lunch. Take it or leave it.'

But I allowed them honour in defeat. They wanted an advance of ten rupees and I let them have it, a singular lack of judgement as it turned out. Grabbing the notes from my hand, they took the stairs two at a time, swaying from wall to wall as they went. 'The clerk will give you mops and a bucket,' I called after them. A burst of derisory laughter and they were gone.

They returned half an hour later and, observing their dramatic entry into the courtyard from the veranda, I knew where they'd been. Poorer by twenty rupees, drunker by a bottle of cheap feni, and now alarmingly up the spout. I thought I knew all there was to know about the demon drink, but I had never in my life seen two men as drunk as this and still ambulatory. They made their way to the car in a lurching fandango, narrowly missing each other, bouncing of a wall here, sprawling into a piece of shrubbery there, buckets and mops abandoned en route, a watery trail marking their chaotic way. They staggered at last to an uncertain halt before the Herald and, overcome by a sense of accomplishment, lay down on the bonnet, crossed their legs, reclined against the windscreen and passed out.

'Hey,' I called out loudly, 'get up.'

Bartholomew opened an eye, woke and moved by a sudden and irresistible need for action, gave Bostao a hearty shove. With a slow flailing of arms and legs, Bostao rolled languidly off the bonnet and landed with a loud thump on the concrete. He rose, in bits and painful pieces, reassembled himself with some difficulty and glared resentfully at the Herald. Then he began to stalk it, taking exaggerated, menacing strides in a clockwise direction around the car, peering intently at this and that. Bartholomew followed close on his heels, Indian style, keen not to miss out on the action. They stopped at the boot, did a smart heel and turn, and stalked the Herald once more, anti-clockwise this time.

Bostao discovered the deflating tyre, took quick offence, aimed a huge kick at it, missed and landed on his rump. Bartholomew followed suit and had better luck. With a sigh, the tyre collapsed. Exhausted by this burst of creative activity, they returned to the Herald, clambered up onto the bonnet and assumed their earlier, restful positions.

Was there a Goan word for rage? I weighed my options: flight; good humour; the Law; a baseball bat; abject entreaty.

There was a deprecatory cough at my shoulder. The desk clerk, leaning on a doorjamb, arms folded, legs crossed, well entertained this fine morning. 'Clowns,' he said appreciatively, then shouted out, 'Malcreados!' The reaction was astonishing. Here was a word I would do well to memorize. Galvanized, Bostao and Bartholomew leaped up as though bitten. Bostao smacked the palm of his hand sharply against his forehead and, guilt-stricken, charged off into the shrubbery. He returned holding a mop triumphantly aloft and began polishing the corner of the left headlamp with great dedication. Bartholomew, meanwhile, was bent on repentant knees before the dead tyre, stroking the treads. Then he shook his head sorrowfully, smacked the palm of his hand sharply against his forehead and disappeared, guilt-stricken, into the shrubbery. He returned with a bucket of water. Bostao tried to get the mop into the bucket, missed, and seized with the humour of the moment, fell about with wild laughter. Bartholomew had even less luck. With shouts of encouragement they urged each other mirthfully on. Then, as one, they grabbed the bucket, swung it forward and backward, shouted, 'One, two three ... ' and hurled bucket and contents at the windscreen, missing, once more, with

A Few Wayward Goan Words

ease. Arm in arm, breaking into gay snatches of a popular mando, they wandered off, immensely pleased with a good morning's work.

The clerk and I watched them as they went. I with awe; the clerk admiringly. He put a comforting arm around my shoulders – I had become one of the family – and laughed.

'Susegade,' he said.

Now where had I heard that word before?

*

I would hear it again, ten years later to be exact, in indignant reproof, on a beach very much like this one. Gita and I had established base in a bungalow on an exquisite headland in the seaside village of Anjuna. We had taken the cottage for a month. Anjuna was the ideal centre for exploration. It lay midway along a coastline extending twenty-five miles from Fort Aguada in the south to Arambol in the north. We took off after breakfast each day in a Maruti Gypsy in search of our perfect acre by the sea. The mornings were wonderfully exhilarating, seventeen degrees, a nip in the air, crisp, clear and fragrant, as near to an Alpine spring day as you were likely to get in the Tropics. Cool enough indeed for our neighbour, Colonel Jeremiah Saldanha, to sport a lively red cardigan and a natty scarf embroidered with crossed sabres and a stallion's head, insignia of his regiment, the Rajasthan Light Horse. The mahogany walking-stick with an ivory tiger's head he had been presented by the regiment on his retirement was an affectation, no more. He took long military strides in a perfectly straight line as though inspecting the ranks, swinging and twirling the cane as he went. The soldier's carriage was never less than erect. Dignity sat well on the slim shoulders. A certain haughtiness to the profile lay claim to distinguished ancestry, as did the thick white moustache curled at the ends, and the careful, measured choice of words. When Colonel Saldanha said, 'And a very good morning to you, Sir,' the Good Lord saw to it that the sky was a bright and burnished blue adorned with just the right touch of fluffy cirrus with an acrobatic flock of swallows swooping and soaring at regulation height.

For the past three days, Colonel Saldanha had paced up and down before his house, hands clasped behind his back, deep in serious and complex thought. The quarter acre before the house was long and narrow flanked on either side by wooden fencing all but hidden from view by a riot of bougainvillaea, cactus and jungle creeper. The hedgerows came to an abrupt end at the far edge of the property, which had been left clear to allow unhampered view of headland, cliff and sea. It was here that Colonel Saldanha paced (twenty measured strides) from the end of one hedgerow to the other. And it was here that I drove past in the Gypsy every morning, stopping briefly to pay my respects.

'Good morning, Colonel.'

'And a very good morning to you, Sir,' – a pause, a courtly bow to Gita, a softer tone, 'Madam.'

'It's a lovely day for beach combing,' Gita said.

'And where are we off to this morning?'

'Tiracol,' I said.

The Colonel approved. 'Magnificent fort. Excellent position. Impossible to storm. Thirty cannon. A thousand yard range. The entire bay covered. Played havoc with Adil

Shah's fleet. Deserved no less, the scoundrel. Best Portuguese coastal fortification in the north. Don't miss the chapel in the central courtyard. Nothing like it in Goa. Splendid beach as well. Good luck to you, Sir.'

The following morning Colonel Saldanha was at it again, pacing away. The mahogany cane had been replaced with a hunting stick. He wore a deer-stalker and carried a sketching pad and a pink felt-tip pen. A reconnoitring mission, no doubt. He walked briskly as usual from one end of the property to the other, along its length, along its width, diagonally, pausing at various points to observe the lie of the land. Every so often, the hunting stick would be planted in the ground. Colonel Saldanha would perch on the open end and make elaborate sketches and notes on his pad. Curiosity got the better of me.

'Planning to build, Colonel?'

'Mongooses,' Colonel Saldanha said, 'killing my chickens in the backyard. Sat up three nights in a row with the Remington. Sight's not what it used to be. Missed the blighter. Six foot wall with an overhang the only answer.'

I had seen mongooses hunting for snakes in the mangrove dunes. They were beautiful animals, superbly muscled, with thick, golden-brown pelts. A full-grown male ran to four-and-a-half, five feet. Sleek, swift and deadly. The unchallengeable predator. Even with excellent vision and a marksman's accuracy, it was next to impossible to shoot one. They moved like shadows, low to the ground, taking advantage of the skimpiest cover and when they attacked it was with the ferocity and speed of a jaguar. They hunted at night, and while they showed a marked preference for wild prey, the larger snakes, bandicoot and hare, they would often raid domestic livestock, killing and carrying away chickens and piglings.

'Do the hedgerows keep them out?' I asked.

'Close packed cactus, wild bougainvillaea. Thorns the size of your thumb. They don't like that. Can't have bio-fencing at the front of the house though. Just not done. Here, take a look at this. Value the memsahib's opinion.'

It was a modest piece of masonry. Fifteen yards long, six feet off the ground with the overhang, two laterite bricks thick. Even with the decorative interlining, sketched in lighter blue lines (an artistic side to the Colonel one would never have expected) it would be child's play to a gang of professional bricklayers: half a day for the trench; a day to dress the laterite stones; a couple of shifts for the laying and cementing and Bob's your uncle.

So much for the innocence of the uninitiated. The next day six strong men and true made their way purposefully down the road and plunged at once into earnest discussion with the Colonel. He had pasted his sketches on large cardboard squares and now held them up one by one, as though at a meeting with his field commanders, pointing here and there with the tip of the walking-stick while he explained each chart. First, the Grand Plan of Action. Then the details: elevation and cross-sections; angle and depth of overhang; the staggered positioning of the laterite bricks at each level. The briefing complete, led by the Colonel in smart military formation, they marched up and down the path where the wall was to be built, peering intently at the ground, taking measurement after measurement with a carpenter's tape which became, every so often, hopelessly entangled with the mahogany walking-stick. The Colonel scribbled furiously in his sketch pad, pausing now and again to take a few quick steps backwards, followed by the team. Then, as one, they shaded their eyes and looked keenly at the horizon beyond the property, before huddling together to begin earnest discussion yet again. Clearly, there were thorny issues still to be resolved. At eleven thirty the Colonel glanced at his watch. It was a signal for instant inaction. The bricklayers assumed postures of grateful ease. The Colonel disappeared into the house and emerged moments later with two brown bottles held by the necks in his left hand, and six tumblers, one into the other, in his right which he held precariously aloft like a juggler at the beginning of an act. The bricklayers responded with alacrity. One by one they came thirstily forward while the Colonel poured generous portions into the tumblers and passed them around. Once more, the bricklayers relapsed on the lawn, while the Colonel regarded them approvingly. 'Good men,' he would say to me later, 'salt of the earth.'

That night I began a fresh entry in my Diary.

Colonel Saldanha's Great Wall ... Day 1

It may be entirely possible that, in the long and chequered history of brilliant human constructions, greater purpose has been displayed in the creation of immortal works. The permanence of the Pyramids of Giza comes to mind, to say nothing of the matchless inscrutability of the Sphinx. The Taj Mahal stands serenely apart, imperishable monument to love's glorious folly. Consider the sheer presence of the Eiffel Tower or the abiding dignity of mankind's most impressive ditch, the Panama Canal. Even the Tower of Babel, however unfortunate the denouement, had its moments. And now we have Colonel Jeremiah Saldanha's Great Wall. The prophetic ring to his given name has not been misplaced. The flourish of trumpets one hears in the distance is well-deserved. We see that mere scale is no deterrent to grand human endeavour. An age-old drama unfolds anew. The Saga begins ...

Colonel Saldanha's Great Wall ... Day 2

8 a.m. Every one of the vaddo's fifty-three dogs begin to bark in a discordant, ear-splitting chorus. The village cocks, who will not be intimidated by a pack of lowly mongrels, take the high ground and begin to crow in the most piercing octave known to man or beast. The cause of all this commotion is the laboured wheezing of a heavy vehicle in heroic if unequal struggle with the gradient leading to Colonel Saldanha's property. Here a motley crowd has gathered in noisy expectation. Ferreting children. Officious matriarchs. Young layabouts. Arthritic elders. They mill about, observing the truck's asthmatic progress, passing rude comments on its age and ability, taking friendly wagers on the likelihood of its imminent demise. But when the vehicle eventually staggers to a halt before Colonel

Saldanha's lawn and settles into the dust with a long shudder and a burst of steam from an overheated radiator, a loud cheer goes up. The truck is piled high with undressed, rectangular laterite stones, well beyond its legal limit of carriage. The six strong men and true sit on top of the bricks with their legs dangling over the sides. They do not smile. Their expressions, full of high purpose, tell us at once that they are on a mission of critical importance to the nation. These are men of the moment. They will seize the day!

Colonel Saldanha meets them at the entrance to his garden. A maid follows bearing a tray with six large mugs filled with hot, sweet, steaming tea and a platter of generously buttered pois. Breakfast takes a leisurely hour but the time is put to good use. Colonel Saldanha chairs an executive meeting. Strategy is formulated. There are furrowed brows, intense debate, pregnant silences. Then the Colonel, the weight of decision-making behind him, issues a terse command. Heads nod. He points to a line on his property. The unloading of the bricks begin. The gang of six forms a chain from truck to storage point; the driver and his boy, crass mercenaries, who have been left pointedly unbreakfasted, stand on the truck and pass the bricks, one by one, to the real professionals. The bricks are swung from man to man and finally hurled with careless violence onto the lawn causing the sod to fly. They work for an hour and a half with toilet breaks, cigarette breaks, water breaks and mysterious, inexplicable disappearances. At the end of it all, one third of the truck is unloaded. Colonel Saldanha calls the proceedings to a halt.

'Time,' he says benignly, 'for lunch.'

Colonel Saldanha's Great Wall ... Day 3

The bricks are being unloaded.

Colonel Saldanha's Great Wall ... Day 4

The bricks are being unloaded.

Colonel Saldanha's Great Wall ... Day 5

Hurrah! They've done it. But there seems to be a problem. One would have expected a round of quiet congratulation. Smiles and happy nods. An air of exuberance. Nothing of the sort. The Colonel paces up and down lost in brooding thought. He barks a command. The bricklayers rush up and surround him. They huddle together like a rugger scrum. Heads are scratched. Shaken from side to side. Eyes register perplexity and a sense of life's injustice. All is not well. I stop the Maruti.

'Good morning, Colonel.'

'And good morning to you, Sir.' But it is clear from the Colonel's tone that the morning has left much to be desired. The bricklayers slouch about gloomily. Gone is the spring in the step, the sparkle in the eye, the swagger in the stride. They form a dejected chain across the road and begin to move the bricks once more. Like Sisyphus they seem reconciled to doing this for the rest of their lives. When I return at five they are still at it. The entire day has been spent moving the bricks from Colonel Saldanha's property to the other side of the road. Like a stricken commander who will never desert his men, he oversees the movement of each brick to its new home.

What is the meaning of this? I have spent the entire day grappling with the conundrum, quite unable to concentrate on my perfect acre, and am no nearer an answer than when I began. Another of life's great mysteries? It will not go unresolved.

'Why are you moving the bricks, Colonel?'

'A small error of judgement,' the Colonel says, a trifle abruptly. 'They were unloaded over the line of the trench. Any fool can see that. Good day, Sir.'

I have been rapped across the knuckles!

Colonel Saldanha's Great Wall ... Day 7

It has taken a day and a half to move the bricks across the road. But this is understandable. Every time a vehicle comes up the road, the chain tears asunder in all the essential places. The bricklayers take a cigarette break and reassemble. The length of the break depends on the nature of the vehicle. Thus, a motor cycle causes only minor disruption; the chain joins again in a matter of minutes. A bullock cart, on the other hand, brings about total collapse. It takes a good half hour before reconstruction begins.

We have decided to postpone our search for the perfect acre indefinitely. The saga of Colonel Saldanha's Great Wall holds us in thrall. Here is history in the making. What a tale to tell our children!

Colonel Saldanha's Great Wall ... Day 8

Something is seriously amiss. Work has come to a complete standstill. The Colonel paces up and down furiously. The bricklayers saunter about to no good purpose and eventually lie down in the shade of a hedgerow for a little rest. The Colonel rushes into the house, emerges ten minutes later, with an envelope. He licks the flap down. The maid is summoned and given peremptory instructions. She rushes off and returns after half an hour on the pillion of a motor cycle driven at great speed up the hill by a young man with a ponytail and homicidal tendencies. The maid seems not to mind. She holds the young man to her bosom in a tight and tender embrace, but quickly puts six inches of modest distance between them no sooner she sights the Colonel. The letter is handed over, instructions given; the demon driver takes off like a dispatch rider behind enemy lines. The Colonel begins pacing furiously again. The bricklayers are asleep.

'Something the matter, Colonel?'

The Colonel gives me a flinty look. Am I pushing my luck?

'A mere trifle,' he says with quiet dignity, 'I had forgotten to order the cement.'

Colonel Saldanha's Great Wall ... Day 10

One learns something new everyday. There is only one way to dress a chunk of laterite brick. It is laid flat on the ground between two bricklayers. Each man assembles chisel, hammer and scraper. They sit, cross-legged, on either side of the stone and run finger-tips ruminatively over its length, sides, front and rear. This takes ten minutes. They exchange notes. This takes another ten. With a sigh (life is grim; life is earnest) they heave the brick over and run ruminative fingers all over it once again. Then they exchange notes. This takes another ten minutes. Now the business of the day begins. One man holds the brick up; the other takes chisel and hammer and with great delicacy knocks off a small chip. The man holding the brick picks the chip up between thumb and forefinger and holds it up for inspection. He turns it every which way, looking keenly to thickness, size, shape, weight, evenness. Then he shakes his head regretfully. The other man scowls and tries again. And again. And again. Finally, the chip passes muster. He chips away for ten more minutes. Then they take a cigarette break and exchange roles. After an hour the brick is done. After three bricks it is time for lunch.

After lunch it is time for a siesta. And when they get up at four before knocking off for the day at five, conscientious men that they are, they find just about enough time to get one more brick done.

The wise man accepts his limitations.
I will never make a good bricklayer.

Colonel Saldanha's Great Wall ... Day 17

Four days to dig a trench!

I am beginning to get cross. Back at the funny farm in Bombay (the endearing expression our creative people use to describe the advertising agency I own), five of us – two copywriters, two art directors, and one chairman wearing his creative director's hat – lock ourselves in a hotel suite for three days and nights to meet yet another impossible campaign deadline. If, at the end of this brainstorming, we are unable to produce a stunning advertising concept for newspapers, television, hoardings and posters (at a cost to the client of anything between ten and twenty million rupees), our jobs are on the line.

It is not a restful way to earn a living.

And here are these carpet-baggers, these rustic con men, these mere ... mere ... masons! Getting away with blue murder.

Never in the annals of bricklaying have so many taken so long to do so little!

Colonel Saldanha's Great Wall ... Day 20

I have had my first run-in with the good Colonel and while I have emerged victorious from the skirmish, I am not at all sanguine about the outcome of the war. The Colonel, I am convinced, is being taken up the garden path with a vengeance. I made an attempt this morning to lead him to the light.

'A slow and expensive business, Colonel.'
'These things take their time.'
'Yes, of course, but each man must cost you twenty-five or thirty rupees a day ... '
'Twenty-five.'
'With their lunch,' – I pause tactfully; offence must not be given – 'and refreshments, thirty I would imagine, or more. That's roughly two hundred rupees a day for the gang. They've been at it twenty days by my reckoning. Four thousand rupees, Colonel, give or take a few. And all you can show for it is a trench and a truckload of dressed bricks.'

The Colonel seems not to have heard. He looks about him vaguely and spots a laterite stone which has escaped chisel and hammer. He points to it.

'Try lifting that,' he says.

A high voltage career in the advertising business is not the best preparation for a snatch-and-jerk with a laterite brick. I haul the stone up; my lower spine begins to sag. I drop it like – well – like a hot brick. There is a naughty glint in the Colonel's eye.

'It's hard work,' he says. 'These men eat well, as they must. A meal's part of the contract. The drink's on the house. Everybody in Goa has a drink or two before lunch. It's part of the culture. So is the siesta. There's a word for it you'd do well to learn if you plan to live in these parts. It's called susegade. Commit it to memory, young man, susegade.'

But I won't let go of it. 'They work five hours out of an eight hour shift,' I say, 'in my book that's highway robbery.'

The Colonel taps me sharply on the arm with the mahogany walking-stick. I take a quick step back. He has my undivided attention.

'George Bernard Shaw,' he admonishes, waving the cane before my nose, 'once said that there are people who know the price of everything and the value of nothing.'

Got you Jeremiah!

'Not G.B.S. Colonel, Wilde. Oscar Wilde.'

'Oscar who?'

'WILDE!'

'Don't confuse the issue. And there's no need to shout. It's time you grew up, young man, and learned the value of things.'

And he turns on his heel, moustache bristling, and marches off.

Crusty. Very crusty indeed.

Colonel Saldanha's Great Wall ... Day 30

We left Anjuna this morning. I loaded the Gypsy

with a sense of melancholy. It came over me whenever I left Goa like the grey pall of pollution I was returning to. I was going back to Bombay, to ten million people on a single, congested island. A few hundred thousand pursued lives of unimaginable luxury, wholly oblivious to the two million who slept on the streets, the three million who eked out an existence, just barely, in shanty towns, the rest who were crowded like rabbits in a warren in mile upon square mile of soulless tenement blocks. Sullenness and resentment lay heavily in the air. The eyes said it all: they were bleak, leached of hope, forsaken, rarely touched by compassion or a smile.

I was glad when Colonel Saldanha held out an olive branch.

'Time for a drink before you leave?'

He did himself proud. The whisky glasses were Waterford Crystal, the decanter Belgian cutglass, the Scotch, single malt. Macallan, my favourite tipple when I could get it. The Colonel knew how to pay his respects to a Highland Malt: he poured us three fingers each. 'You look like a man who knows his scotch,' he said, smiling, 'but you can have ice and water if you want some.'

I raised my glass.

'Cheers, Colonel,' I said, 'your wall's come along nicely.'

'Not bad going,' he said; then, with a touch of regret, 'it should be up any day now barring the gate.' For a moment or two, he was lost in thought. Then he perked up a bit. 'I shall have Father Anthony bless it, of course, and a party for the workers, a few good friends from the village. Make a jolly evening of it. Pity you won't be here.'

'Sorry about the song and dance on wages, Colonel,' I said. Macallan's like that. 'No offence meant.'

'None taken,' the Colonel said amiably. 'I remember when I was a young man in a hurry' – he laughed – 'ended up chasing my own tail. Goa taught me that getting there is much more fun than arriving, once you learn how to make the most of the journey. Good lads, these workers. Known every one of them, man and boy, twenty-five years. Their fathers built this house. Look at the masonry, the workmanship, the woodwork. Last forever. So will my front wall. Taken its time of course, but the fun we've had! Another drink.'

'Well, perhaps I ... '

'Long journey ahead,' the Colonel said, 'getting there should be fun.' He poured another three fingers of Macallan into my glass. He inclined his head courteously towards Gita, and when she said, 'Thank you, Colonel. Half as much,' he beamed. The Colonel liked a lady who could hold her drink like a man.

We raised our glasses again.

'Took three years to build this house,' the

Colonel said. 'No road then. No trucks. Had to carry every blessed thing up the hill by head load. The noise, the confusion, the dust, the sheer excitement of it all! Cobras and kraits popping up all over the place when we dug the foundations. Impossible to dig a well. Solid rock. Six months before we struck a watershed. Couple of furlongs from the site. Pump too weak for the gradient. Head loads again. Buffalo-skins to a tank at a half-way point. Had to organize a field kitchen for the workers. And ten litres of feni a day. Tremendous fun!'

There is nothing like Macallan to clear the mind. The cobwebs blew away. A fine understanding dawned. I laughed out loud. The wall was an excuse! A grand subterfuge. A wonderful reason for four glorious weeks of fun and games. Had there ever been a mongoose? I sought to make amends. 'Colonel Saldanha,' I began – would I find the words? – 'you are an officer and a gentleman. You have maturity, patience, understanding. In a word ... '

'Simpatica,' Gita said triumphantly.

'I take each day as it comes,' the Colonel said, 'and I try to make the most of it. The army taught me that a straight line is the shortest distance between two points. In Goa I discovered that it's great fun to doodle. Takes time though. Have to unlearn a lot. One day, my young friends, you will learn that simpatica is the only way to be.'

The Colonel walked us to the Gypsy. He shook each of our hands in turn, bowing to Gita as he did so.

'Come again,' he said, 'mea casa, tua casa.'

'My best regards to the mongoose, Colonel.'

The Colonel chuckled.

'If I ever find the blighter!'

... if and when you do, Colonel, I suspect the Remington will miss again. Blame it on simpatica. It has taken me a while to make the word my own, twenty years or so, and there are times still when I'm not quite certain I've lived up to it. But you were right, my honourable Colonel, there is no better way to travel ...

The Sea Wolves Take a Bath

Goa's chequered history is peppered with lively incident and vivid moment. In this colourful miscellany, a handful of rousing encounters of the more unusual kind have become a part of Goan folklore and continue, irresistibly, to engage the public imagination. One such, celebrated in book and film, and vividly recalled in burnished anecdote by eye-witnesses to the event, concerns the Calcutta Light Horse and its German enemy, the Sea Wolves, when, for one stirring fortnight, Goa became the focus of the wrath of a world at war.

I was lucky to be in Goa when the film was made, and luckier still to find myself included in an inner circle of most favoured journalists. In the best tradition of Goan logic, I shall begin where the story ends, high above the windswept reaches and crumbling laterite fortifications of a Portuguese fort, at the highest crest of a hill. It is the last place you would expect to find a tombstone. The inscription spells German names, and the bones which lie in unhallowed ground know only the cry of the kestrel, the blind fury of monsoon storms, the lonely vigil of the cliffside lighthouse. Yet in this last, lost monument to the ruthlessness of a handful of Germans and the implacable courage of their enemies lies a tale well worth the telling.

Euan Lloyd had every intention of doing so. The urbane

Boon Companions

The Sea Wolves Take a Bath

producer of *The Wild Geese* sipped a beer on the manicured lawns of the Fort Aguada Beach Resort, and waved an expansive arm towards six miles of virgin beach, emerald palms, crystal surf and azure sky. 'Isn't that magnificent?' His voice carried a congratulatory, somewhat proprietorial air, as well it might, for he had brought a team of international stars to Goa – Gregory Peck, David Niven, Roger Moore, Trevor Howard, Barbara Kellerman and Patrick MacNee, and was enjoying himself hugely making *The Sea Wolves*. The film was based on the book, *The Boarding Party* by James Leasor, and retold a World War II episode of crackling voltage and derring-do. All the ingredients of a box office bonanza were there: spies, treachery, beautiful women, ruthless heroes, roller-coaster action, a plot of sufficient density to transcend the cliched and, of course, all of the lush splendour of the Goan environment.

'We have appropriated the cottages on the hill for the duration,' said Lloyd, and indeed they had. Mr and Mrs Roger Moore, a party of seven with seventeen suitcases, were comfortably settled in Cottage No. 2 within neighbourly distance of Mr and Mrs Peck and Mr Niven. 'I'm glad I settled on Goa,' Lloyd said. 'We considered Mauritius but I spent two weeks in Goa last year and that was it. Clever of me.' A master stroke that everybody found most agreeable. The stars loved their cottages and spent their evenings companionably together in cane sofas on the lawns.

One such evening of moonlit serendipity was rudely disturbed by a large, rather unwieldy Dutch friend of mine, wandering the world and now, sense of direction somewhat impaired by four large caju fenis, lost among the cottages.

He heard voices raised in pleasant camaraderie, sallied gladly thither, tripped over an ornamental bush and landed bruisingly on all fours. Gregory Peck offered him a solicitous arm. Roger Moore brushed him off. 'Lost, I gather,' David Niven observed keenly, 'and looking to find your way. It's quite simple really. Turn left at the second rose bush down the path, mind the snake, leap lightly across the open well, allow the panther a wide berth and give or take a jackal or two, there you are right by the pool!'

Niven is made of sterner stuff in the film. He played Lt. Colonel Bill Grice, second-in-command to Gergory Peck's Lt. Colonel Lewis Pugh. Together, laughably assisted by what one historian refers to as 'a band of middle-aged, pot-bellied British boxwallahs' they scotched the murderous activities of a nest of German spies in Goa.

'Isn't it extraordinary,' said Major General Lewis Pugh, C.B., C.B.E., D.S.O. in mild astonishment, 'that the Germans who survived the raid and settled in Goa haven't met each other in twenty-five years.' He sat across from me in a small hotel room in Panjim, now in Goa as technical consultant to the film. A slim, erect figure, carrying his years lightly. The blue eyes were gently reminiscent as he recounted, in the imperturbable tone of a master of ceremonies at a flower show, of the German spy, Trompeta, and of his own role in a saga of death and retribution.

A lieutenant colonel at thirty-five, head of the Secret Operations Executive for South East Asia, ensconced in deadly anonymity in a small office in Punjab, he plotted subversion, sabotage and assassination against the Rising Sun. 'We had to clear a statement of objectives with three

The Sea Wolves Take a Bath

people at the top,' General Pugh chuckled lightly, 'they always ran a red line through the word "assassination" and pencilled in "termination".'

1943: the myth of Japanese invincibility had yet to be shattered. Enemy legions stood poised for an invasion of India. Allied armies and morale lay in shreds. Mountbatten surveyed the wreckage and prepared for a long, hard war. Men and supplies were of critical importance. But the Indian Ocean had become a death trap. Allied shipping was lost to the torpedoes of the Sea Wolves, German U-Boat raiders, at the rate of a vessel a day. A traitor in the shipping office in Bombay leaked classified information of ship movements, with deadly accuracy, to the German spymaster in Goa, code-named Trompeta who, in turn, radioed the data to the submarine fleet. Trompeta had to be 'terminated.'

'Easier said than done though,' said General Pugh thoughtfully, 'Portugal was neutral. Even so, they allowed us port facilities in the Atlantic. There were three German ships in Goa and we couldn't touch them. They may as well have been in Hamburg for all the good it did us. The largest, the Ehrenfels carried the secret transmitter. Trompeta had to go, and it had to be a clandestine operation performed, so to say, in mufti.'

Pugh and a major from the S.O.E. planned and executed a daring raid into Vasco da Gama, a major Goan port city. They kidnapped Trompeta, eluded Portuguese border patrols and returned to Bombay. 'Gavin was supposed to cosh him and I had to give him an injection to put him to sleep. He had a hard head, that German. Gavin kept hitting him but he refused to behave. 'Well,' – a small sigh – 'I took the cosh and gave him a mighty whack behind the ear and that did the trick. Out like a light. His wife was screaming her head off by this time and the neighbours were beginning to wonder what the fuss was all about. We bundled him into the back seat of the station wagon and took off in rather a hurry.'

Our heroes returned to Bombay with Trompeta in tow who disappeared in due course, dispatched no doubt with terminal prejudice. But the spying continued. So did the destruction of allied shipping. There was no question about it, the Ehrenfels had to go. Enter Lt. Colonel Bill Grice, alias David Niven, and that redoubtable fighting force, the Calcutta Light Horse. Seeing what it did to the hapless Ehrenfels, let us pause a respectful moment or two with the Light Horse. It was a territorial unit, manned by civilians and set up by Robert Clive. A distinguished fighting force in the days when Imperial history was being made now, alas, a pale shadow of its former self, given over to sundowners at noon and restful ease. No more relaxed bunch of boxwallahs knocked back their burra pegs this side of the Suez Canal. Drawn from the leisurely ranks of the mercantile community, it would have taken the keenest, most optimistic military assessment to anticipate the honour and glory that awaited it. 'Middle-aged?' Indisputably. 'Pot-bellied?' Oh, well ... 'Fire in the belly and rarin' to go?' Look what happened to the Ehrenfels! In the event, when asked to volunteer nary a man said no. Hundreds of disheartened rejects watched enviously as eighteen volunteers were selected and put through a rigorous training schedule. They acquired arcane and deadly skills, and embarked from Calcutta on a rusty, leaking barge, the Phoebe, of distressing vintage.

The Sea Wolves Take a Bath

After a hair-raising trip around Cape Comorin in horrendous weather, set adrift for half a day with a broken engine, they finally arrived at Cochin on the Malabar Coast. There the Phoebe picked up the other half of the raiding party which had made its way over land from Calcutta, and proceeded urgently and noisily to Goa. At two in the morning, all lights off, arms and ammunition primed, they drifted into Murmugao port, with the Phoebe's engines at lowest revs. Limpet mines were attached to the German ships. The boarding party grappled its way up the sides of the Ehrenfels. Outnumbered five to one, but with surprise on their side, the boxwallahs emulated the Light Horse's very first action in 1759 in Calcutta. In an engagement which was 'short, bloody and decisive' the enemy was routed. All the German ships were blown out of the water, scattering bits of transmitter and other nastiness all about Goa's harbour, while the Phoebe and every one of her gallant crew returned to Calcutta, triumphant and unscathed, to a rousing welcome.

'It was a neat little action as these things go,' said General Pugh, 'and luck of course was with us.' He leaned forward, serious and intent as never till now. I prepared myself for one final cataclysmic revelation. 'Would you be so kind,' he said, 'as to order me a fresh lime and soda?'

Stronger refreshments were shared between me and the Goan film executive in charge of production. He wore several hats with Lloyd's team, some of them very hard indeed: fighter of brush fires, wily negotiator, keeper of the unit's peace, patient and creative interpreter. He made sure that Goa produced what was sought, on time (no mean feat this) and with goodwill and fair reward among all. He began by assuming responsibility for the selection of locations which the producer insisted should be no further than a seven kilometre radius from the capital, Panjim.

It was a task which called for the tact of a diplomat, the bargaining skills of a Levantine and truly heroic stamina. 'There's a scene which takes place on the evening of the attack of the Ehrenfels,' he said, 'where the local bar girls offer their services free – courtesy, Lt. Colonel Pugh – to the sailors in the harbour to keep them out of the way of the action. The diversion, of course, was bank-rolled by His Majesty's exchequer. We found just the right sort of house and began negotiating with the woman who owned it. At our first meeting she settled for the painting of the exterior and five hundred rupees. The next day she added a hire charge for the furniture on the front porch. Three days later, having read the fine print in the contract, she swore by all that was holy that she would never allow the ancestral manse to be put to such low and libidinous use. The next day she settled for fifteen hundred rupees. Just for a minute's footage.

'We shot a major scene at the Vasco railway station. A madhouse. Five thousand people milling about as we shot the station first as Cochin, then as Calcutta. For the Calcutta sequence we managed to get a group of Bengali extras; for the Cochin sequence they loosened their dhories, converted them into wrap-around lungis, the women combed their hair out and we were in business with a crowd of instant Keralites. There were a few hairy moments. Goa's general election was on in Vasco and a local candidate surrounded by some of the toughest political thugs I've seen, threatened to break up the set because we were keeping thousands of people from voting. Touch and go that. We just managed to save the day.

'And I shall never forget the occasion when Barbara Kellerman was not attacked by a fierce German Shepherd. We had booked Goa's finest police dog for the role. On the day of the shooting he was fifty miles away in the jungle, hot on a trail or whatever police dogs do in the line of duty. We sent radio messages, dispatch riders, jeeps. No dog. McLaglen, the Director, was not amused. He wanted a dog, like now, so we got him a dog. A lanky, decrepit Labrador of advanced years. "Make him up," McLaglen roared. We made him up to look like a big bad dog. He was supposed to leap at Barbara, fangs bared, growling in his throat. But like the rest of the unit, a glance, and he was madly in love with her. Never in my life have I seen a dog behave so foolishly. Belly down, tail going like a metronome, fawning all over her and making small pleading noises. Couldn't really blame him but the shot had to be scrubbed.

'It's a good unit. One couldn't ask for a nicer lot. They love Goa and the Goans have, as they usually do, been friendly and helpful. All of us have enjoyed the experience.'

Euan Lloyd and the Light Horse will be fondly remembered in Goa. They left behind much goodwill and an abiding mystery. To this day no one knows who refurbished the forgotten tombstone on the hill above the fort. The names of the dead have been etched afresh. The marble is polished to a brilliance and it catches the last amber light of the fading sun with a translucent, elegiac grace.

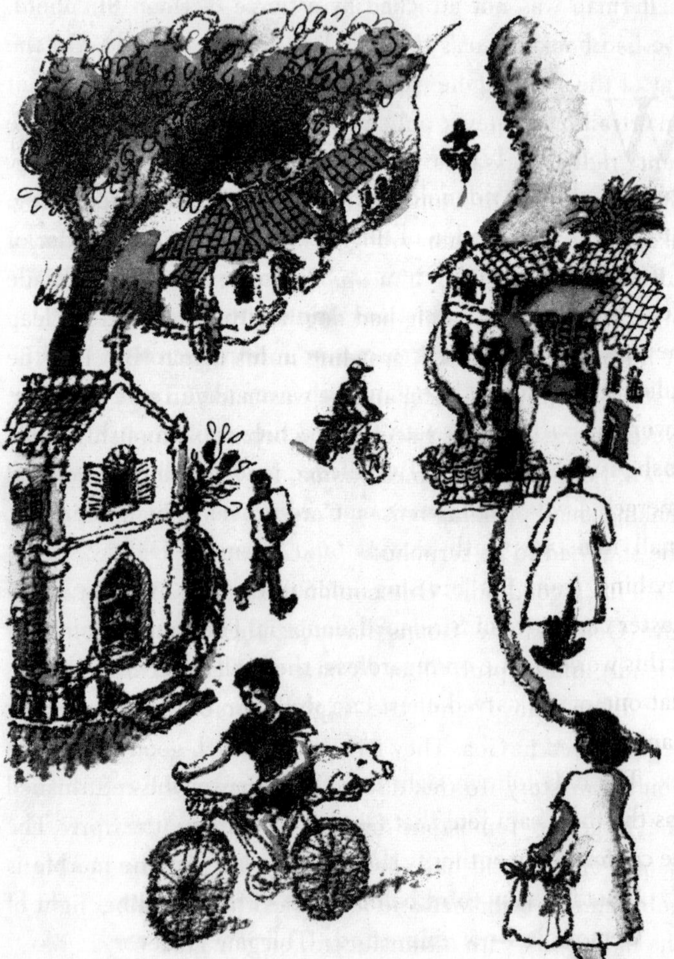

Bernie Finklebaum Jr. Learns a New Word

Whenever I hear the nasal twang of the American abroad, raised in adenoidal protest at some real or imagined outrage, I am reminded of the hapless Bernie Finklebaum Jr. A couple of Colonel Jeremiah Saldanha's gentle lessons in Goan etymology; a Christmas drink with Gerson and Jude, the redoubtable Public Prosecutor and Inspector General of Police whom I came to regard with awe as the Two Just Men; a working partnership with those geniuses of the perfect car wash, Tweedledum and Tweedledee; and Bernie would have emerged a wiser and better man, equipped to confront life's small injustices with a wink and a smile. Did he learn anything from his bruising encounter with Aloysius, the master carpenter of Siridao? I doubt it. The Finklebaum Jrs. of this world hurtle on regardless; they will never understand that one man's carved chest can well turn out to be another man's folly.

The only folly in sight this fine Christmas Eve morning was the third caju feni that Gerson was urging upon me with the commanding authority that only the law can bring to bear.

'That'll be my third before noon,' I protested.

Gerson was not impressed. 'The law is never an ass,' he pronounced grandly, 'when it comes to drinking before lunch on Christmas Eve. Drink up, it's going to be a weekend.'

Jude, the Inspector General of Police poured me three fingers of caju, added a splash of cold water as an afterthought, and said, 'How else will you keep your strength up?'

Gerson's is the final legal word in the sixty thousand kilometres of Goan territory; it does not, however, extend to the kitchen. His wife Anna's voice rose above the clatter of pots and pans. 'Not a drop more unless you eat something. Won't be a minute.' And true to her word, in moments, large platters of fried prawns and Goa sausage turn-overs appeared. We ate as Goans do when they enjoy their nosh, in reverential silence. And Jude had a point; it was wise, if not imperative, to keep one's strength up.

In Goa the Christmas spirit begins to shake a glad leg, quite literally, at brunch on the 24th and proceeds, in ever swifter good cheer, to the early hours of the 26th. In between there are lunches which begin at three in the afternoon and end weightily at seven, and dinners which commence alcoholically at one in the morning and seem to go on forever. A pause for midnight mass (sung – the strength now well and truly up – vigorously off-key) and on to the first Christmas party of the day. A refreshing catnap as dawn breaks, then up and stirringly about at ten when the day really begins with a round of visits to friends and distant branches of the family, a lunch to test strong men to their limits, a grand ball that night at the Clube Nacional, and home to bed as dawn nuzzles the night. Everybody collapses on Boxing Day.

Bernie Finklebaum Jr. Learns a New Word

I raised my glass, 'Down with law and order.'

Jude chuckled. 'There's not much of that about over Christmas. Crime seems to take a holiday.'

'Strange, I should have thought just the opposite.'

'Soused,' Jude said, 'out of their minds. Thieves break into empty houses; pickpockets try it on police inspectors; smugglers land contraband at customs wharves. Very few arrests though.'

'Why is that?'

'The forces of law and order,' Jude sighed, 'are as human as the rest of us. Let's be charitable and say that the spirit of peace and goodwill reigns.'

'Except,' Gerson said cryptically, 'when it comes to pigs.'

They exchanged mischievous glances and laughed. I had known them for ten years; one would, I reflected, be hard put to find two more good-tempered, mild-mannered and heartily feared men in all of Goa.

Now they were agreeably relaxed, feet up, toasting the yuletide spirit, and inclined to frivolity.

'Pigs?' I repeated, intrigued. A Tall Tale was in the offing. 'Tell me more.'

Gerson turned to Jude. 'Tell Frank,' he said, 'about the case of the purloined pig.'

'That shouldn't count really. It happened on 23 December.'

'Near enough,' Gerson said.

'Despite the forensic abilities of the best minds in the business,' Jude said, 'the case of the purloined pig remains stubbornly unresolved.'

'We strongly suspect,' Gerson added, 'that one man's purloined pig became another man's sorpotel, but there isn't a shred of evidence to prove it.'

'As these things go,' Jude said, 'a tragic ending.'

'A grave miscarriage of justice,' Gerson agreed, 'yet not without drama. Like all sensational crimes, it has everything. Grand larceny, hot pursuit, violence, lynch law and, at the end of it all, a mystery that has never been solved.'

They were beginning to enjoy themselves.

'The suspense,' I said, 'is giving me a thirst.'

I helped myself to a jumbo feni; so did they; then Jude settled back and told us the tale of the purloined pig.

Two days before Christmas, seized by one of those inexplicable impulses that only occur at this time of peace and goodwill to all men (and women!), Jude decided to be nice to his wife. He would shoulder the burden of the day's household chores and buy the fish himself. He met his wife's solicitous suggestion that he lie down till the urge went away with dignified silence and, feeling particularly virtuous, he walked to the village tinto. It was a morning to lark about without a care, a nip in the air, a gentle breeze from the sea and a sky which would remain a clear blue forever. The village was making ready for Christmas, red and green buntings adorned front porches; holly and mistletoe set the sophisticates apart from the hoi polloi who made do, poor things, with Chinese lanterns and intricately wrought Stars of Bethlehem. But social distinctions seemed not to matter; there was an energetic bustle wherever you looked, much excited too-ing and fro-ing, a glad and generous feeling to the day.

The village square was in the process of waking, a scene of positively bucolic arousal which unfolded each morning in movements so slow as to induce mesmerized slumber. The

Bernie Finklebaum Jr. Learns a New Word

exquisite reluctance with which Da Silva, the grocer, put his shutters up evoked a sleepy sympathy; the achingly ponderous movements of Barboza the baker as he placed loaf after loaf resentfully on the counter touched one to the drowsy core; the morose resignation of Mendonca the cold storage merchant as he put down the Kwality Ice Cream sign struck dreamy chords of fluffy fellow-feeling. The thought of a day's work – the last, thank God, before Christmas – lay heavily upon the morning.

As if on cue, the Holiest Family in the Village, led by a Pious Elder, eyes averted from all of this irreligious disorder, disdain for lesser mortals in every stride, made its way to the Church for Mass, pointedly ignoring the day's first drunks quenching unquenchable thirsts on the steps of the tinto's taverna. The drunks couldn't have cared less. They exchanged ribald sallies with the fisherwomen, bright as peacocks, exchanging colourful and inventive insults as they pushed, shoved and jostled for the best sales positions. Looking on in various attitudes of imminent collapse, propping up walls, tree-trunks, road-signs and shop fronts, was that energetic component of the village youth which laboured diligently every morning at its favourite activity: standing and staring. Bullock carts trundled by; motor cycles ridden by murderously dangerous young men skidded and zoomed about the square. Cyclists rode and chatted amiably, four abreast, blocking everyone's right of passage. Then a young boy, no more than thirteen, made an appearance on a bicycle. He rode alone, with a pig lashed to the carrier, taking the animal to the Mapusa bazaar.

Boon Companions

There are only two sounds capable of penetrating the noisy hubbub of a village tinto: the first is the squealing of a pig being taken to the market; the pig knows that no good is going to come of it and protests mightily with squeal after porcine squeal of doomsday anguish; the only other sound to equal, indeed surpass by several decibels those of the hapless porker, are the bellows of rage when a pig is found to be purloined. They now rent the air in a frenzied torrent from a very fat, very old woman who rushed into the centre of the tinto, stopping the traffic, glaring wild-eyed this way and that, brandishing a club and screaming at the top of her voice, 'WHERE IS HE? WHERE IS HE? THE FATHERLESS MALCREADO! HE'S STOLEN MY PIG! THE MISBEGOTTEN SON OF A SOW HAS STOLEN MY PIG!'

Nothing arouses the native ire like the theft of a pig. Breaking and entering is considered a minor peccadillo, more so as the only houses worth breaking and entering into are owned by extortionist landlords who eminently deserve and can amply afford to be parted from some of their ill-gotten gains. Crimes of passion are discussed philosophically, with a world-weary resignation: such things will happen; the heart has its reasons; Cupid does not discriminate with his thunderbolts. The surreptitious shifiing of a boundary stone by the dark of the moon prompts sage and legally inclined debate, when the merits or otherwise of the shifting are seen in proper ancestral and historical perspective: past injustices, unrepaid loans, mortal insults, an unlikely pregnancy, the disappearance of mangoes and coconuts, and suchlike. But steal a pig and passions are set violently aflame: rough justice is the order of the moment, and woe to the thief!

Bernie Finklebaum Jr. Learns a New Word

Like the Keystone Kops in fast forward, every single mother's soul in the tinto leaped up and rushed about in different directions, shouting all at once as loudly as they could. 'I have never seen such chaos,' Jude recalled happily, 'not even at a bull fight when the favourite bull loses.' The chaos was showing signs of developing into a small but moderately violent riot when Barboza the baker, showing unexpected qualities of leadership, grabbed hold of Mendonca, the cold storage merchant's Kwality Ice Cream sign and waving it above his head like colours retrieved in battle, charged to the aid of the Victim, with Mendonca and Da Silva the grocer, all thought of work gratefully abandoned, close at his heels. The layabouts and the fisherwomen brought up the rear (while the tinto's cats made hay among the fish) and the drunks, pausing for quick refills, sought, however unsteadily, to aid and abet.

They gathered supportively around the old woman, patting her shoulder, making sympathetic noises, looking around, about, under, above, as though the pig might have taken wing, but she would not be consoled. The first rush of rage was replaced by wailing grief. She sobbed hysterically, tore at her hair, beat her breast with clenched fist, called upon the saints to witness her plight, beseeched the heavens: Was she not a virtuous woman? Had she not lived a God-fearing life? Did her neighbours not know her as the very soul of honesty? Had there been a day, a single day, when her life had been anything less than pure and blameless? What had she ever done to deserve such a calamity? Never in her life had she reared a sow of this stature, Madre de Deus, with her own two hands like a child!

And the way her pig had bred! Litter after litter popping out like peas. What could a poor widow like her do now?

Heart-rending wails, sorrow to make strong men weep, a soaring grief which only immediate and vengeful action could put to rest. Find the thief! Bring the rascal to justice!

There was an investigative quiver in the air, a sense of urgent, manic enquiry. Barboza the baker, now a fearless leader unafraid of the odds, led the way.

'How big was the pig?'

Quick to grasp the general trend, Mendonca the cold storage merchant, asked, 'Was she black, white or spotted?'

'She might,' Barboza said shortly, 'have been brown. It's been known to happen.'

But, as any fool could tell, there was more to a purloined pig than its colour. Da Silva the grocer went off at a clever deductive tangent, 'When did you last see her?'

One moment snuffling happily, as only a well-beloved pig can, the next gone, vanished into thin air, not a hint of hair nor hide, gone, gone without a trace. The old woman crossed herself. The largest of the fisherwomen, moved as fisherwomen rarely are, to tearful sentimentality, enquired with great tenderness, 'Was she an amiable pig? Warm-hearted? Affectionate? A member of the family?'

A tactical error. The past tense prompted a fresh outburst of wails, lamentation, gasping sobs and wringing of hands. The investigation was getting rapidly nowhere until one of the drunks, with a leap of inspired lateral thinking, showed the way.

'The boy on the bicycle,' he shouted, waving his glass about triumphantly and spilling the contents down the

Bernie Finklebaum Jr. Learns a New Word

shirtfront of Barboza, who seemed, for a moment or two, to be less of a Man among Men than a very wet and angry baker. Heedless, seized with the joy of revelation, the drunk shouted again, 'The boy with the pig on the bicycle. There he goes, the swine!' As one, the crowd looked up the road. A few hundred yards ahead, pedalling calmly and leisurely, as though without a care in the world, the wicked boy, the brazen felon, the ... the stealer of sows! was making off with the old woman's purloined pig.

'AFTER HIM!'

'I have never in my life,' said Jude admiringly, the recollection mint-bright as the day, 'seen such a swift and purposeful pursuit of a villain. Well worth writing up in the training manual. Before you could say, "Save the sow" they were off in a howling mob, some on cycles, others on foot, picking up sticks, bricks, anything they could lay their hands on as they went. The boy on the cycle with the pig at the back was a bit thick. He heard the commotion, turned, looked back, thought nothing of it, pedalled along whistling, heard the baying behind him get louder by the minute, looked over his shoulder again, realized with horror it was him they were after, shot up straight in the saddle as if he had sat on a live wire and hared off down the road. Big mistake. Here was guilt, no question about it, with a capital 'G.' Would an innocent man flee in this fashion? Howling lustfully, like a pack of hounds closing in on a fox, the mob went after him.'

A simmering shoot-when-you-see-the-whites-of-his-eyes excitement descended on the tinto. There were oaths in the air and blood in every eye. Weapons were being assembled. The old woman sat against a wall, grief replaced by quivering intensity. She held the club in her right hand, white-knuckled, testing its weight, heft, balance, smacking it thoughtfully into the palm of her left hand every so often. The fisherwomen had removed their chappals and placed them within easy arm's reach, ready to leap up and belabour the stealer of pigs at the first opportunity. The drunks were stocking up on Dutch courage with the urgency that comes over men about to enter into battle.

They heard the moans of the villain well before the mob reached the tinto. At first all was a babble of confusion, and cries of pain to the sound of crisp thwacks, and 'Take that you rascal,' 'Break his head!,' 'Rub his nose in dung,' and other equally inventive suggestions. Then the voices of those in command could be heard above the din.

'To the police station with him,' – Barboza the baker leading, as always, from the front.

'Take him to the church. Let the padre pass judgement,' – the Pious Elder, conscience troubled no doubt at having forsaken early morning mass for a spot of mayhem.

'He would have made five hundred rupees on this pig,' – Da Silva the grocer, deductive to the bitter end.

'It's a black pig,' – Mendonca the cold storage merchant who, once he got his teeth into an issue, never let go.

And then a small voice, touched with tears, bewildered and – good for the rascal! – edged with terror, pleaded to no avail, 'It wasn't me. I haven't stolen anybody's pig.'

'Liar!' And he was cuffed about the ears. 'Turn him upside down and beat the soles of his feet!'

'Throw him into the well!'

'IT WASN'T ME! IT WASN'T ME!'

Bernie Finklebaum Jr. Learns a New Word

The fisherwomen had risen as one, ominously, scowling, muttering vile abuse, chappals clutched, ready for action. The old woman stood four-square, holding the club with both hands over her shoulder/head lowered, shuffling her feet like a bull about to charge. The layabouts were rolling up their sleeves dramatically, massaging their biceps and taking deep, significant breaths. The drunks focused carefully on the centre of the mob, rushed forward, lurched this way and that, caromed into each other, tripped over the fisherwomen's baskets and their own feet, then, overcome with the confusion of it all, rushed back to the taverna to top up one last time before the fray.

Jude sighed; in seconds he had ceased to be the father of a family of four doing his good deed for the day, and become Goa's Inspector General of Police at the scene of a pignapping, the only cop present at the caper. Duty called. He climbed onto a convenient beer barrel, rolled the day's *O Heraldo* he was carrying into a makeshift megaphone and issued a command, crisp and compelling, 'Police. Stop this nonsense at once!' He was recognized immediately. Nobody would look him in the eye. Feet were shuffled. Throats were cleared. The layabouts sought urgent flight. The drunks fled into the darkest recesses of the taverna.

Holding the old woman firmly above the elbow ('She seemed quite demented by now,' Jude said, 'and capable of anything') he led her to the edge of the mob. It fell apart hastily. Only the baker, the grocer and the cold storage merchant stood their ground. They held the boy by his wrists, the back of his trousers and the scruff of his neck. He had been in the wars: the bruise on his cheek was a promising purple; the black eye was well on its way to an early ripening; the shirt had been torn off his back; he had been rolled several times in the mud which, for good measure, had been liberally applied all over his hair. The pig, stricken dumb by the drama of the past hour, now remembered the purpose of its journey, raised its snout to the sky and squealed to high heaven, as if stuck prematurely in a tender part. The old woman took one look at it, shook her head in disbelief, smacked her palm against her forehead, sat down on the road, stood up, pointed at the pig and whispered, 'That's not my pig ... '

'Not your pig?' – Barboza.

'THAT'S NOT MY PIG!'

'How could it not be your pig?' – Da Silva.

'It's a black pig, anybody can see that,' – Mendonca, obsessed to the point of no return.

'My Esmeralda,' – sobs, wails, fresh heights of biblical grief – 'is pink and white, with a black patch over her left eye.'

For long moments, there was a guilt-stricken silence. Then the Pious Elder turned an inquisitor's relentless eye on the boy, 'God will punish you for this, you scoundrel!'

'Why did you run off in the first place?' Da Silva wanted to know.

'Leading us on, eh?' Barboza accused.

'Your idea of a joke, you wicked boy!' – Mendonca fumed. 'We'll teach you a joke!'

'MALCREADO!' The mob, furious at the injustice of it all, was once more in full cry. Jude's patience was at an end. He threatened mass arrests on the spot, incarceration and bread-and-water over the Christmas holidays. The mob fled. Jude led the boy off, reflecting on the impossibility of reconciling justice with the law, and walked him home, a good half hour to the vaddo where he lived. The pig, saved to squeal another day, and quite undone by all the excitement, fell asleep. The boy's family and friends – a clan of ramponkar Figuerados – swore vengeance and sought to assemble a war party and plunge into battle with the louts at the tinto. Jude calmed them down. This took another hour. Then as gallant saviour of an innocent young life, a drink or two was pressed upon him. It would have been ungracious to refuse, or to say no to one for the road. By the time he got back to the tinto, all the fish had been sold. The cats were licking their chops.

'My wife,' Jude concluded ruefully, 'was not best pleased.'

'Did they ever find the old woman's pig?' I asked.

'Fat chance,' Gerson said.

'You'd be surprised at the number of pigs reported missing in Goa every week,' Jude said, 'and never recovered.'

'Perhaps,' Gerson suggested, 'you could consider a Missing Pigs Bureau. Identity cards for pigs, at five rupees a pig, a snip. From this day on, nobody will own a porker without its picture. I can see the posters up, Jude, in every tinto in the land. Missing porker. Answers to the name of Percy. Beloved member of the Fonseca household. Black wart above left eye. One cauliflower ear. Imperious snort. Engaging smile. Last seen midnight November fifth in lustful pursuit of Angela, the next door neighbour's sow.'

Gerson was in full, hilarious flight. He would have gone on in this inventive vein till inspiration collapsed, but the doorbell rang, an unwelcome interruption. It rang insistently. Once, twice, thrice.

'Who is it, Anna?' Gerson called.

Anna answered in a troubled voice, 'Raoul Pimenta's wife, dear, with the children.' A pause. 'She wants to meet you. Shall I send her in?'

'No,' Gerson said, banter forgotten, a slight edge of regret in his voice, 'I'll be out in a moment.'

Jude went with him. I was intrigued. I heard a woman's voice, speaking rapidly in Konkani, the emotion barely in control, rising in pitch and intensity, breaking into muffled sobs. Anna consoling her. Gerson calm, patient, comforting. Jude adding a sentence or two with a gentleness quite at odds with his reputation and position. The front door was at the end of a long corridor and it was difficult to hear what was being said, more so as the woman spoke very rapidly, in obvious distress, and was answered in low tones. Every time she raised her voice, Anna shushed her as one would a child. Then I heard one of the children cry out, 'Please, patrao, please. Only for Christmas day.' Footsteps returning down the corridor. Gerson's voice in English, 'Take them to the kitchen, Anna, and give them something to eat.' Jude popped his head through the doorway. 'We won't be more than five minutes, Frank, help yourself to a drink.' He disappeared into the corridor. Serious conversation again. Measured, objective tones. Long, thoughtful pauses. A sense of debate on issues of consequence. Here were two professionals about their business. Finally, a conclusion.

Bernie Finklebaum Jr. Learns a New Word

Gerson's voice rose unwittingly, gladly, 'All right, let's do it. You tell her, Jude.'

'Public prosecutors aren't expected to shirk their responsibilities,' Jude said. 'Go on, set a good example. You tell her.'

'I suppose I'd better,' Gerson's voice faded towards the kitchen.

Jude came in and made straight for the feni, poured himself a large drink and said, 'This one I've earned.'

'What's going on?' I asked.

Gerson came in just then, sighed mightily, attacked the bottle, did himself generously and collapsed into an easy chair. He raised his glass and said, 'Merry Christmas, Raoul Pimenta.'

'This is no way to treat a guest on Christmas Eve,' I said, 'what was that all about?'

'Raoul Pimenta,' Gerson said, 'is in the Fort Aguada jail serving a fifteen-year term for manslaughter.'

'It's a mandatory sentence,' Jude explained, 'for the crime.'

'But the man is not a criminal,' Gerson said, 'no criminal record, not even a misdemeanour. A ramponkar, liked by the other fishermen in the vaddo. Happily married. Two kids. He was young when it happened, twenty-nine or thirty I think, and even with time off for good conduct he's going to be locked up for ten years.'

'It's not too bad a place,' Jude said, 'the villains call it the user-friendly jail.'

'That sounds nice.'

The guards and jailors are both there for the long haul. They strike up friendships. Small favours are exchanged. The guards fetch and carry. Hot meals are smuggled in on weekends, with a bottle or two of feni. They borrow from each other when they're short. And conspire when they think no one's looking. It's not entirely unknown for prisoners to disappear from their cells at lights out and reappear mysteriously when the morning gong goes.'

'How,' I asked, 'did Pimenta get into trouble?'

'A nasty piece of luck,' Gerson said, 'and on the one occasion, poor devil, when he had every reason to celebrate. After six months of the old run around, he had finally managed to get a loan from the village co-operative bank for an outboard motor. He and his crew heard the good news one morning while bringing the boat in from a night's fishing. Excited, they rushed off to the bank, as they were, bare-bodied, in langotes, to confirm that the loan had been cleared. A celebration, quite naturally, seemed called for. No sooner said than done. They descended, en masse, at the local taverna, and went at it with a vengeance.'

'Seems perfectly reasonable to me,' I said, remembering Joaquim and his Merry Gang, the catamaran which grew up to become a Motor Boat, and the monumental binge that followed masquerading as breakfast.

'It wasn't his day,' Gerson continued, 'as luck would have it, a gang of out-of-state labourers were knocking it back at the next table. Surly bunch. Everybody seems to have drunk too much too quickly. One of the labourers poked fun at Raoul's langote. Hot words were exchanged and they came to blows. The ramponkars are a tough lot and once the blood's up, difficult to control. Raoul hit the man on the temple. His skull cracked. He went into a coma and never

Bernie Finklebaum Jr. Learns a New Word

regained consciousness. Died three days later. There was a postmortem. The blow had caused a blood clot in the brain, and that led to a stroke. Death by cerebral haemorrhage. In a word, manslaughter. Fifteen years in the slammer, without benefit of parole, but with time off for good behaviour. He's just about completed a year.'

'Was that his family?'

'His wife,' Jude said, 'a gem, and two lovely children. But the boat's in his name and his crew work it. They are well provided for. Still, it just doesn't do for a family not to have a man about the house.'

Two plus two made a golden four fit for Christmas.

'I suspect,' I said dryly, 'that there will be, shall we say, a temporary accommodation.'

'What on earth are you talking about?' Jude threw his hands up in mock horror; Gerson rolled his eyes heavenwards.

'Only for Christmas day, patrao,' I said.

'How could we ever do a thing like that?' Gerson said gravely.

'It would be against the law,' Jude added.

I laughed out loud. 'Since when,' I asked, 'has the law had anything to do with justice?'

'If even a hint of this slanderous accusation got out,' Gerson said, 'it would be as much as our jobs are worth.'

'However,' Jude chortled, 'the law is not without compassion.'

'Particularly,' Gerson said, in his I-will-not-be-trifled-with Public Prosecutor's voice, 'if a prisoner is deemed to be critically ill. It is then left to the discretion of the authorities concerned whether or not he is granted temporary leave of absence – under strict vigilance, of course, to spend a day or two with his loved ones.'

'Whose discretion?'

'Ours,' they said.

Just then a young woman and two children, radiant as rainbows, rushed in breathlessly, exclaimed, 'Happy Christmas, patrao!' – in English yet. The woman went on her knees to touch Gerson's feet. He would have none of it; he pulled her up gently and said, 'Merry Christmas. Off you go now.' And off they went, in winged flight, feisty as angels, straight up to Cloud Nine.

Simpatica!

Here is a Christmas tale, I thought, to save for my children's children!

Embarrassment was writ large in Gerson's self-deprecatory smile, and Jude's eyes refused to catch mine. They were trying hard to appear modest and nonchalant, going off on all sorts of unnecessary tangents in order to put Raoul Pimenta behind them. But I was without mercy this Xmas Eve.

'Lovely word, simpatica,' I said, 'one can't have too much of it.'

'Where do you plan to go on the twenty-fifth?' Gerson asked Jude.

'The Clube Nacional,' Jude said. 'They have two new bands on for Christmas.'

'From the big, bad city,' Gerson's eyes lit up, 'and a genuine Egyptian belly dancer. That should stir up the city fathers.'

'Not, I hope,' Jude added chuckling, 'our old friend, Isabella from Porvoreim.'

Bernie Finklebaum Jr. Learns a New Word

Tsk, tsk, pale pinkherrings. Did they really think I'd take a rain check on my very own true tall tale?

'Did Mrs G,' I said, 'have any belly dancers on the List?'

Gerson scratched his head and looked vaguely troubled. 'You shouldn't believe everything you hear,' he said.

'Rumours,' Jude admonished, 'will be the ruination of Goa.'

'After this morning's work,' I said, 'what's left of your reputations is in shreds. It's time to come clean, but I must admit, from what I've heard, your handling of the List was a neat piece of action. Very nifty indeed. Warms the cockles of one's heart. Courage beyond the call of duty, etc.'

Jude glanced at his watch. 'Must rush,' he said, 'early lunch. Wife will be furious if I'm late.'

'You did say, Frank,' Gerson glanced at his watch, 'that you were expected home by one.'

'Not,' I said, 'before I get to the bottom of this. I want the truth mind, nothing but ... ' And I launched into my own True Tall Tale.

*

If Mrs G hadn't existed, it would have been necessary to invent her. Illustrious daughter of one of the nation's Founding Fathers, she walked tall in his footsteps, took up the political inheritance like a duck takes to water (or, as her unkinder critics would have it, as a shark to a feeding frenzy) and ruled the land with an iron hand in an executioner's glove. Cabinet Ministers trembled in her presence and were dismissed from office in the time it took for their knees to knock; Chief Secretaries fell by the wayside in droves; State Governors found themselves roofless between breakfast and lunch; civil servants were decapitated by the trainload. But Mrs G GOT THINGS DONE. She was a perfectly reasonable Prime Minister so long as you did it her way.

But, as all know, the processes of democracy are maddeningly irresolute: opposition parties are cussed beyond belief; the press, when it is not illiterate and misinformed, is up to all sorts of mischief and rabble-rousing, being polite only to its proprietors; that seditious bunch of no-gooders, the civil libertarians, may not be locked up without due process of the law and one could grow old waiting for justice to appear to be done. A disgraceful situation, fraught with peril for the nation. One morning, a National Emergency was declared.

The black shadow of dictatorship had fallen like a shroud over eight hundred million Indians. They were the lucky ones. The thousands who had the misfortune to incur the wrath of the authorities were hauled off in black Marias in the dark hours of the morning and deposited in the nearest jail without benefit of charge-sheet or trial, there to languish till their future was decided. No bets were being laid. The Emergency proceeded with ruthless efficiency and astonishing speed. Lists of enemies of the state – real, imagined, national, marginal – were drawn up for immediate arrest and incarceration, with a fine disregard for the niceties of cause, proof, bail, trial, defence, prosecution, and all of the unessential impediments which, until then, had come in the way of true and radical patriotic action.

Bernie Finklebaum Jr. Learns a New Word

Indeed, a fine democracy was very much in evidence. The Lists were wholly without bias or discrimination: members of the ruling party shared cells with communists and other subversives; Captains of Industry rubbed shoulders behind bars with leader writers; smugglers found themselves sharing bed and board with Members of Parliament; film stars and bureaucrats were forced into reluctant intimacy; contract killers sent delicate shivers down the spines of couturiers. Judges were jailed; maharajas and maharanis showed no clemency; prelates put away without a thought. It could hardly be helped if a few babies went out with the bathwater. The blameless, the innocuous, the merely idiosyncratic, they too, in fear and trembling, awaited the rumble of the tumbrils.

As we all know, in operations of this nature, conducted on such a dramatic and operatic scale, swift timing is of the essence. Thus it came to pass that at noon on the morning of that fateful day, a thick manila envelope, marked, 'HIGHLY CONFIDENTIAL & TOP PRIORITY' arrived in Goa by special aircraft, was rushed from the airport by motor cycle courier, and placed on the desk of the Public Prosecutor. At exactly the same time a copy was handed over to the Inspector General of Police.

The conversation which followed between the two has not, so far as I know, been officially minuted, but the gist, I believe, is faithful to the spirit of the exchange:

Gerson : Did you get it?
Jude : Just this moment.
Gerson : Daft.
Jude : Bonkers.

Gerson : Certifiable. Have you gone through it?

Jude: You must be joking. There are hundreds of names here. Alphabetically. Neat. Just like the telephone directory. Gerson : A regular Who's Who. Jude : A regular Who's Hit. Gerson : Is this an open line? Jude : Which planet are you on? Gerson : We'd better meet. Jude : Right on. If I'm not with you in ten minutes, you'll know I'm behind bars. Gerson : Very funny!

They pored over the lists in a silence broken only by exclamations of wonder, awe, bewilderment, disbelief.

'Everybody who's anybody is in here.'

'Except the village idiot.'

'They've gone haywire.' Jude said. 'Why on earth do they have Julian Fernandes down? He's in the organic manure business.'

'Creates a stink!'

'Good grief. Umberto Miranda. But he's a pig farmer.'

'And about as political as a peanut.'

'The Count of Asagao.'

'Mistaken identity. It's the great, great, grandfather they want. He was put away for sedition by the Portuguese.'

'Treason in the blood, the sod!'

They scanned Page Two.

'No more mando festivals. They've put the finger on Victor Coehlo.'

'Dilip Kamat as well.'

'But he's in trucks and barges.'

'Strategic transport I imagine.'

'The Director of the Carnaval? Subversive?'

'You think that's odd. Here's the Harbour Master.'

Jude chuckled. 'Alberto Figuerado. They have got something right.'

'Since when has owning a restaurant been a crime?'

'Have you eaten there lately?'

They leaned back. Thirsty work this. Two more large fenis to get the incarcerationary zeal going. No such luck.

'This,' Gerson said, 'is going to be difficult.'

'Can you see Lousito Braganza in the Aguada lock-up without four course meals and a wine list twice a day?'

'Or Aloysius Sequeira without his guitar and his girlfriend.'

'Utterly fiendish,' Jude said, quoting from the Most Urgent memorandum attached to the list, 'ARREST AND IMPRISON IMMEDIATELY. REPRESENT GRAVE THREAT TO NATION. NOT TO BE RELEASED UNDER ANY CIRCUMSTANCES. STAND BY FOR FURTHER INSTRUCTIONS.'

'They haven't left us much choice.'

'Still, we can do the decent thing.'

'It would be inhuman to arrest them before lunch,' Gerson said.

'Or without warning,' Jude said.

'Perhaps if each of us phoned ten of them ... '

'... And asked each of them to call ten others. Brilliant.'

'Give them time to put some decent food together, pack a toothbrush, light reading, a bottle or two, that sort of thing ... '

'And at a civilized hour.'

'Certainly not during the siesta.'

'Unthinkable!'

Boon Companions

While chauvinist historians are strident in their claims that the Portuguese legacy is corrupt beyond hope of redemption, it must be said that in the matter of the siesta, the Portuguese knew their onions. There is no more civilized and rejuvenating preparation for sunset and evening star. The length of the siesta is fair measure of the generosity of the meal which precedes it, and it is not unusual for the siesta to extend from two hours to four or five in the afternoon. You disturb the Goan in his siesta at your peril. Goa slumbers and may not, short of natural calamities and Acts of God, be stirred. Judges take to bed; politicians snooze; tycoons take their restful ease; carpenters down tools and assume horizontal positions; prelates put their feet up; even the pigs get in forty winks.

Gerson and Jude made their phone calls before lunch. Goa's telephone system was exercised as never before. One hundred and fifty would-be arrestees sat down philosophically, and with whetted appetites, to groaning boards (How soon would they see another?) which the women of the household had put together with exemplary speed and inspiration. Would the Emergency disturb their siesta? Perish the thought. They slept the sleep of the just, the innocent, and the magnificently fed.

One may only speculate on the high drama of the actual arrests, but I like to think that it was a friendly and relaxed scenario, unfolding with courtesy and good grace. A uniformed figure ambles up to the houses, pauses to admire the bougainvillaea, knocks gently at the door. It is opened without undue haste. Pereira, the Harbour Master, well rested and in excellent humour, stands in the doorway.

Bernie Finklebaum Jr. Learns a New Word

'Good evening, Officer. There you are then. Do come in. Take a seat.'

'Packed and ready are we? Bit of a nuisance this.'

'Can't be helped, I suppose.'

'Out in no time, I expect.'

'Can't take any chances though. The wife's got a small hamper going. Won't be a minute. You in a hurry?'

'Not at all. Take your time.'

'One for the road?'

'Sounds like a very good idea.'

'There you go.'

'Great stuff. Where do you get it from?'

'Arpora.'

'Thought as much. Well, cheers.'

'Mud in your eye!'

*

'Well?' I said.

Gerson and Jude did not quite writhe, but it was a near thing.

'Outright slander,' Gerson said.

'The very stuff of libel,' Jude said.

'Dare breathe a word of this nonsense to anyone,' Gerson promised, 'and you'll face charges.'

'It should be fun to arrest you,' Jude said.

'I shall thoroughly enjoy the prosecution,' Gerson said.

'The selection of a judge will be a matter of some delicacy.'

'Judge Saldanha?'

'Judge Saldanha will do nicely.'

'He owes us one.'

'A hanging judge, but there ... '

'Who cares,' I said, 'so long as he's simpatica!'

Then, for no reason at all, I thought of Bernie Finklebaum Jr. There were three words in this delightful morality play that Bernie would have done well to take to his acquisitive little heart; three words doing yeoman service – susegade, alegria, simpatica – come gloriously together in common cause. And, I suppose, yes, stretching a definition by a siesta, you could include that most generous of nouns, phale, as well ...

*

Why is Goa so unfortunate in its American visitors? At a distance they seem harmless enough, a bit too large for my liking perhaps, with the avoir du pois thoughtlessly distributed, and the accent – somewhere between a whine and twang – doing nasty things to the inner ear. The uniforms put me off as well. While I appreciate the fact that Bermuda shorts were invented for the Budweiser boyo – the six-pack/Big Mac folk hero of all those depressing TV commercials – it must be said that having seen one pair, one has seen them all. And were Hawaiian shirts really necessary when all about you lay a world created by Gauguin and commissioned by God? All, however, was not lost. The horizon, as far as the eye could reach, was serenely unafflicted by a MacDonalds sign and Coke had yet to insult the fragrant purity of a great caju feni. But I was less sanguine after my encounter with the Finklebaum Jrs. With Bernie and Babs trampling about ham-footed in a distant

Bernie Finklebaum Jr. Learns a New Word

hamlet like Siridao, could the New World Order be far behind?

Every couple of weeks I make the hour-long journey to Siridao, much in the manner of an indefatigable prospector in search of a lost motherlode. Hope springs eternal. Perhaps, who knows, this day is The Day and I will have the stupendous good fortune to return with The Chest. Aloysius, the master craftsman, who has a fine sense of humour and appreciates a good joke when he sees one, smiles broadly no sooner he catches sight of me, draws up two packing cases, produces a bottle and glasses like a magician. And then, with dramatic flair, he explains why his art has failed, yet again, to reach an exquisite consummation. I sympathize with great sincerity. Art must await inspiration. Even if the surroundings fail to inspire boundless confidence; indeed, they prompt grave misgivings. Lathes of venerable provenance lie about at odd angles; saws, which, like their owner, have said farewell to the odd incisor years earlier, prop up a wall; flat stones and pieces of wood encourage antique planes to find a level; araldite and scotch tape keep heirloom chisels from falling apart. Distinctly unpromising: one's faith in Aloysius begins to falter until one catches a glimpse, in dark corners, of carved chests of utterly preposterous beauty and elegance awaiting, alas, other owners.

I arrived to find two outsize pairs of Bermuda shorts, stretched tight over rumps of heroic heft and thrust, bent over a chest, while their owners examined the intricate carving with growing confusion and unease. A piercing twang rent the air. Aloysius winced.

'Is this our chest, hon?'

'I'm not sure, Bernie. They all look the same to me.'

'Hey, what's your name, bud?'

Aloysius looked over his shoulder, caught my eye, shrugged, sighed, shook his head. Bernie poked him in the chest with a hard forefinger.

'I'm talking to you, fella. This guy talk English, Babs?'

'He did, hon, the last time I was here.'

Aloysius looked at the forefinger. He would have liked to do it grievous harm, but desisted. What was the protocol in America? Should he stroke it? Shake it? Poke back at its owner?

'He wants to know your name,' I said in Konkani.

'My name?' This was easy. Aloysius produced his best English, short on articles and pronouns, long on consonants, lingering lovingly on vowels; it took time, like his chests, but was well worth waiting for.

'Name Aloysius Braganza,' he said.

'Right, Al, now we're getting somewhere.'

'No Al. Aloysius.'

'Al's good enough for me.'

'You better call the man by his full name, hon.'

'You ever hear anybody call me Bernard? Al's good enough for me.'

Bernie Finklebaum held out a hand the size of a baseball glove. Aloysius, alarmed, took a quick step back; Bernie took a quick step forward. Aloysius, retreat cut off by a lathe, offered two fingers and a thumb. Bernie seized them with a glad cry and thumped them up and down vigorously.

'Bernie Finklebaum Jr.,' he boomed.

'Aloysius Braganza.'

Bernie Finklebaum Jr. Learns a New Word

'I know that, Al, you tole me. How you doing?'

Ask a Goan how he feels and you can write off half an hour of your life. Aloysius massaged his stomach and groaned.

'Loose motions,' he said, and groaned again.

'What did the guy say, Babs?'

'I think he's got the runs, Bernie.'

'See what I mean, Babs. You drink the water, you're dead.'

At the word 'drink' Aloysius perked up. Out came the bottle. Dusty. Cobwebbed. Infectiously corked. Glasses, liberally finger-printed, which hadn't been near water for a week.

Mrs Finklebaum Jr. shuddered.

'I'm a Budweiser man myself, Al,' Bernie said.

'Good feni,' Aloysius urged, 'have drink, Mr Flickinbim.'

'Finklebaum.'

'I understand, sah. Fickle … bum.'

'FINK – LE – BAUM!'

'Bum?'

'Baum!'

Was there a wicked glint in Aloysius' eyes? They widened as understanding dawned, then closed briefly in gratitude. The frown disappeared; an expression of ineffable beatitude took its place.

'I call you Fink,' he said happily. 'Have drink, Fink.'

'Enough already,' Bernie muttered through clenched teeth. 'My wife ordered a carved chest from you three weeks ago. You promised it in two. I take off from this burg Toosday. Not too soon for me, if you get the drift. Where's my chest?'

'What chest?'
'The chest, dummy, my wife ordered three weeks ago.'
'Oh, that chest.'
'Yeah, that chest.'
'Why you don't take this chest? It's a nice chest.'
'That's not the chest I ordered, hon. I wanted the fleur-de-lis. I lurv fleur-de-lis.'
'You hear that, Al. Fleur-de-lis. Babs here lurvs fleur-de-lis.'
'I made this chest for German hippie, live in Anjuna. It's very good chest.'
'How come you wanna sell it?'
'The German is always drunk.'

Bernie Finklebaum Jr. took his wife aside. In a loud whisper that set the thatch quivering, he said, 'I'm gonna kill this guy.'

'Bernie, hon, you know what Doc Horowitz said about your BP.'

Bernie took a deep breath.

'You guys drive me up a wall,' he said, 'but I'm not gonna lose my cool, bud. You got a problem with my chest?'

Aloysius buried his head in his hands for a moment, then raised tragic eyes. The pity and the sorrow of it all...

'You think, Fink, I no have problems. I go Cuncolim buy wood for Mrs Fink's chest on Saturday. No, no, no, stupido! Not Saturday. Saturday I spend in Saligao with cousin brother Vincent. It was his wife's sister's daughter's birthday. First baby, first year. How we celebrate. We all got very drunk. So I sleep Saligao two days and by the time I get to Cuncolim, what to tell, man, that rascal Fernando has gone

Bernie Finklebaum Jr. Learns a New Word

to Dona Paula for feast of St Theresa. Proper dumb bell. Thick in head. Like plank. He takes key of woodshed with him. The wood for Mrs Fink's chest is in woodshed. I stay two days in Cuncolim my cousin Raul. No, no, stupido! Pedro. I eat too much prawn balchao. Arre! What to tell! Three days I make loose motions. Such motions, madre de deus, every hour, run! You never know what you are eating in Cuncolim. You take life in hands. That's Goa for you. Gone to dogs. Feni not fit for pig. Nobody cares. Bad prawns! Can you imagine, bad prawns in Goa. Then Fernando turns up, rolling drunk, and loads wood into cart pulled by cow in full heat, I swear by my mother, and at the creek, D'Souza's bull smells the cow, breaks the fence and tries to mount her, and the cow and the cart and the bull and Fernando and Mrs Fink's wood all end up in the creek. Dear God, now Anton my brother arrive from Saudi with family and new dog. We all going Calangute for week on beach. The children like the sea and...'

Would Bernie Finklebaum Jr. bite his tongue?

'JESUS H. CHRIST. WHEN YOU GONNA DO MY CHEST?'

Aloysius looked thoughtful, riffling no doubt through the rich lexicon at his command, but I knew, even before he uttered the magic word, that there would be joy this morning but not, sadly, for Bernie Finklebaum Jr.

'Phale!'

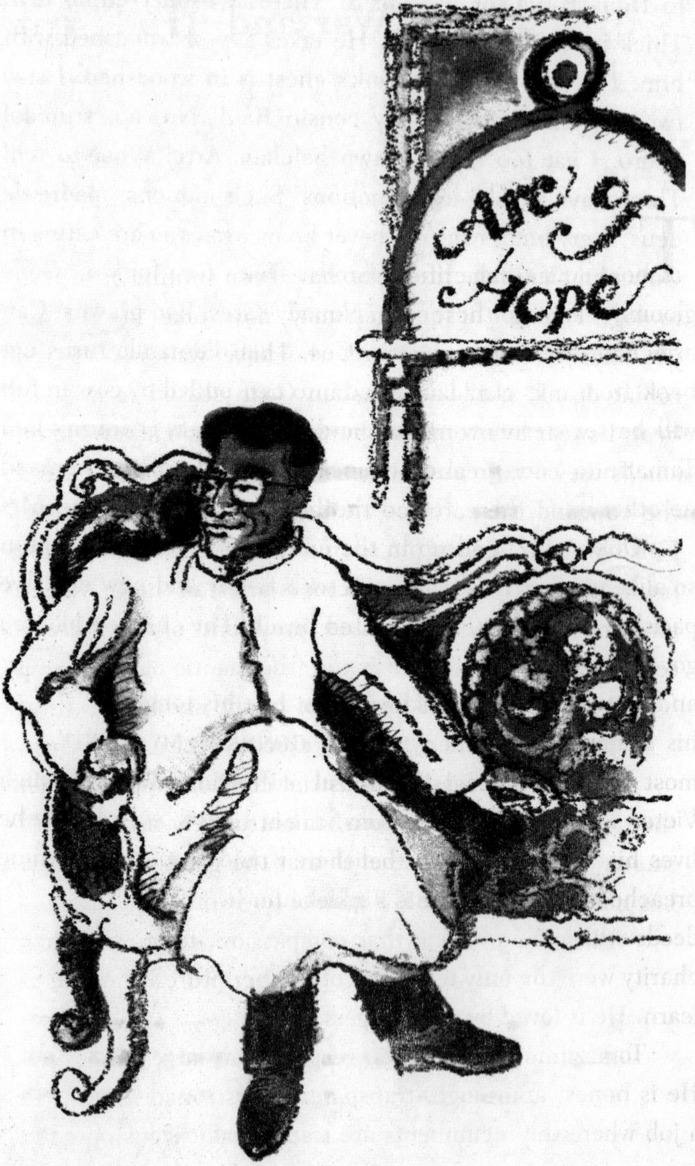
Arc of Hope

Peace, War and True Grit

Those dour Goan critics who have been snuffling about so gloomily among these pages may now take heart. The armchair hedonists out there who have wallowed in the book from one glad bacchanalian Goan season to another will be set sternly to rights by this chapter. Father Victor, Tomazinho Cardozo and Shivanand Salgaocar would have it no other way.

One would be hard put to find three men so different or so alike in all of Goa. Father Victor is priest of the Candolim parish, Tomazinho the elected president of the village governing council, and Shivanand (the mantle of leadership and responsibility thrust upon him by the sudden death of his distinguished father) is chief executive of one of Goa's most brilliantly successful industrial conglomerates. Father Victor is spare, gently spoken, unobtrusively ascetic, and lives his life in the sound belief that the good word is best preached by example. He is a man of few words and splendid deeds who once told me that compassion, forgiveness and charity were the only teachings of the Scriptures I needed to learn. He is loved by the villagers.

Tomazinho has won their respect in as large a measure. He is honest and tough, transparently just, incorruptible in a job where the incumbents are traditionally accustomed to accumulate assets out of all proportion to their declared incomes, and is willing to commit himself to battle against impossible odds once he believes the cause is true. He is about as easy to manipulate or coerce as a river in full monsoon spate and, when the occasion demands, can be just as intractable. But he tempers the letter of the law with the wisdom of experience, and he is scrupulously fair to friend and foe, Catholic and Hindu, persons in high places or low. If he is at all partisan, it is to the greater glory of Candolim, the village of his birth.

Shivanand, like his father before him, has won his spurs in the cut-and-thrust of international trade, negotiating huge iron ore contracts for his mines with inscrutable Chinese communists in Beijing ('The toughest capitalists,' he told me recently, 'I've ever done business with'), Japanese Samurai masquerading as executive clones in Osaka boardrooms, and Korean Black Belt Chief Executives in Seoul steel companies, he seems to thrive on it. When he isn't flying off in all directions at once, he is kept out of mischief in Goa by a score of industries, a workforce of two thousand, family charities which range from Goa's first College of Law to a state-of-the-art hospital and medical research centre, and a charming family – quite naturally, in reverse order of priority. Once you meet Ranjana, his wife, and the children Swati and Toto, you understand why.

The circumstances in which I first met Father Victor (I have mentioned this briefly before) could not have been more improbable. When we laid the foundation stone at Rockheart, an elaborate puja was held. A senior Pandit and a junior Pandit performed a ceremony which took all of an hour with a lack of urgency which put my patience to a severe test: raw rice, marigold flowers, an assortment of fruit (five kinds), pedas, kum-kum and agarbatti were arranged artistically with subtle, thoughtful adjustments of placing here and there, on a gleaming copper tray; a sacred fire of sandalwood sticks was lit; holy oil was blessed and liberally dispensed; the chanting of mantras drifted among the palms; and I was made to break a coconut, which I did to sighs of relief (you could never tell with a Christian!) in one strike, into two perfectly hemispherical and auspicious halves. The Senior Pandit beamed as if it was all his own work. It was then that I noticed a Catholic priest (Gita, hedging her bets, had invited him to bless the stones as well). He had arrived early and now stood at a discreet distance from our puja group, looking on with polite interest and making perfectly clear from his expression that he was not about to pass judgement. He wore a spotlessly white soutane with a surplice about the shoulders, a silver holy water dispenser in his hand, patiently awaiting his turn.

Father Victor. Tall and lean, with a profile chiselled out of old, warm laterite, and a look of mild benediction which said to all who cared to take note, 'All faiths may find shelter in the House of the Lord.' The Pandit's look, on the other hand, as he completed the puja and threw a quick, dismissive glance in Father Victor's direction, indicated without any possibility of doubt that he considered holy water and a surplice very small potatoes. And the thought struck me – as it irreligiously does on such occasions – that the piousness of a Pandit may be measured instantly by the generosity of his girth, while, with a priest of the church, the precise opposite seems to be the case. Large notes, discreetly folded, passed from Gita's hand to the Pandit's and disappeared into the folds of his voluminous dhoti. Then Senior and Junior Pandits made what may only be described as a significant exit.

Father Victor's turn after this was a bit of an anti-climax. He came forward, opened his missal, delivered a short Latin invocation with grave authority, sprinkled the stones and – with pointed emphasis – us! with Holy Water, and was done. Then he accepted our invitation to coffee.

I was comfortable with the protocol. I knew that a small donation to a parish charity was par for the course, but it wouldn't do to be crass. I would only make him an offer he couldn't refuse when the moment was right.

'Do you plan to live here when the house is ready?' Father Victor asked.

'As often as we can,' Gita said.

'Can't be too often for me,' I said cheerfully.

'Well,' Gita said, by way of explanation, 'whenever Frank can take a few days off from his company.'

'Company,' I said, 'which company?'

Father Victor laughed.

'I gather,' he said, 'from friends of mine who live there that Bombay can be a burden.'

The innocuous but loaded understatement, as I was to discover in due course, was just one of Father Victor's many gifts. So was subtlety.

'We have our problems in Candolim as well,' he said, 'but it's a large village and we tend to keep them out of sight.'

I could appreciate an opening when it was offered.

'If I can help in some way, Father. A donation perhaps.'

'A donation,' Father Victor said, 'is always welcome. But ten minutes of your time would be even better.' No sooner said ... He glanced at his watch. 'The matron should be there about now. We can leave right away.'

'Very well, Father.' Gita began gathering up her things.

'Where are we going?' I asked.

'To pay a visit to a few old ladies,' Father Victor said cryptically and not a word more till we arrived at the Arc of Hope.

The name had been painted many aeons ago, in blue and gold, on a wooden plaque. The paint had long since flaked away; the letters were faded and hard to decipher, only the outlines – like a hazy memory at the distant edge of recollection – told of their meaning. The plaque was seamed and cracked in a hundred places and hung slightly askew from rusty hooks on the remains of what had once been a magnificently carved front door of Burma teak. The house it once protected was a very old mansion, formerly a grand and aristocratic residence, now, like so many others in Goa, left to dereliction and ruin. The marbled facing of crushed seashells worked with oil to a thick hard crust had peeled off in ugly swathes exposing pitted and broken laterite stone. Green moss and lichen had taken root in the cracks and spread in patches of ugly fungus on the walls. Huge portions of the roof were without tiles. The wooden beams and a good part of the loft, eaten through by white ants, sagged dangerously where they hadn't broken apart. A far cornice had crumbled and I was reminded of sunlight on a broken column in the ruins of my father's ancestral house in Colvale.

The Arc of Hope was no misnomer. Only hope in the face of hopeless odds would have kept this desolate shell of a house erect. The quarter acre of garden – such as there was – was overgrown with wild cactus, jungle grass and clumps of bamboo among the dying, untended palms. At the far end of the property were two rough sheds, a cooking place and an outdoor latrine. An open well with a cast iron bucket and rope attached to the handle lay under the frugal, cobwebbed shade of a parasite tree. It did not flower or bear fruit; the branches were gnarled and misshapen with spiky dark green leaves; the roots went deeper and wider into the ground than any other tree, draining all water from the soil in an area many circumferences wider than its own; in that circle of drought not a single other green thing grew.

I thought of the house – nothing stinted; no expense spared – which would rise on the foundations of Rockheart, and I felt guilt and depression, and a sense of my own mortality. Gita avoided my eyes. There seemed little point to conversation. Father Victor, with an equanimity which showed that he was no stranger to the Arc of Hope, looked about him with an air of expectation. I heard the distinctive, throaty growl of a Harley-Davidson revving in low gear – there is no other sound in the world like it – then the huge motor cycle swung into view around the corner and came to a racing stop within arm's length of us. A lithe, athletic figure, tall in the saddle, held out a hand. A glad smile creased dark, compelling eyes.

'Meet our Sarpanch,' Father Victor said in a tone of quiet self-congratulation as though Tomazinho Cardozo was his very own idea, minted and gift-wrapped specially for the occasion.

'Glad to have you in Candolim,' Tomazinho said. 'I'm told you're rebuilding an old house in Simer,' he chuckled, 'and paying a visit to one about to fall down.' He turned to Father Victor, 'Not if we can help it right, Father?'

'Lead the way.'

Father Victor pushed hard against the door; it creaked open a foot or so and jammed. Father Victor went in sideways, swiftly and neatly; he had done this before. Cautiously Gita and I followed. Tomazinho brought up the rear. 'Just a moment,' he said, paused, turned back to the door, examined the hinges, held the door top and bottom by its edge, lifted it and with a short grunt, heaved it fully open and flat against the inner wall. Then he dusted his hands off on the back of his pants. Here, I thought, was a man who would never let a problem pass him by. Candolim was well served in its sarpanch.

The interior was dark, fitfully lit by sunlight which filtered through the broken roof and barred windows. Deep shadows lay like the scars of old wounds on the cracked Italian tile, the ornamental mouldings and pelmets of what had once been a formal entrance hall. A woman came through the door at the far end. She walked towards us hesitantly and stopped in a shaft of sunlight. It lit up a face of rare serenity and gentleness; there was a radiance about her, a sense of loving kindness you wanted to reach out and touch and, within the fragility, a quiet strength of purpose you would never make your own.

'Azelia,' Father Victor said, 'she cares for the inmates.'

'It's very good of you to come,' Azelia said, 'I'm afraid they take a nap at this hour. They have very little strength left you see, and even for those who can be up and about, I'm afraid there's nothing to do.'

She led us through dank corridors to the right wing, the largest room in the house and the only room where the ceiling had remained in one piece. The women lay on reed mats on the floor. Ten or twelve very old women clearly at the end of their lives. They reminded me of nothing so much as rag dolls arranged by a child in attitudes of repose, curled up like foetuses, covered in the summer heat with cotton sheets drawn up to the neck; crumpled, abandoned heaps of utter inconsequence, faces turned to the wall, a hair's breadth away from their journey's end. Pray God, let it be soon enough. I was ashamed the moment the thought came to mind, but it persisted; it lay like an arctic chill upon the heart, a bleak and insistent summons in that mansion of despair. Father Victor bent down on one knee, smoothened a wisp of grey hair from a pale forehead, murmured a few words of what might have been comfort or prayer. The woman stirred; there was no recognition in the faded eyes. She raised her head with difficulty, took Father Victor's hand in hers and pressed the palm to her lips.

Father Victor spoke to me without looking up.

'Will you help us build a new Arc of Hope for our old people,' he said.

With astonishment I heard myself say, 'I'll try, Father.'

Where had the words come from?

*

We gathered in Father Victor's personal quarters in an annexe to the school. Spartan and frugal. A single bed, a cupboard and chest of drawers, a desk and chair drawn up (a single concession to personal indulgence) to a window with a view of fields of emerald paddy fringed by sentinel palms and, in the distance, pale hills cloaked in a fine violet haze. Pastoral beatitude. Good for Father Victor. He seemed to have made do excellently without a television set, a tapedeck, a radio. But how did he manage in this heat without a refrigerator? My respect for Father Victor increased at once by several orders of magnitude. Now, he gave us a short preamble to the business at hand.

'The present home,' he said, 'is a temporary accommodation. The owners live in Panjim and while they would be very happy to deed the house over to us, under Portuguese law – which, incidentally, still holds good in Goa – a legal agreement has to be drawn up and signed jointly and severally by the entire family. The daughters are in favour of doing so, but there's a son in Toronto who refuses to part with the house.'

'It's coming apart at the seams,' Gita said.

'Why doesn't he have it repaired?' I asked.

'He can't afford to,' Tomazinho said. 'It's the old Goan story all over again. He would rather see it fall to pieces than give it away. Ass!'

Azelia smiled. 'He does have reasons,' she said, 'sentimental reasons. He wants to keep his ancestral home in the family.'

'You know what they say about sticks and stones,' Tomazinho said.

'Come now,' Father Victor said, 'fait accompli. There's no point arguing about it. We can't have the house. Our lease runs out in a year. In any case it wouldn't do us much good if we could keep the place. It isn't large enough. There aren't any facilities. The kitchen's thirty yards away. Wood fires under brick and the child who cooks can barely cope. She has to feed twelve inmates and three nuns.'

'The toilets,' Azelia said, with a depth of understatement that Father Victor would surely approve of, 'are really hard on the old dears.'

'Quite impossible in the monsoon,' Tomazinho said.

'They prefer to stay in,' Azelia said, 'till the rain stops. But quite a few are incontinent anyway and it's hardest for them.'

A disquieting thought; for a moment, my mind held the image of one of those frail old women negotiating that horror of a garden, in pitch darkness and a rainstorm, to answer the call of nature. It was not something to have on one's conscience.

Action then; swift and decisive. 'Right, Father,' I said, 'let's get down to brass tacks, shall we? Have you quantified the requirement?'

Father Victor smiled. 'I like that word, quantified,' he said, 'it has a nice mathematical ring to it. I must remember to work it into one of my sermons.' He turned to Tomazinho, 'How does this sound, "Have you quantified your sins for the week, my children."'

'It might work even better at the next meeting of the Panchayat,' Tomazinho chuckled. 'Have you quantified the number of times the building laws were blatantly flouted in your vaddo?'

Gita added, 'Now if only Frank quantifies the fenis he knocks back before dinner, we'd be getting somewhere.'

Chastened, I said, 'What I meant was … '

'We know what you mean,' Father Victor said benignly. 'We have to build a new home for forty inmates, a ground floor and a first, with provision for a second as time goes on. Toilet facilities and a pantry on every floor. Well-equipped central kitchens and staff quarters. A recreation hall and a proper examination room for visiting doctors.' He paused for an essential afterthought, 'A quarter of an acre of garden, at the very least, with benches and a friendly dog or two. Elderly dogs, we can't have puppies prancing about all over the place.'

'How much will all this cost?' Gita asked.

'A million not counting the land,' Tomazinho said.

'How much have you raised?' I said.

'Not a paisa,' Father Victor said cheerfully.

I was well and truly up against it.

As if on cue, Azelia, who had excused herself ten minutes earlier, returned bearing a large tray with teacups, a steaming pot and a platter of Goa's most popular tea-time treat: light, fluffy rice-and-semolina pancakes fatly stuffed with grated coconut and melted jaggery with a hint of cinnamon. They were delicious. Here was a lady of many distinguished parts. I regarded Azelia with renewed respect. Was there no end to her virtues? Three pancakes and two cups of tea later, a cautious optimism seemed to be in order.

'A million,' I said, munching thoughtfully, 'will take some doing and a fair amount of time,'

'I'm sure the villagers will help,' Father Victor said.

'We shall put it to them,' Tomazinho said, 'forcefully.'

I was beginning to recognize that tone of voice. And I remembered the short shrift given to the Burma teak door at the Arc of Hope. Forcefully? I would bet long odds on it.

*

That evening we were invited to a tiatr 'under the stars' at the village football ground. 'A comedy,' Father Victor explained, 'written by the best Konkani playwright in Goa, in celebration of an award he received the other day – his umpteenth – from the Kala Akademi. You must come. I promise you won't be disappointed.' I said that I looked forward to it. I was not being polite. The tiatr is Goa's most enduring form of local drama raised to scintillating heights by highly skilled itinerant amateur and professional groups. Konkani is a language enriched by an oral tradition and best appreciated when spoken. Phonetic rendition – ranging from the subtle to the dramatic – changes meaning, adds fresh dimensions to emphasize and enhances plot and character at will. In the hands of an accomplished playwright and actors, the language becomes notation, the players the orchestra and the performance a symphony as imaginatively and finely wrought as anything you are likely to see on stage. The tiatr began at nine that night. An exuberant audience several hundred strong sat impatiently before a wooden stage artfully created from planks of mango wood, bamboo, painted wings and backdrop. The light boys armed with coloured cellophane filters perched on high ladders set slightly behind the wings. Now and again a tousled head popped up to genial cat-calls and affectionate cries of 'Cut his head off!' 'Down you clown!' and 'It's that monkey Mario,

Peace, War and True Grit

he's going to fall off any minute.' Behind the drawn stage curtains silhouetted figures could be seen rushing this way and that like marionettes, arranging props and furniture with great urgency, a few collisions (which the crowd greeted with cheers), more than a degree of confusion, and the odd, stifled curse. Then a gong sounded, loudly. The spotlights which played on the audience from the perimeter of the football field went off without warning. Sudden darkness; an excited hush faded into an expectant silence. The curtain parted and I noticed for the first time that the stage was open to the night sky. Under a million stars, the tiatr began.

It was a village satire, as wicked a piece of tiatr as playwright ever put to pen. The plot was dense, bewilderingly swift, as involuted as a French farce, with dramatic twists and turns, thorny pitfalls and hilarious prats, red herrings and dead ends. It was a delightful, rip-roaring send-up of the traditional village icons: the pontificating Headmaster whose ignorance left little to be desired; the Magistrate who was not beyond the discreet peccadillo; the slit-eyed Landlord, the fastest man with an eviction order in the village; the rapacious Hotelier who cut profitable corners at the expense of a hapless American tourist played by the darkest member of the troupe in – surprise! surprise! – Bermuda shorts, a Hawaiian bushshirt and a baseball cap with mirrored sunglasses that reflected the spots like laser beams; and the most oleaginous shyster of them, the Sarpanch. He was fat and sly and brilliantly unworthy, was our Sarpanch, full of chicanery and guile, pompously good words and heinously wicked deeds; he raised cynicism and insincerity to an art form, ruthlessness to stratospheric heights, rapacity and greed to a glitteringly beguiling philosophy. How we awaited his exposure and comeuppance. And when he was finally led off by the Law, manacled and sweaty, hurling dark vengeful glances and imprecations all about him, the audience jeered and catcalled until it was hoarse.

It was well up to midnight; the play was over but the credits had still to roll. Rousing curtain calls, wolf whistles at the heroine, loud kudos for the simple but honest hero, a thunderous fanfare for the assembled troupe as they took bow after bow. Then the erstwhile Sarpanch stepped forward, called for silence, made a brief speech and concluded fulsomely, '... and we, the players, would like to give special thanks tonight to the genius of Goa's greatest playwright. We are honoured that he chose to direct this evening's performance. Let's give him a big hand!' A dramatic moment or two; all eyes were turned towards the wings (where was the playwright?); then rapturous applause as Tomazinho Cardozo, Sarpanch of Candolim, walked modestly onto the stage ...

*

The phone rang at seven in the morning. I opened a reluctant eye, and picked up the receiver. Why do I wake in Bombay feeling like a three-day-old dog's breakfast, while in Goa I am up and blithely about at the crack of dawn, one with the larks?

'Frank Simoysh?' This is the way they say my name in Goa; I shall never get used to it; it makes me sound like an exotic brand of sausage.

'This is he.'

'Father Victor. Good morning. Have I woken you?'

Perish the thought. I've just returned from a five mile jog, done fifty push-ups, taken a cold shower and read five chapters of War and Peace.

'Not really, Father.'

'I have news for you, Frank. At three in the morning – hardly, you will agree, a Godly hour – we had what at first appeared to be a celestial visitation. The wrath of God, no less, just outside my window. A thunderous roar approaching at speed. Just when I thought the object, whatever it was – a thunderbolt perhaps – would bring the house to the ground, it stopped just short of the window.'

A dramatic pause. Why was Father Victor so histrionic so early in the morning? Or was all of this waffle leading up to something?

'It was a small truck, or van,' he continued, 'difficult to tell at that hour of the morning, with a presence out of all proportion to its size. The noise, even with the engine idling, was astonishing. Families within a radius of five hundred yards had woken, rushed to the spot en masse in various stages of undress, and now stood at a respectful distance from the machine waiting for something to happen. It wheezed, hissed and refused to be quiet.'

The penny dropped; I squirmed a bit; Father Victor was enjoying himself hugely.

'Father Christmas,' he said, 'rather early in the year, but who am I to look a gift horse? No sleigh or reindeer. Sad, but there you are. Technology catching up with the old boy. Happily, the truck expired just then and four large men emerged and brought forth ... '

Boon Companions

'It was Gita's idea,' I said lamely.

'Such an unChristian thing to do,' Father Victor chuckled, 'but what can one expect from a Hindu? You, I gather, were staunchly opposed to the thought.'

'I have never known you to talk so much, Father Victor.'

'I have not been moved to such eloquence in a very long time,' Father Victor said, 'but you must admit I have reason. A refrigerator with three doors, separate temperatures and it defrosts itself! I have never seen such a machine in my life. Please thank the anonymous donor for me.'

'Selfish motives, Father. Now you can offer me a chilled beer when I next visit.'

'Or as much ice as you'd like in a caju feni or two.'

'Or three – charity, Father, charity.'

Father Victor laughed. 'The machine has been kept in the corridor which connects the teachers' room to my quarters. Now all of us can use it. The Headmaster has written you a thank you letter. I am having it couriered today. He has just been elected President of the Headmasters Association of Goa. Don't forget to congratulate him.'

'As sincerely as I know how, Father. Take care. Thank you for calling.'

'God be with you, my son.'

The letter arrived at lunch; I opened it and was disconcerted to find myself addressed by my first name by someone I had never met.

Dear Frank,
  On behalf of all of the teachers of St Joseph's High School, many thanks to you and Gita for such

a thoughtful gift. Summer is beginning to settle in and it is nice to know that, from this day on, we shall have only ourselves to blame if we get hot under the collar!

Father Victor tells me the machine was conjured up out of airy nothingness at three o'clock in the morning. Amazing grace! With influence of this order at your command so early in the day, can a mere million take more than a week?

With every good wish,
Yours,
Tomazinho Cardozo

PS: *A bottle of Candolim's noblest caju feni cools, chills, frosts, etc., in the machine even now, awaiting your arrival!*

Tomazinho Cardozo wasn't the only Goan who could dash off a nifty letter. I replied by return of post.

Dear Tomazinho,
I am in a quandary as to how you should be addressed.
1. Dear Sarpanch
2. Dear Principal
3. Dear Playwright
4. Dear Actor & Director
5. Dear President of the Headmasters Association of Goa.
Whew!
Please clear up this confusing situation at once.

> *Tick off no more than or no fewer than five of the above.*
>
> *Just to be on the safe side, Gita and I send heartfelt congratulations to each of you.*
>
> *Take care.*

*

Airy nothingness, indeed. A million was a great deal of money, even by the standards of Bombay's overflowing coffers. Charity here was an industry, but there were two conditions a genuine donor insisted upon. The first was the tax-exempt status of the charity, failing which the gift would be added back to the donor's income (whether individual or corporate) and taxed. The second – and perhaps most important – was the legality of the charity. Was it genuine – a trust registered and monitored by the government – or did it lie in that grey area which cast a pall over the entire economy of the country: the hyperactive industry which converted white money to black? Scores of shell trusts and charities existed for this purpose alone. The most common wrinkle occurred in donations out of company profits. A donation of a hundred thousand, for instance, would be made untaxed out of income (if the charity had tax-exempt status) and ninety thousand would be returned, cash in a bag, the trust keeping ten; the donor became richer and the exchequer poorer by sixty thousand rupees. There were no end of ingenious creative twists to the original scam. The one most in demand saw the donation in rupees appearing, by inexplicable sleight of hand, in a Swiss or Bahamian bank in sterling, dollars, francs or Deutsche Marks, take your pick.

It was a financial minefield where legitimate companies and individual donors had to tread very carefully indeed. There were many strikes against the Arc of Hope, and I listed them down gloomily:
1. A trust would have to be set up.
2. It would take a year to acquire tax-free status. Could we wait that long? No.
3. Candolim? Where on earth was that?
4. Did the plight of a handful of destitute old women matter in a country with tens of millions of poor, lame, blind, deaf, dumb, diseased and underfed children?
5. Frank Simoes? Who cares!

Here was a product which didn't exist which I had to sell to people who couldn't care less if it did. Ho hum. That had a familiar ring to it. The advertising business trains one well for this sort of thing. First things first. I set about preparing lists of the well-heeled and philanthropically (?) inclined:
1. Senior and junior Captains of Industry from the register of the Indian Society of Advertisers ('Social Responsibility' was their new buzz word; let them put their money where their slogans were).
2. Diners Club members (fat cats, and I was, after all, only asking for a thousand rupees a go. One measly lunch at a five-star watering hole).
3. Those splendid chaps, the Rotarians (One had only to ask? Fool!).
4. My friends in the arts (poor as church mice; generous as gods).
5. My enemies in the advertising business (Conscience money!).

6. Rich Parsi dowagers dripping with the stuff (where would I find them?).
7. Newspapers and periodicals the length and breadth of the land to which my advertising agency contributed astronomical amounts of revenue annually (put up or else!).

A net which spread far and wide – pleasingly democratic and commendably endowed; it presented a single problem. I hadn't the faintest idea of what to say to them.

Radhika found me one morning grappling with the Appeal, moping at the Underwood and snarling at the cat.

'What's wrong, Dad?'

I told her. Children have a wonderful clarity of vision.

'Just tell them what you told me when you came back that morning. Do you remember?'

'You shed a tear or two.'

'I did no such thing.'

'Sorry, you sniffled.'

'I had a bad cold.'

'Quite right. The simple truth, no more, no less. Avoid frills and dramatis personae. No Harley Davidson. Not even Azelia.'

'Have a go dad.'

So I did. Dottore Luiz da Gama Rose, wherever he was, cast a kindly eye and a purposeful wink in my direction. Carl Jung, chuckling at the innocence of it all, lent a helping hand: shafts of synchronicity swung my way. The stars rearranged themselves in beneficent disposition. The luck of the Simoeses held good and true. The cheques began coming in, first in dribbles, then a flood. My Chief Accountant was not amused.

'Seven hundred thousand rupees,' he said resentfully, 'our income tax officer will have a question or two to ask when we file our returns. And I will have to answer them.'

'That's the least of your problems, my dear chap,' I said, restraining a ferocious glee (it wasn't often that our accountant was hoisted with his own petard), 'how will you explain away the donations in kind?'

'They will have to be valued,' he said gloomily, 'before we send them off to Goa, and I doubt we'll be allowed the trucking costs as an expense.'

'Life is hard.'

'Give-in-kind-if-you-can't-give-cash' was my very own idea and I was proud of this little bit of inspired lateral thinking. It had reaped rich if unpredictable dividends.

We had pledges for fifty coir mattresses, but no pillows; four dozen pillow cases but only a dozen bedsheets, a perpetual supply of toilet paper (somebody out there was really concerned). A cosmetic company had written in offering, with a straight face, a year's supply of anti-wrinkle and moisturizing creams, 'just past their sell-by date but guaranteed to be 100% effective for the next twelve months'. A manufacturer of breakfast foods gave us a choice between muesli and oats, recommending the oats strongly, ' ... an excellent nutritional supplement for the aged. The fibre promotes regular pain- and strain-free bowel movements' (ouch!). A jam manufacturer brought a creative solution to breakfast spreads: 'We can ring the changes from season to season. Mango preserves in summer, for instance, strawberry jam in winter and (triumphantly) guava cheese right through the year.'

The nation's largest purveyors of toiletries promised an 'on-going supply of essentials – soaps, talc, toothpastes, provided the requirement was certified, individually and severally, by all the members of the trust and an independent firm of chartered accountants, and supported by an audited balance sheet at the end of the financial year'. ('Go the whole hog,' Gita said, 'send them notarized identity cards, baptismal certificates and clean chits from the police. Finger-printed!') I had reservations about the canned foods on offer; problems loomed large: was corned beef generously marbled with fat quite the ticket for an octogenarian diet? Would ninety-year-old taste buds leap joyfully to the fray at the sight of a can of eels in brine? And surely pork vindaloo would offer scant encouragement to livers of such venerable provenance?

'Accept it all,' my accountant said, with a let's-pick-the-bones-clean look in his eye, 'what they can't use they can sell at a discount.' The pharmaceutical manufacturers displayed a sense of confusion. Vitamin supplements, antibiotics and suppositries (geriatric expertise of dazzling depth!) – a thoughtful gesture that would never have come to mind – were very welcome indeed. But testosterone capsules? I was somewhat mystified at the offer; did they know something about old people that I didn't? My favourite music company had donated a stereo system, with a touching note and a cheque, 'To stock up on their choice of Goan songs and melodies.' I would see to it that they did.

There is no logic to generosity or the lack of it. Small

Peace, War and True Grit

firms, unheard of and unsung, sent in ten thousand rupees and more; conglomerates refused to help; a dozen companies – at the top of the Indian corporate ladder – sent in a measly thousand rupees each with a curt covering letter from a grudging minion who maintained a disapproving distance from such disgraceful behaviour, 'On instructions from our Managing Director (I am no party to this foolishness) ... Please receipt our contribution by signed revenue stamp (or else!)'. But I was happy to have been wrong about the Rotarians; they came up trumps.

The donations added up to six hundred and ninety thousand rupees. The gifts and pledges in kind ran to six foolscap sheets. The last entry, scribbled in a neat and familiar hand, read:

From Radhika Simoes: A Christmas Tree.

I phoned Tomazinho with the good news.

'How,' I asked, 'do I get a Christmas tree from Bombay to Goa?'

'By refrigerator truck,' he said, 'but not, if you can help it, at three o'clock in the morning.'

'And seven hundred thousand rupees?'

'In a plain bag,' he said, 'in trench coat and dark glasses at the last stroke of midnight under Abbe Faria's statue in Panjim. You will be met by Father Victor disguised as an Archbishop. Please memorize the passwords. He will say, "Feni?" You will reply, "A triple and spare the water."'

'You are wasting good money making bad jokes on a trunk line. When will you grow up and begin to behave like a sarpanch?'

'We have not allowed the grass to gather underfoot,' Tomazinho said, in the stern but kindly voice he assumes when addressing his Panchayat. 'At the end of High Mass on Sunday, Father Victor made a passionate appeal to the parishioners – the creamy upper layer who will only attend High Mass and no other. You would have been proud at the manner in which our pastor quantified the problem!' – Would I ever live that down? – 'His oration, there's no other word for it, went on for fifteen minutes and at the end of it, you couldn't find a dry eye in the church. We were thoroughly ashamed of ourselves when he made his final point. That clinched it.'

'Fire and brimstone if you don't deliver?'

'Could we do less for our old people than hard-nosed city slickers from big, bad Bombay?'

'Hardly hard-nosed.'

'Only in a manner of speaking.'

'And shortly to become a villager in partial residence, in case it's slipped your mind.'

'You will be overwhelmed by our welcome. Seriously, wonderful things have happened. We have collected two hundred thousand. One of the best architects in Panjim has offered his services free. A contractor has pledged the labour, again at no cost, and a widow not noted, shall we say, for her boundless generosity, has seen the light. She's donated an acre of land, a few minutes down the road from the church with a magnificent view of the paddy fields.'

'That leaves us two hundred thousand short.'

'Never fear. You'll find a way.'

'I shall apply what's left of my mind to the problem,' I said, 'without benefit of the local brew.'

'Our prayers,' Tomazinho said, a hint of laughter still there, 'will be with you.'

*

Then I remembered Shivanand Salgaocar, the second son of that great and mighty oak of a Goan, Vasudev Salgaocar. When his father died suddenly and prematurely, at the age of sixty-seven, the mantle of a legend was thrust upon Shivanand and his younger brother Raj. Shivanand was a little over thirty at the time. Overnight, he was thrown into the ruthless maelstrom of global commodity trading, negotiating multimillion ton contracts in boardrooms in Tokyo, Peking, Hamburg and Seoul. 'They don't give an inch,' he said to me years later. 'It's all thrust and parry, move and counter-move, every advantage is pushed to the limit, no quarter given and, in all fairness, none expected. It's not as if they are ruthless or unscrupulous men. This is simply the way they do business. They know no other.' The men across the table were a good twenty years older than Shivanand and, by his own admission, he was still wet behind the ears. But he prevailed. If, today, Shivanand is the first standard bearer of the House of Salgaocar, Raj at his shoulder, is its inspired commercial and political entrepreneur. He has taken the group into activities as far removed as publishing and real estate and, with determination and commitment, led the political movement in Goa and New Delhi which culminated in the official recognition of Konkani as one of India's national languages.

Boon Companions

    I had met Shivanand briefly on social occasions while his father was alive, but we were no more than casual acquaintances. Then, in the unlikeliest of circumstances we began what was to prove an enduring friendship. Goa's creme da la creme gather together once a year on 26 January, India's Republic Day, to take tea with the Governor. I laid no claim to belong to that exalted company, and had been invited as a polite afterthought: a house guest of the Governor was a friend of mine. Feeling somewhat lost, I cast about for a familiar face when a hand touched me lightly on the shoulder from behind. Shivanand. He does not stand out in a crowd. He is slim, neat, quietly centred and perfectly certain of himself. 'I've been meaning to talk to you,' he said and got to the point without preamble. The family sought a biographer for his father. Would I accept the assignment? There were reasons for the request. As a Goan I would bring a greater depth of understanding to the subject but, what was more important, his father and I had been friends. So we had; I was proud of the friendship, and glad to agree.

    By the time Fare Forward Voyager was published, Shivanand and I had become friends; so had our families. We worked closely in the year it took to put the material together for the book – hundreds of interviews, months of desk research, a great deal of travelling, the excerpting and indexing of hundreds of files of correspondence, memoranda and documents. In the process, I became an infernal nuisance. I demanded unconditional access; I got it. I'd phone Shivanand at all hours of the day and night. When the pressure got to me, and I snarled and snapped at anything that moved, he was unfailingly understanding, good-humoured and helpful. Boon companion in that daunting time, ever encouraging and supportive, never once drawing attention – no matter how tactfully – to the fact that I was well over the deadline. When I sat down at the typewriter to compose the final paragraphs, I felt as close to him as a brother. They are worth reproducing; they give some slight indication of the weight of responsibility that became his:

Vasudev Salgaocar's body was cremated at 5.30 p.m. on Sunday, 14 October 1984, on the open ground before the Salgaocar Medical Research Centre.

To this day, no one can explain how word could have spread so quickly. But they came, the people of Goa, in the burning heat of the noonday sun; singly, in twos, threes, small groups of ten and twenty; then in their hundreds until well over fifteen thousand mourners stood silent and unmoving paying their last respects. They came from the southern mining villages and the far-flung hamlets of the north, from town and countryside, by road, rail and bullock-cart-fisherman and farmer, priest and politician; bargeman and shopkeeper, friends of his youth and trading years, compatriots from his pioneering ventures into Goa's virgin mining territories, powerful colleagues drawn from the very summit of Goa's elite. Never in living memory – not since Chief Minister Bandodkar's death – had so many Goans gathered together in prayerful silence to pay homage to one of their own.

To thousands, with tears in their eyes, it was a death in the family.

Shivanand, in this the most despairing moment of his young life, blood shaking his heart, sought his father's courage even as he put flame to pyre and destroyed his mortal remains.

*

I tried to get hold of Shivanand at Vasco da Gama, the company's headquarters but had no luck. The family was vacationing in Europe. Summer was upon us and the great annual exodus to cool watering holes in India and abroad had begun. Schools closed for the seven week holiday; offices ran on skeleton staffs; the government limped along, the bureaucracy now with a real excuse to sit on its hands. Power and water shortages plagued the cities. Those who could fled the heat; the less fortunate sweltered in temperatures which stayed above a hundred and prayed for an early monsoon. I said goodbye to Tomazinho and Father Victor. The Arc of Hope was put on hold till October, when the rains would end. Gita, Radhika and I took swift passage to London as we did each year and settled like a small, brown, migratory flock in the well-watered pastures of St James Court Hotel at Buckingham Gate. We took an apartment there each year where, after initial forays into Fortnum & Mason, Selfridges and Marks & Spencers, I assumed the role of Michelin Chef manque, providing light relief to an unappreciative family until, driven by frustration and gloom, I sought refuge in pork pies and room service, glad of the opportunity to complain about somebody else's cooking.

Peace, War and True Grit

Our first Sunday found me in an attitude of disgracefully sybaritic repose, in pyjamas, dressing-gown and bedroom slippers, deeply sunk in that most perfectly inspired of English inventions, the over-stuffed sofa, feet up, sharing Breakfast with Frost over a tulip of Moet de Chandon and a bowl of chilled strawberries. Frost and the champagne were in sparkling form. I was well on my way to getting there. Gita and Radhika were off feeding the ducks at St James park, a barbarous insult to a Sunday morning; but there's no accounting for the antic behaviour of Indian tourists in London. The doorbell rang. Resentfully, I opened it. Shivanand, Swati and Toto stood in the doorway. They were dressed in the hi-tech protective gear Indians employ to keep the treacherous English summer at bay; from ankle, to wrist, to throat, the children were enwrapped as for a winter in Helsinki; Shivanand wore heavy-duty Levis, trainers, turtleneck and a chunky Shetland sweater knotted snazzily about the waist. An umbrella was draped over one arm, under the other was a collapsible stroller with the *Sunday Times*, neatly folded, firmly wedged in the seat. For good measure, he sported a jockey cap worn back to front. Ready for the blizzards. I thoroughly approved. My own pyjamas discreetly hid all signs of the second most perfectly inspired of English inventions: silk long Johns. No Indian who cared for his goosebumps would go to bed without them.

'What on earth are you doing here?' I asked.

'We are here,' Shivanand said grandly, 'to invite your delightful family to Sunday brunch at Spolinski's Balloon. If you're very nice to me I may take you along as well.'

'How did you know we were at St James?'

'Ve haf vays of getting at the truth!'

'Have you been drinking, Shiv?'

'It's the spring air and the prospect of a glorious fortnight in Scotland. On yon bonny banks ... '

'Who is Spolinski? And why does he have a fetish about balloons?'

'You will be a wiser and happier man for the experience,' Shivanand said. 'Where are the better half and the light of your life?'

'Feeding ducks in the park.'

'While you wallow in sloth and strawberries.'

'I waved at the champagne, 'Wallow away.'

There was a triumphant shout from the master bedroom. Toto had discovered the second television set. Within seconds, the Masters of the Universe began to tear the morning apart. Regretfully, I picked up the remote control and vaporized David Frost. Shivanand closed the drawing-room door gently, helped himself to some champagne and nibbled at a strawberry.

'A chilled mango,' he said, 'would have brought out the flavour better.'

I said farewell to a halcyon Sunday.

'I suppose I'd better get dressed.'

'Spolinski's are a liberal, broad-minded establishment,' Shivanand said, glancing at my ankles, 'but they may draw the line at long Johns.'

In the event, I doubt they would have done any such thing. Spolinski's was a theme restaurant for kids of all ages. Glittering baubles, neon buntings, trick mirrors and fairy lights at every twist and turn of the circular wrought iron staircase. A Pierrot and Pierrette gave away enormous gas balloons free. A lady clown, tripping the light fantastic, led us to a long table for ten. Shivanand had invited friends. The children scrummaged for the best seats. We took the last two in the corner, backs to the wall, and looked about us warily like gunfighters at a Wild West Saloon.

There was a stage at the far end of the restaurant, and a show was on: tumblers and jugglers dazzled with their antics; clowns fell over their feet; three Pekes jumped through hoops, climbed ladders, walked tight ropes and found hidden things until, suddenly, one of them ran around in little circles, barking furiously, found a post and raised a contented leg. The children cheered. We were served the best junk food I have eaten this side of Big Mac and Colonel Sanders. A young woman, in a tiger-striped jump suit with a tail and whiskers, came across and without so much as a by-your-leave painted the children's faces with day-glo, making them over, with uncanny realism, into characters from the musical Cats. Toto began to miaow loudly. And when the Chairman of the Bank of England strode magisterially to our table (to complain, no doubt, about the din; Shiv and I unlimbered our gun hands!), he turned out to be Mr Mike MacDuff, magician extraordinaire, who conjured up coloured eggs out of thin air, shining half-crowns from young ears, caused wedding rings to disappear off fingers only to retrieve them from a bread basket and brought starspangled smiles and yelps of glee to little cat faces.

'It would be nice,' I said to Shivanand, sotto voce, 'if we could take Mr MacDuff back to Goa with us in a doggie bag.'

'When do you return?' Shivanand asked.

'Three weeks from today. And you?'

'At about the same time.'

'You must,' I said, 'spend an evening with us in Candolim. There are a few old friends I'd like you to meet.'

Nice phrase, 'a few old friends.' Ambiguous. Yet truthful to the core. It would have won Father Victor's instant approval. Shivanand came as near to an indignant snort as he would ever get.

'News travels fast in Goa,' he said, 'I know all about your old friends.'

'We are two hundred thousand short.'

'You have all of my moral support.'

'Two hundred big ones.'

'I doubt if even Mr Macduff could manage that,' Shivanand said, 'you won't get a rupee out of me, but let's wait till we meet in Goa. I have' – he chuckled – 'a few tricks up my sleeve.'

*

The tricks were huge tipper-trucks, sturdy work horses normally used to transport loads of iron ore from the mines to the loading barges along the river. Now they carried cargoes of generosity and goodwill from Vasco da Gama, the Salgaocar headquarters, to the site for the Arc of Hope in Candolim: long shafts of building steel painted a bright, rust-proof ochre, planks of strong, seasoned mango wood, hundreds of coils of insulated electrical wire, ton-loads of laterite bricks (dressed!) well beyond our needs ('You'll have to build a wall; two wells, elevations for the raised flower-beds,' Shivanand said, 'and no garden is complete without a gazebo. Face up to it, Frank, you will never make a builder'). The trucks were unloaded with the speed and efficiency for which the Salgaocars were renowned, Father Victor, his finest hour upon him, moved in and out of the clouds of dust like a happy wraith, settling a point here, giving a swift instruction there, examining, with a keen if unprofessional interest, the contents of every truck; beside himself at the arrival of a truck with incidental furniture; quite overcome by another with bathroom fixtures and odds and ends; and rendered speechless (as I was) when the last truck turned into the dirt-track bearing a young gulmohar tree, a team of gardeners and a note from Shivanand, 'Replant this at once in a corner of the site. There's nothing like a flowering gulmohar to cheer everybody up.'

Now why hadn't I remembered to tell Shivanand that we would be happy to accept kind for cash?

Ask a Goan to work for a cause and he will labour mightily without thought of rest from dawn to dusk; ask him to do the same work for a wage and it's best to bring in Colonel Saldanha as a consultant. Astonishing application attended the building of the Arc of Hope. The labour went at it like inspired dervishes. I couldn't make any sense of the clouds of dust, the confusion, the vast amounts of material scattered at random all over the place, and why was the huge cement machine placed dead centre of the site? But method emerged from all of this madness. Before you could say 'Pass the pickaxe,' the foundations had been excavated; within days, the stones were laid and cemented; within a fortnight the structure began to take recognizable shape, like an unfolding mirage against the palms and the rippling velvet lakes of young paddy. The Harley-Davidson put in an appearance from time to time, its throaty growl cutting cleanly through the clatter; Tomazinho would cast a cool, professional eye over the chaos, nod approvingly, and roar off. Father Victor made an inspection every day. I visited as often as I could.

And one fine morning the Bishop, no less, came along with his entourage on his annual visit to the parish.

He was well pleased. There was a lunch at the school hall, put together with great pride by carefully selected ladies of the village chosen as much for their culinary skills as for subtle restraint (none of the unbridled excesses of a festal groaning board here!) and preceded by an aperitif trolley from which the Bishop helped himself to a large Black Label, the rest of us following suit, with the exception of Father Victor (who chose to remain noticeably abstemious). Then the Bishop made a small speech. He congratulated us on the Arc of Hope. It was, he said, a fine example of Christian endeavour at its unselfish best. In the twilight of life, there was no finer succour for our less fortunate brethren than shelter, care and a loving hand. Then, with a twinkle in his eye, he concluded wryly, 'And I am certain that those among you who have worked hard to raise funds for this noble cause will have applied their minds to the small matter of the upkeep of the home. We must do justice, in the years ahead, to the very generous beginnings of the Arc of Hope. I have asked Father Victor to work out an estimate of the annual costs' – Father Victor avoided my eye – 'Thank you all.' And the Bishop blessed us for past – and future! – endeavours.

A small cloud on a perfect horizon.

Darker, heavier clouds would gather in the years to come, breaking with sound and fury over the lives of my three friends. Father Victor would be transferred, shortly after the inauguration of the Arc of Hope, to a poor and remote parish in the south of Goa, where an undeclared war had broken out between a renegade priest and a tough, unforgiving community of ramponkars. Tomazinho would go forth and do battle for his political life against impossible odds. And Shivanand would be struck down without warning to be brought into brutal confrontation with his own mortality.

*

In the fifteen years in which Tomazinho Cardozo had been thrice elected sarpanch of the village of Candolim, he had won the hearts and minds of its five thousand families, tempering the law of the land with compassion and understanding. His authority, sanctioned by the electorate but, in large measure earned, went well beyond its legal definition. He had become friend, confidante, father-figure, arbitrator in family disputes, marriage counsellor, and godfather so many times over that he had long since lost count. At the best of times, the governance of Candolim was no easy proposition. A villager's first loyalties, deeply rooted and fiercely upheld, are to the immediate family; next to the extended clan; to lesser degree but still staunchly defended, to the vaddo in which he resides; and only then to the village at large. It is a closed, rural community, basically agrarian and often medieval in its attitudes and behaviour. Tomazinho had pursued a single principle as sarpanch: he would not, if he could help it, allow the greater good of his villagers to be subverted by any one individual or group. And while at the beginning of his tenure as sarpanch, this stance, as troublesome as it was refreshing, caused resentment, over a period of time the people of Candolim came to realize that Tomazinho's way was in the best interests of all. They closed ranks behind him, and when Gita and I began the construction of Rockheart, I was glad that we had an honest and committed sarpanch as head of the village council, and I only wished, on this pleasant December morning, that our first meeting could have come about under happier circumstances.

Our property was unfenced and the evening before, Radhika, two years at the time and playing on the sand had come within a heart-beat of sudden death: I have mentioned her encounter with a cobra before. Only Jimi, hackles up, growling deep in her throat, stood between my daughter and the black cobra, its ribcage spread wide, the spectacled hood quivering, lower body coiled taut as a spring, ready to strike. A carpenter's boy screamed and the cobra moved swiftly across the sand and into the mangroves along the dune.

Our neighbours in the fishing hamlet where Rockheart was being built were generous with all manner of exotic advice, from the planting of a Mosandas tree (there wasn't a snake which didn't flee in disgust at the scent) to the services of Mohan Kandlikar who had a special way with cobras, the ritual handed down for generations from father to first-born son. Kandlikar's Poisonous Snake Puja was guaranteed to cause all manner of slithering beastie to depart our acre post-haste, never to return. I thought it best to take a third opinion. My forestry officer friend said, 'Superstitious nonsense. You need a six foot snake wall with a forty-five degree overhang, coated with a special weatherproof glazing and with a curved hemispherical trench all along the outer base. Or you can keep a mongoose or two, but the neighbours won't like that.'

I had asked for a meeting with Tomazinho with some misgiving. The law had banned all new construction within two hundred metres of the high tide mark and half of our acre lay within that point. I had to have my wall; the law said I could not; it was a judgement that would have taxed Solomon.

Tomazinho said, 'I know why you're here. It's about the cobra on your property last evening.'

'Touch and go,' I said, 'six feet from Radhika and ready to strike.'

'Part of the ecology,' he said, 'but they very rarely come out before nightfall. The construction work may have unsettled it.'

'I've had a word with the Forestry Department,' I said, 'a wall is the only solution.'

'Half of your property lies well within the two hundred metre line.'

'I know, but I can't take a chance. My daughter is two years old and you know how they are.'

Tomazinho laughed. 'Perpetual motion,' he said.

'And quick. You can't take your eyes off them for a minute.'

'Well, let's have a look at the plans.'

He spread the survey map on the table and studied it carefully.

'If memory serves, we've given you permission to rebuild on an existing house.'

'That's right.'

'It was originally owned by the Figuerido family in Cortalim. Very rich and distinguished. Old money. They took every care when they built. And walls, strong, stout walls, kept encroachers out. So there had to be a wall around the property. Let me check. We may have an earlier survey map on file.'

A dusty box file was brought in. Tomazinho and his clerk pored over the contents. Yellowed, fragile paper, worn like parchment, the ink faded and indecipherable, the outlines of property, houses and walls blurred, broken and quite beyond resolution.

'Here we are,' Tomazinho said, studied the survey map carefully, then sighed. 'No luck I'm afraid. Now we do have a problem. Let's assemble the master minds.' He turned to the clerk, 'Any of the panchayat members in?'

There were; Tomazinho made the introductions.

'The best minds in the village,' he said, 'will now offer a solution.'

'Piece of cake,' said the first member.

'A concrete and brick wall upto here,' said the second.

'And bio fencing,' Tomazinho added triumphantly, 'the rest of the way around.'

'A bio fence?' I said, unable to keep the misgivings out of my voice.

'Nothing like it,' Tomazinho said, 'six feet high planks of mango wood, three inches thick, packed tight, with a cactus barrier all around the outside.'

'And will that keep snakes out?'

'Anything that slithers,' Tomazinho laughed, 'grass snakes, pythons, anacondas, take your pick.'

'A brick wall,' I said, 'which grows into a mango wood fence and sprouts a cactus hedge. Will wonders never cease!'

'Send in an official application,' Tomazinho smiled, 'and a small piece of advice, if I may. Why don't you have the snake puja done as well? You never lose by hedging your bets.'

'You're going to like Candolim,' said the first member.

'Snakes and all,' said the second.

'I have a sneaking suspicion,' I said, 'that I will.'

*

But ten years later I had reason to fear for Goa's future. In that decade, Candolim, like the rest of Goa, saw more turbulent change than in the previous half-century. International tourism had discovered the green and pleasant land of my ancestors. Candolim was one of the most beautiful coastal villages in the north, a plum, ripe and rich for the picking. Powerful corporations, with an established national presence and much clout in the corridors of power in Goa and New Delhi, moved in like sharks for the kill. They bought large tracts of agricultural property and obtained residential conversions in the time it took to put pen to paper (for the most part illegally), and sought to bend the construction laws to their advantage by bribery and coercion. Irresistible force, till they encountered an immovable object in the person of a sarpanch on a Harley-Davidson! Worse, the last of a near extinct species, an honest official in power; a sarpanch moreover, beleaguered and in conflict with his own government for Tomazinho had made enemies among powerful figures in the administration. By the time the fourth Panchayat elections came to be fought, the battle lines were drawn.

I was in Bombay during those tumultuous weeks, and quite unaware of the dramatic events taking place in Candolim. Months later I was able to put together, piece by critical piece, the violent mosaic of the momentous election. The forces of reaction had never been stronger or more determined. For the first time in the history of Goan village politics, politicians in high places in Panjim threw themselves into the fray through surrogate contestants. The elections were keenly followed by political observers in every village in Goa, and no one was prepared to lay odds on Tomazinho's survival. Powerful electoral machines, massively funded, took to the rural hustings with every dirty trick in the book. Overnight, posters sprouted on tree trunks, shop fronts, bus stops and village tintos. A whispering campaign was launched against Tomazinho, but there were no chinks in his armour and his opponents made rough weather of it. At their wits' end, they accused him of corruption and worse. Rumour spreads and gathers embroidery in Goa in the time it takes for a calumny to pass between two people. The financial chicanery attributed to Tomazinho ran true to form, and took wild flights of fantasy as time went on. Tens of thousands of rupees under the table became, overnight, hundreds of thousands in kickbacks from construction licenses. A pig farm tucked away in Belgaum was discovered in his brother's name. Bungalows and acres

Peace, War and True Grit

of property in Pune and Bangalore materialized out of thin air. A prawn hatchery in Ratnagiri was thrown in for good measure. But there were those who would have none of this nonsense. Tomazinho, they said, had simply salted the stuff away in a numbered account in a bank in Zurich.

The man with illegal millions, pig farms, prawn hatcheries, palatial residences and a numbered Swiss bank account lived in a house so small, I had to bend at the knees to get in through the front door. His personal life was beyond reproach (though this did not prevent his enemies from spreading the nastier kinds of slander); he and his wife earned their living as school teachers, and for twenty years his only means of transport had been the trusty Harley-Davidson. But throw enough mud and some of it begins to stick. Doubts were expressed about Tomazinho's integrity by villagers who had so far been loyal supporters. The whispering campaign was lubricated by large sums of money judiciously distributed, by threat and intimidation where cash offered no possibility of coercion. And when a large corporation with a major investment in the village threw its considerable financial and organizational support behind one of Tomazinho's major opponents, the tenor of public opinion began to tilt, imperceptibly but surely, against him.

Tomazinho had no organization worth the name. His supporters and well-wishers from every vaddo in the village did their bit, but their funds were nowhere near enough to make an impression. For every poster they put up the opposition had a dozen. Under cover of darkness, their posters were defaced, pasted over or torn down. For every public meeting they were able to hold, Tomazinho's opponents organized a handful; for every leaflet distributed they sent out a hundred. As the deadline for the elections approached, Tomazinho's supporters were in near panic. His cause seemed not so much lost as irretrievably stifled. Then Tomazinho decided to take the fight in person to the people; every villager would hear his voice. 'I decided to go on my own to every hamlet in every ward,' he said to me later, 'and put my case to the villagers.' Word was sent very late the night before, so that the opposition would have no time to disrupt the meetings. At first light, Tomazinho would kick start the Harley-Davidson and begin the day's Mission Impossible. His message was simple and direct. It had the clarity of truth and he never deviated from it. 'When I could help,' he told the small gatherings, 'I did so. When I could not, I told you why. I have not been able to do everything you wished, but I have done a great deal, and I will continue to work for you if your trust is placed in me again.'

The votes were cast and the ballot boxes opened and counted under armed guard. Tomazinho had won an overwhelming victory. He was elected to a record fourth term as sarpanch by a margin of 4,700 votes, the highest in the history of Panchayat elections in Goa. At the victory rally held on the night the results were announced, trucks with lathi-wielding goons drew up in the dark with their lights off. Armed with tyre irons and clubs, dozens of shadowy figures moved through the palms towards Tomazinho and his people. Tomazinho went forward alone. Three of the leaders came at him, swinging their clubs. 'It was touch and go,' a village elder recalled later, 'but Tomazinho stood his ground. He said, loudly, for all to hear, "If you want to spill blood, you will have to start with mine." The cowards, not one of them had the balls to raise his hand. They slunk off and left.'

They still talk about the War of the Vaddos in Candolim. It has found a treasured place in folklore and memory, a victory for all times and all seasons, a victory for the people.

*

I was visiting my mother early on the morning Shivanand came to face the furies. We stood on the balcony watching the flock of herons which nested in the tamarind tree in winter feeding their young. 'Three more eggs hatched last night,' my mother said, 'look there.'

I heard the twittering but couldn't see a thing. 'Your sight,' I said, 'is a good deal better than mine.' Then the phone in the sitting-room rang. It was Gita, greatly distressed. I felt a chill breath along the spine, a premonition which augured ill.

'Ranjana called,' she said, 'it's Shivanand. He's in intensive care at the Hinduja hospital.'

'How bad is he?'

'Something to do with his heart. It's very serious, Frank. She said he was critical and they had to operate immediately.'

'I'll meet you there,' I said, 'it shouldn't take more than half an hour.'

'Shivanand,' I said to my mother, 'he's at Hindujas. A heart attack, I think. I must rush.'

After I left, my mother pulled a trunk out from under her bed. It was a large, unwieldy trunk and she met with some difficulty, but by pulling and pushing in turn, she finally managed to get it out and into the centre of the room. In the trunk was a wooden box which she carried to the altar in the sitting-room. The box contained twelve hand-made blue and white candles. Blue and white plaits of wax, the colours of the Blessed Virgin; candles consecrated at the Church of Our Lady of Joy in Old Goa. She lit a candle, placed it on the altar and marked the time. Nine. Then she went down on her knees and began the first of twelve novenas to Our Lady. Each novena and each candle would last an hour. She would pray till all twelve candles and novenas were done, rising briefly at the end of the hour to light a candle afresh. She would pray for the life of Shivanand Salgaocar.

The night before Shivanand had woken with his heart in a vice, in an agony so intense he was barely able to reach for Ranjana before he passed out. He regained consciousness at the Salgaocar Medical Centre and was flown at once to Bombay. The angiogram at Hindujas revealed major blockages in the arteries feeding the heart. The surgeon, flown in from Madras, had yet to decide between bypass surgery and an angioplasty. Eventually, he settled for the latter and began the angioplasty at eight that evening, at the very moment my mother lit the twelfth candle and began her last novena. The operation was monitored on a computer screen and as the catheter with the furled balloon at its tip moved through the last of the cardiovascular system towards the muscles of the heart, the surgeons discovered to their astonishment (checking twice with the angiogram to make sure) that the earlier blockages had shrunk by half.

I am an agnostic. I do not believe in miracles, but facts

do not lie. And while the Miracle of the Twelve Candles (as Radhika calls it) does little to convert a hardened disbeliever like me, I have to concede that half of a blockage in the heart isn't something one can wish away ...

*

It is a winter's morning of such astounding brilliance that even an agnostic could be forgiven a doubt or two. Joaquim has just dropped in and departed leaving behind three plump, glistening pomfrets. Father Victor has scootered two hours on his ancient Vespa from his once recalcitrant parish in the south, now pacified and tranquil. He seems as fresh as a daisy at dawn. How does he do it? Tomazinho is modestly resolute as he refuses to tell us, yet again, how the unGodly were brought low in the War of the Vaddos. He takes refuge in a small – very small – Director's Special. Shivanand does himself well. I allow myself an extra finger to celebrate the great good fortune of my friends. We talk about the Arc of Hope. A lady of means has weazled her way in 'for the sake of the company.' She shall be unceremoniously ousted. The fat cat tour operators in the village have been brought vigorously to heel. They wear a lean, hungry and fearful look. Shivanand has bought a piece of land along the beach and is building a house on it. And Ranjana, he tells us unable to keep the pride out of his voice, is writing her first book.

'Here's to the author,' I say, and we clink glasses.

They leave shortly after. I am sorry to see them go but happy in the thought that we shall meet again soon. Shivanand takes a ride on the pillion of the Harley-Davidson. Why? Where is his Mercedes?

'I want Tomazinho to have a look at my property,' Shivanand says.

Tomazinho laughs. 'He wants permission for a wall,' he says, 'but there seems to be a problem. Half of his property is well within the two hundred metre high-tide line.'

I can't resist the last word.

'Tell him,' I say, 'about the unalloyed joys of biofencing.'

'And the pleasures,' Tomazinho says, waving goodbye, 'of a small python as a pet!'

Three Thunder-Boxes and a Mandolin

My friend, Remo Fernandes, is a man of many admirable parts. I admire his character, informed as it is with the finest of Goan virtues, held in tempered, understated balance. I am in awe of his success in India and the world at large; it has given fresh meaning to the phrase, 'self-made'. His knowledge of Goan esoterica never ceases to amaze me. His commitment to family, friends and the good Goan earth is as unwavering as my own. I strongly applaud his love of the simpler pleasures: good food and drink, the company of children, dogs and books, a twilight evening alone by the Siolim backwaters with a meditative flute. But there is one thing about him I shall always envy: his childhood; it was the stuff of happy dreams. We played a game once at Remo's birthday party. Each of us had to recall two of our first memories, the happiest and the funniest. When he was six years old and his musical talent had begun to be seriously noticed, his parents gave him a birthday gift of a mandolin. It was the happiest moment of his life and his joy was unconfined. He and the mandolin were inseparable. He mastered the instrument in months, as well he might, given practise of such dedication that it began early in the morning

Boon Companions

while he sat on one of three thunder-boxes in a shed above a pigsty out in the yard. Then, as now to a great extent in rural Goa, sanitation was brutally elementary but ecologically sound; loos were located well away from the main house above a trough where the family's pigs fed. One eased oneself, in Remo's words, 'to the soothing rumble of pigs at breakfast.'

The morning's ablutions presented him with his first funniest memory. The commodes were placed on a single platform two feet apart. Remo, his father, perhaps an uncle, shared the loo while engaged in friendly evacuation. Remo strummed on the mandolin; the older men began their day with a companionable chat, a bit of gossip, a quick run through of the headlines in *O Heraldo*, a review of the day's agenda. A felicitous arrangement. It suited the pigs, as well, splendidly: three breakfasts at one serving. Their contented grunts, according to Remo, was a sound as easeful to the spirit as to the bowels.

Then, a foreign guest, 'a most proper Austrian gentleman' came to stay. It was his first visit to Goa and his arrival was celebrated in the grand manner – mea casa, tua casa – with a feast of truly impressive proportions, a groaning board long on fish, flesh and fowl but, sad to say, short indeed on essential roughage. Spurred on by three large caju fenis, a good half bottle of wine and two coffee liqueurs, the Austrian did himself generously. The next morning, a wee bit the worse for wear, perplexed by Remo's father's invitation, but keen to enter into the spirit of the occasion, off he went, with Remo, his father (the mandolin and *O Heraldo* in tow) to the communal loo. 'It may have been the dinner,' Remo recalls, 'or the unusualness of the surroundings, but the poor man was making rough weather of it.'

Indeed, the Austrian displayed every sign of growing unease. He shifted his weight from buttock to buttock, made small despairing sounds, rocked ever so slightly forward and backward on his heels. It was clear that there was to be little joy this morning. Then the porker below his thunder-box, disappointed at the lack of adequate sustenance, grunted loudly in annoyance, and decided to investigate the cause of this unusual deprivation. It poked a hairy snout up the bottom of the commode, squealed mightily, and snuffled this way and that. The Austrian glanced between his legs, swore an incomprehensible oath in a strange language, leaped off the commode, and rushed across the yard, struggling with his trousers. That morning, claiming urgent and unavoidable business, he departed, bag and baggage, for Panjim and was never heard from again. Had Remo composed a neat little ditty to honour the event, I asked, a musical ode to the Goan commode? Remo smiled. His lips are sealed. We shall never know.

Thirty years on the only porker in sight is on a buffet plate. The venue: the Regal Room at Bombay's Oberoi Inter-Continental, ever-so-correctly sanitized for an exclusive celebration, the star-spangled tenth anniversary of Aroon Purie's elitist Bombay magazine. The guest list: Bombay's best and brightest (if you aren't invited, you don't exist). The evening's main attraction: Remo Fernandes, Goa's supremely gifted rock star and, arguably, India's finest entertainer.

Remo is not particularly sanguine about the success of the show. He faces a motley assortment of socialites, high-

Three Thunder-Boxes and a Mandolin

flying journalists, business tycoons, film stars, celebrity authors, the mandatory flutter of catwalk models and a brace or two from the current crop of artists in vogue. Bombay's creme de la creme make an incestuous, blase gathering. They are the chosen: cheek touches cheek; languid greetings fly about the place; the Scotch and water flows; the canapes are ignored, as is a group of hapless entertainers (Bombay's premier jazz ballet ensemble) which could well be invisible. Generously lubricated, the buzz of chatter rises as the evening wears on. Then, with no warning, the lights soften. There is a thunderous drum-roll and Remo appears centre-stage. He moves on the balls of his feet, with a cat's fluid grace, tracked by a single golden spotlight. His fingers race along the guitar strings in a medley of explosive chords, a superbly controlled riff. His magnificent voice – a voice for all seasons – hurls a challenge that echoes across the Regal Room, 'Are you ready for the magic?' A moment's silence. Then the city's elite, on their feet, cheering, respond with a joyful chorus, 'Yeah!' Bombay's movers and shakers will swing into the wee hours of the morning.

Remo Fernandes is India's most charismatic rock star, a rare combination of riveting stage presence and electrifying performance. Precociously talented as a child (he led his own school band), and entirely self-taught, he has pursued his vocation for forty years with the dedication of a Trappist monk and the kaleidoscopic talents of a Renaissance polymath. The press has labelled him, inelegantly, 'a one-man band' and 'a music industry,' but there is no question that he is a musical phenomenon. From concept to concert, he does it all: composes the music; writes the lyrics; plays a range of instruments; arranges the score; mixes and records; designs the album cover and the advertising; and celebrates the final creation on stage and film.

It is a singular pleasure to spend an afternoon with Remo, his French wife Michele, their two young sons, Jonah and Noah, and to discover that the family honours are evenly distributed. In fine Gallic style, Michele presides over a memorable lunch: a cheese souffle that rises triumphantly to the occasion, a roast ox tongue with a clever Provençale sauce, a fragrant prawn pulao (how does Remo keep his figure?), a salad Nicoise with impeccable credentials and as sublime a chocolate mousse as you are likely to meet this side of the Eiffel Tower. Later, over coffee and cognac in the flagstoned garden – a riotous melange of flowering plants, a gulmohar tree, recent litters of kittens and puppies, canvas recliners to fall asleep in – Remo plays a tape from an album in progress on Mother Theresa.

His studio occupies a separate room in this lovely old Goan house (the ancestral home, sold and bought back within the week by Remo, who has an abiding love for the place and finds ingenious excuses not to move). It was here that he created the albums that were to make his name an inspirational icon to the young of all ages, wherever rock reigns in India. Drawing on the rich motherlodes of his Goan heritage, with roots in the Konkan mando, the Portuguese fado and the Indian classical tradition, taking his talent farther afield to the fertile pastures of Europe and North Africa, and, finally, fusing all of his experience and musical knowledge into personal art, expressed in original compositions of enduring virtuosity.

Three Thunder-Boxes and a Mandolin

He is tall, slim, with the proportions and grace of a ballet dancer, and looks a good ten years younger than his age. Understated and soft-spoken in private, he performs with the kinetic energy of the early Mick Jagger, and an incandescent stage presence that will brook no authority other than its own. His audiences will have it no other way. At his favourite gig, the Haystack in Anjuna village in Goa, where, in season, the faithful gather under the stars every Friday, Remo comes on close to midnight. This is not polite, creamy Bombay, but local, highly vocal Goa. A roar of joyful expectancy from hundreds of loyal fans greets his arrival. They are never disappointed and, within minutes, have fallen under his spell. The range, power and timbre of his voice are astonishing; more so, when one learns that he perfected the art busking in the great cities of Europe – Paris, London, Venice, Rome, Madrid – where, down and out, he literally sang for his supper. Tonight is not so much performance, as reverential communion. We have heard most of the songs before, but they are, in some wonderful way, fresh and new again. He draws on a repertoire that goes back ten years and a bit, selecting old and new favourites from a half dozen albums that have made Indian recording history.

But no bets were being laid when Remo began his long odyssey; indeed, in 1983, when he made the rounds of the established labels with his first album, Goan Crazy, the odds were dismal by any reckoning and he was given short shrift. 'No one,' he was told curtly by a producer who has lived to eat his words, 'wants to hear original songs in English composed by an Indian.' But hope springs eternal in the Goan psyche. Unfazed, Remo decided to go it alone. He set up a production company, Goana, in his house at Siolim. By a charitable suspension of disbelief, the recording equipment could, perhaps, have been described as archaic. The distribution network, as well, was distinctly modest: it consisted of Remo on a yellow scooter, a sight that would soon prompt wry affection the length and breadth of Goa. Goans love happy endings. Goan Crazy proved a runaway success. It brought Remo to national attention and, more importantly, to the discerning eye of the country's best film producers. His work for the cinema – entire scores, theme songs, orchestration for dance ensembles – was widely acclaimed.

Remo had arrived. Ten years later, with a shelf-full of national hit albums to his credit and scores of live appearances the world over, he was awarded the Grand Prix at the Dresden Festival, where, the previous year, he had won three major awards competing against the world's best from twenty countries. His latest album, *Politicians Don't Know How To Rock 'n' Roll*, sold out in days and augurs well to set yet another national record. Remo would be noticeably embarrassed if I were to refer to him as a musical institution, but his career speaks for itself. He is India's leading performer at home and abroad. The year 1985 saw him at the head of a cultural troupe at the Festival of India in Hong Kong and Macao. Three years later he was invited to sing at the 'Save the Children' extravaganza in London. In Moscow, he performed before the Presidents of the USSR and India and an audience of 120,000 at the closing ceremony of the Festival of India (within the week 3,000 Muscovites bought Bombay City). That year, he sang at the grand finale of the

Three Thunder-Boxes and a Mandolin

Soviet Festival in New Delhi, before Rajiv Gandhi and Mikhael Gorbachev, prompting one press report to describe him as 'the most popular Russian of the evening.' On 31 December, he brought in the New Year on national television.

Yet his career has never been far from controversy. Some of the more savage of his satirical lyrics have struck to the bone: he has exposed cant, corruption and hypocrisy, causing grievous offence in high places, where the accumulated scores of years awaited settling. Opportunity came when Rajiv Gandhi visited the territory. Remo performed for him at a public function. Goa's Governor, Cabinet and power elite were in highly visible attendance. Remo sang the cheeky hit, 'Hello Rajiv Gandhi' from his first album, Goan Crazy; Goa's top brass – not best pleased – sat in stone-faced silence. The storm broke the next day. Remo a disgrace; his performance cheap and vulgar; Goa had been shamed. For weeks, Remo was pilloried by a section of the press and public – attacks as ugly as they were unjustified – until a certain person decided that enough was sufficient, and Remo received a crested letterhead in the mail.

It read:

Dear Remo,

> *We had a pleasant evening and enjoyed both your songs and all the other items in the cultural programme. So long as you are sincere in your art, I do not think you should let a little criticism in the press upset you.*

> *With best wishes.*

Boon Companions

It was signed by the Prime Minister of India, Rajiv Gandhi.

To this day, no one knows how the letter leaked to the press on the same day Remo received it: newspapers across the country printed Rajiv Gandhi's letter with glowing editorial approval.

For Remo Fernandes, Goa's minstrel with the golden voice, ever 'sincere to his art,' there would be no looking back, except, once in a while, to three thunder-boxes and a mandolin...

Grandfather's Silver Rupee

A placebo is a small white sugar pill that does nothing for you except make you well. My grandfather, whom we met earlier on in the book, would not have been surprised. He was a Doctor of Medicine in the true spirit of the words. It was an article of faith with him that the real process of healing began in the deepest recesses of the human psyche, well beyond the reach of the pills and potions of his time. He practised medicine with a wayward democracy – among the rich ('I steal from them my son, as God is my judge!'), and the poor, whom he treated without charge and, of course, on me, his favourite grandchild, though he'd never have you know it. His appearance at my sickbed made me feel better at once. He made a grand entrance, all six feet of him, in immaculate white ducks and a sola topi blancoed to a dazzling shine, twirling a short cane with a nimble dexterity worthy of the music hall. His moustache and French goatee were trimmed to a neat jauntiness and his opening remark was full of good cheer, 'Gone and done it again, have we?' He maintained, with some truth, that whenever a new germ appeared in the neighbourhood, I'd find it, make friends and bring it back home.

His way with the language was as winning as his way with patients. He attended my birth and, according to my

Boon Companions

mother, passed thoughtful judgement: 'A trifle large in the head and there's a certain crumpled effect, but I suppose we shall have to make do.' At the age when little boys eat everything in sight, he enquired politely as I reached for my fourth hard-boiled egg at breakfast, did I eat them or had I started a collection? He held firm and jaundiced views about the ability of the local Jesuits to educate his grandson and I can see him now, monocle in place, scrutinizing my monthly report, not – even by the most wildly optimistic assessment – an encouraging document. 'Padres,' he'd say coldly, investing the word with immeasurable scorn.

He was an ardent student of life and all of life's creations. He believed that the universe was profoundly sacred and purposeful: the hieroglyphics of an infant's brain and the star spirals of receding galaxies were written by a single mighty hand. Friend, guide, philosopher king, he undertook my education with high seriousness and a strong sense of preference, leavened with wit. 'That,' he said to me once, pointing to the Sahara in an atlas, 'is a desert. Never get lost in it. Sand all over the place and there is no way to satisfy an honest thirst.' Whereupon, the French goatee perking up as though at some happy and wholly unexpected congruence of ideas, he reached out for a merry brown bottle, roughly corked, which arrived (and woe if it did not!) with strict regularity from Saligao. I was allowed a sip from his glass 'to build up strength against infections.'

He had a child's sense of curiosity: discussing the intricacies of a frog's anatomy or the mysteries of the Holy Trinity, he informed his forays into the manifold splendours of the universe with wonder, awe and a sense of delight. He taught me that personal honour gave a measure of meaning to a man's life; that before one could love one's neighbour it was essential to learn to love oneself, 'damnations and all.' 'Do not expect perfection,' he said to me once, 'least of all from yourself.' Yet all of his life, as I remember it, seemed to be a striving towards compassion, justice and order, and an honest correspondence with his fellow human beings.

My education was in his hands and no one dared interfere. We sallied forth one morning by tramcar on a secret mission. 'A city must eat,' my grandfather said cryptically and introduced me to the exotic joys of Crawford Market where, after a grand tour, he made me a gift of a young squirrel. 'You are now responsible for another life,' he said, well pleased, 'it is an education in itself.' Latin conjugation held no fear for me at school. Apart from my grandfather and myself (and perhaps one or two others) who else was privy to its origin: the mystical suckling of Romulus and Remus and the magnificent empire that began with them on the Seven Hills of Rome? He discussed the news with me after breakfast each morning, seriously, as between one well-informed adult and another, and I always left for school with the conviction that the world would be much better managed if placed in the care of my grandfather and – well, yes – myself!

Now he sat on my bed and played a little game. He gave me an ancient stethoscope which I plugged into my ears. I placed the other end on his chest. My grandfather sighed. 'You will never reach great heights in the medical profession,' he said, 'that's my spleen.' Long moments passed. I was, on solemn promise, never to repeat a diagnosis and there was a time limit. Serious, absorbed, he paced me on a gold pocket watch. In the past, I had run through chicken pox, flu, malaria, German measles, gout (a famous Goan affliction) and, shamefully, runny tummy. I had precisely two minutes left; inspiration had fled; all at once my grandfather began to behave very strangely indeed. He took off his sola topi, flung it aside, mopped his brow vigorously, wiped his neck, patted his cheeks, huffed and puffed and murmured in a voice weak and trembling with some instant, terminal illness, 'I feel faint, dear God, it's the heat, the heat ... ' 'Sun-stroke,' I shouted triumphantly, and a smile tugged at the corners of his mouth: 'Let's have a look at you.'

His examination was careful, gentle and thorough, and when it was over, he chuckled and poked me in the ribs, 'You'll live, provided you follow instructions.' They came in two parts: the first, a bottle containing a vile purple brew with a paper cut-out for the three daily doses stuck on; the second was a magic talisman, a silver rupee fresh from the mint; it shone and glittered with a hundred points of light, potent with meaning and promise. 'Under your pillow,' said my grandfather, 'day and night. And you'll be as right as rain in no time.' He was never flippant about the silver rupee. It was given to me with a sense of ceremony, a particular reverence, and in the sacramental moment when our eyes met and he laid his hand on my cheek, I knew with a certainty beyond reason that all would be well.

The silver rupee never failed me. I remember a critical night when I was near delirious with fever and my bedclothes were damp with the sweat of an illness that had gone on all week. There was a bruised look to my mother's eyes and my grandfather, for once, was grave and silent. I was to be 'cupped' as a last resort. The paraphernalia for this arcane ritual lay neatly to hand: six small wine glasses, slices of onion, pieces of camphor. I clasped the silver rupee tightly in my hand – round, hard, comforting. One by one, the slices of onion were placed in two parallel rows on my chest, a piece of camphor in the centre of each. The wine glasses were made ready, the candle was lit. Flame to camphor, a wine glass quickly upturned, a sudden vacuum sucking at the skin, the inverted glass clinging to my chest, mysterious vapours swirling within it, while the skin beneath swelled, turned an angry red. Six sharp wasp-stings and it was over. I was made to lie still while the 'cupping' took place. I got well, of course, but only my grandfather and I knew that the silver rupee had, once again, turned the tick.

Thirty years after my grandfather's death, the retina in my right eye tore and detached: sparks, flashes, jagged forks of white-hot light, a celestial fireworks. There were seven out of ten chances that I would go blind. I sat in silence and terror, pupils dilated with atoopine, the vision fogged, while the surgeons argued my case. They reduced me to an object, to an eyeball, to a broken retina. The universe of my being had shrunk to the torn and shattered blood vessels of an eye. They talked options and procedures: they would puncture the eyeball; they would go into the eye with sharp knives, with laser beams, with liquid nitrogen.

They never used my name.

And no one offered me a silver rupee.

4

'Boa Festas!'
Food, Feni and Fun

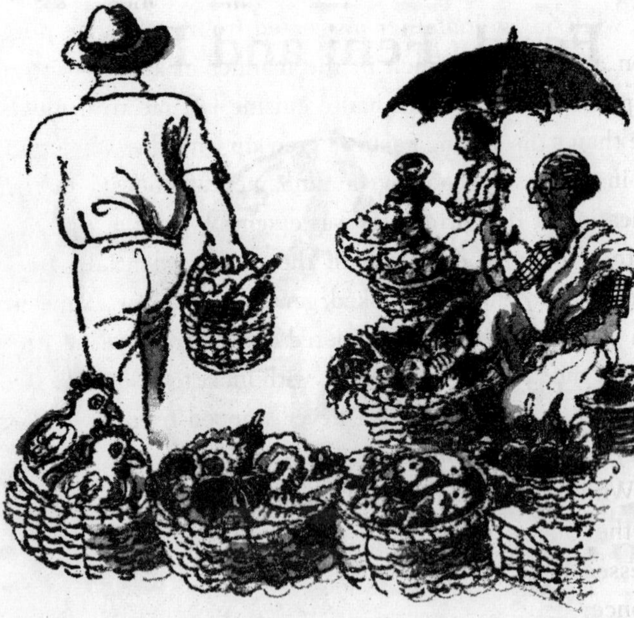

Who's Afraid of a Little Cholesterol?

If, today, I can tell the freshness of a fish by peering under a gill, or the goodness of a lady's finger by breaking off a tip, or never allow an indifferent mango to slip by unremarked, I give thanks to my grandfather's inspired scholarship. He taught me to cook; more correctly, my mother taught me to cook while my grandfather instructed from a distance, feet up on an armchair, much in the manner of a guru with a disciple. These lessons in haute cuisine left me with much more than a discerning palate. I grew up with the conviction that in life, as in cooking, a fundamental honesty in the application of first principles was essential. Even a fried egg had to arrive at the table with the right credentials: free-range, laid on the day, cooked gently over a low flame in fresh butter, salted and peppered just before eating and never in the kitchen. One could, with luck, fool some of the people all of the time (and I never stopped trying!), but in the frying of an egg lay the moment of truth.

With tutelage of this high order, it comes as no surprise that the Goan's response to good food and drink may be expressed in that single, hallowed phrase, 'I pass this way but once.'

'Boa Festas!' Food, Feni and Fun

The proper education of a young Goan gentleman begins at a tender and impressionable age. Master Desiderio or Simplicio or Innoceno, as the case may be (given names in Goa tend to combine, in equal measure, piousness with the pompous flourish), learns the great and immortal truths of life at his mother's knee: First, God is good and just. He knows precisely what sort of mischief each of His creatures is up to at any given point of time. Give praise! Second, nothing begins to compare with the grandeur of being Goan except, naturally, the supreme grandeur of being Saraswat Brahmin Roman Catholic Goan (I shall try, though I cannot promise, not to repeat this). Third, food and drink are at all times serious and sacred, deserving of thought, care and appreciation.

The reputation of a household rests to a considerable degree on the quality of its table; slipping up is considered immorality of the unholiest kind. A young lady's marriage prospects are assured if she is merely rumoured to be 'an excellent cook,' never mind the moustache. Recipes are regarded as priceless heirlooms, jealously guarded, and handed down from mother to daughter unsullied by experiment or improvisation. In short, food, God-given, is a matter of talent, honour and fierce pride.

But God and his omniscience was not a conclusion you would easily reach, observing the feckless, guileful antics of the local fisherwomen at the Mapusa market. Brazen hussies, puffing on vile home-rolled cheroots, without qualm or conscience; indeed, bereft of all norms of ethical behaviour, they would, given half a chance, attempt to foist off old fish preserved in ice and dethawed that very morning as the real article, ancient mutton-dressed-as-lamb lobster, and other such abominations. With a slit-eyed ruthlessness that would have done my Saraswat ancestry proud, I poked, prodded, pried, sniffed, and generally made an unholy nuisance of myself.

It must be said that this tough-minded expertise was expected, indeed enjoyed by the fisherwomen in an ironic and savage sort of way. Its absence was seen as the worst kind of ignorance and answered with a weary contempt and twice their usual profit. Sardonic chuckles and ribald comment greeted my inspection of the merchandise, calling into question the sanity of my ancestors and suggesting improbable futures. Would I go about selecting a wife in this unseemly manner? And if so, where, pray, would I prod first? No matter. I maintained a dignified silence. The offending pomfret had a gill pressed firmly down, the flesh just below the spine investigated with a rigid forefinger, the white of the eye keenly examined. Flesh and fowl were subjected to similar indignities. I knew the precise meaning of colour, texture, touch, smell, and could tell in a moment or two, the general well-being (or otherwise) of all kinds of provender. Freshness is a cardinal principle of good Goan cooking, for Goans literally live off the land. Fresh pork and unpolished rice are the only year-round staples. Virtually all else is seasonal. I have eaten baby squid in Goa for breakfast just off a fishing boat, and flesh-frozen baby squid prepared the same way in Bombay. The difference left me stricken and brooding.

Here I must confess – and no Goan worthy of his free-range pork would fail to do so – that vegetables leave me cold and unmoved. There is little virtue to the legume. To the best of my knowledge, no Goan has ever encountered a cabbage with character. The artichoke, much touted by the cognoscenti, is all work and no joy. Ditto the drumstick. And no matter how you regard the carrot, dismal root, it is difficult to suppress the conviction that rabbits are the only answer. As for the squashiness of the eggplant, there are certain things one simply does not discuss in a book for the general family. And while I feel no shame (only mild depression) at admitting that half my family is vegetarian, I personally hold that a few seconds' swift work with the rear mandibles for a mouthful of undistinguished fibre is no cause for celebration. Having got that little lot off my chest, no more caveats, I promise.

Freshness then; the application of subtlety in selection, finesse in preparation and, above all, the intelligent exploitation of potential. Consider the coconut and the mango. In its infancy, the tender coconut offers a flesh of delicate flavour and pleasing texture. The water within the coconut makes for a refreshing drink with a light pleasant flavour. The soft creamy flesh is eaten plain or cut into strips, dipped in melted sugar and used to decorate pastries and desserts. As a young adult, the coconut is firm enough for thick grating, mixing and blending, and is used in bread, cakes and for savoury and sweet fillings. The mature coconut is one of nature's small miracles. The husk provides fuel, coir for rope, the dried flesh called copra is processed into coconut oil, even the half-shells are used, fashioned into ingenious ladles while the sundried fronds of the palm tree are put to a myriad uses – from thatch for roofing to stout fencing and wind- and rain-shields during the monsoon.

The mango is no less ingeniously employed. Tiny raw green mangoes are used in curries, sauces and in an inspired pot-pourri of pickles; water-and-salt, vinegar, the fiery miscut; semi-ripe, the mango is cubed for sweet chutney, and converted (by sheer leger de main with the flavour as rich and natural as ever) into jams and cheeses. No Goan in his right mind would experiment with the fully ripe Alphonso or Malcurada. Golden and ambrosial, tribute is paid to this magnificent fruit as nature intended. They are lightly chilled, sliced along the seed and eaten down to the last morsel, a deeply satisfying if somewhat untidy business.

Add to the virtues of ingenuity, freshness and finesse, an absolute commitment to cooking as a minor art form, and you have a cuisine, or more properly cuisines, extending from the deceptive simplicity of fishermen's fare to the elaborate menus of the landed gentry. I lived alone for six blissful weeks in a fisherman's home in a beach village sufficiently remote to be without electricity and running water. Cuisinart would have been ill-pleased with the kitchen. It consisted of two rows of laterite bricks placed on a platform three feet high. A single cutting, scraping and grating metal implement, put together with the genius of simplicity, attached to a wooden platform by means of a swivel, and supported by a couple of knives and a stone grinder were all the fisherman's wife had to work with. More than ample as it turned out, for she produced small, exquisite miracles each day. All of the food was cooked in earthenware vessels made by hand by the master potters of

'Boa Festas!' Food, Feni and Fun

Bicholim, from red clay which fired true and hard and lasted a generation and more. Wood fires provided a nutty, aromatic flame. Baking was accomplished by the simple expedient of placing a lid over a pot and covering it with hot embers. An equal circulation of heat was thus created above, below and – by the judicious placing and removing of bricks – all around.

I ate like a prince. A typical day's menu would find me breakfasting on scrambled eggs with Goa sausage, bolo and mangada. Two sausages had been neatly excised from a string hung high above the kitchen fires to cure these past six months. Into a pot with a large onion and well water to cover, brought quickly to the boil, then simmered till all the water evaporated. The sausages (hitherto shrunken, much put upon fingerlings which usually prompt grave misgivings in the uninitiated) were now twice their original size. Lovely, savoury aromas filled the kitchen. Sliced down the middle, the meat – diced pork, pork fat and spices marinated in palm vinegar – was quickly mixed with the scrambled eggs just as they were beginning to set. A whisk or two. Onto the table. The bolo was a sweet country bread baked that very morning, made from whole wheat flour, molasses, fresh toddy and a smidgen of bran. The mangada – soft, moist, irresistible – Goa's celebrated mango cheese.

Lunch consisted of unpolished rice, crisp and nutty, grown in the paddy fields outback, kingfish curry (I had seen my host hauling the kingfish out of his boat at the crack of dawn). Generous slabs of the fish were stewed to perfection in a sauce of finely ground spices, thick coconut milk, red chillies, cumin seed, garlic and a touch of ginger, splendidly bound with tamarind juice and whole green chillies slit along their length. The kingfish was a lady well in the family way, and a perfect roe, unadorned, accompanied the meal. Lightly salted, fried over a low flame, firm to the fork, crumbling on the tongue. Yams for dessert – from the back garden, where else? – baked in the hot ashes of the kitchen fire, smothered with melted black jaggery.

Dinner began with an ambrosial vegetable soup (to the back of the class, minestrone!) followed by fist-sized chunks of succulent roast pork, marinated overnight in a devilishly cunning paste of garlic, ginger, cloves and the purest palm vinegar, with small new potatoes (parboiled, fried quickly in pork fat, rubbed over with garlic, sprinkled with rock salt); for dessert, inch-thick diamonds of the toffee which the Goans call dos da grao. Made from gram flour, grated coconut, sugar, and flavourings; the crust is crisp and firm, yielding to a thick centre the consistency of caramel and infinitely more gratifying.

Peasant fare? Praise the Lord and pass the feni.

Fine food and feni truly come into their own on festive occasions – christenings, weddings, first communions and grand annual festivals such as Christmas, Easter and the pre-Lenten Carnaval. Cobwebbed bottles of vintage feni are ceremoniously dusted off and uncorked. Wines are generously sampled by the male members of the family before the festival selection is made. The poorest of village families will go without for weeks so that, on the day, the groaning board is traditionally complete; each main course – fish, rice, pork – must be presented in a variety of different recipes. The women of the house (often assisted in wealthier households by professional cooks) are totally absorbed for days before in the serious business of creating this feast among feasts.

If you have the good fortune to be invited to a family banquet of such generous disposition, respond with gratitude, skip breakfast and sally forth. You are about to experience a gastronomical tour de force, and are expected to perform as never before; the slightest flagging of appetite will be met with genuine concern and grave enquiry into the state of your health. Exquisite rendering of the three great culinary strains that influence all Goan kitchens will be presented with care bordering on reverence: simple but excellent fare from Hindu Konkan Goa; the richer, more elaborate variations offered by Hindu and Christian Saraswat Brahmin cuisine; and, finally, classic Portuguese cooking made brighter by the ingredients and flavours of the tropics.

Resist the impulse to indulge in an orgy of mass consumption; this would be not merely intemperate but distinctly unwise. Generous helpings by all means, but what is essential is a careful orchestration of texture, colour, taste and balance – from first sip to last nibble – if the raison d'etre of the banquet is to be wisely celebrated.

Begin by clearing and stimulating the palate with a generous copito of palm or caju feni over ice with just a drop or two of fresh lime. On then to the hors-d'oeuvres. A difficult choice what with the guisado of oysters, the stuffed, spiced crab in the shell, the prawn balchao and soupa catalina making equal and urgent claim to your attention. A second copito is essential at this stage to clear the mind so that a happy decision may be reached. You decide, wisely, on the apa da camarao (do not stint with the portion) and young mangoes in brine. The apa is done to perfection. A pie of impeccable pedigree, fiendishly tricky in the baking (layer upon alternating layer, with a semolina, egg and coconut dough and a savoury, delightfully sweet-and-pungent prawn filling. And how does one get the prawns to stay so succulent in a hot oven? Do not ask!). Light conversation with your neighbour at this juncture may be your last chance for small talk; with the entrees a chomping silence descends on the room.

Begin with the pulao cooked in chicken stock and half a pomfret reacheado (sliced above and below the bone, stuffed with tiny shrimp marinated these past twenty-four hours in a sauce whose provenance shall forever remain a family secret; the pomfret then tied, brushed with the same marinade and shallow fried over high heat so that the flesh flakes softly on the tongue under a crisp and crunchy skin).

A glass of white wine, perhaps, with your rice and fish, Adega da Velha, sec. And no wistful regrets, for there will always be another time, another occasion, to enjoy the pleasures of the chicken cafreal, the steamed king prawns, the stuffed baby squid, and you have yet, remember, to partake of the main entree of the evening. Sorpotel – inevitably and gladly – the great Goan pork dish; cubed pork, liver, heart, blood, blended to triumphant perfection in a superbly orchestrated base of spices and vinegar, simmered for hours over a slow fire, sealed in its earthenware pot for three days to cure. It is eaten with sanas, the round, steamed bread made from a dough of rice and dal flour fermented overnight in toddy. Washed down by a glass or two (or three) of the robust red wine of Monte de Guirim. A longish pause before dessert is recommended. Conversation may be resumed, however sluggishly. Sample if you wish from a bewildering variety, but you will, as we all do, settle eventually for a royal portion of that monarch of desserts, bebinca, my mother's recipe for which begins, 'Take the yolks of forty country eggs ... ' (It takes hours to bake by the traditional method, layer upon layer, with hot embers above and below, so that every one of the twelve layers melts as easily, as equitably, on the tongue.) And as you settle this magnificent repast with a coffee liqueur of honourable lineage, you may be forgiven if a defiant little cloud hovers on an otherwise perfectly tranquil horizon, 'Who's afraid of a little cholesterol?' And so to bed ...

Use Your Loaf

Let the French keep their baguettes. Who cares if the Germans, poor devils, labour under the delusion that pumpernickel is the real thing? Let Hovis pursue its uninspired and dreary subversion of the British breakfast. And pity the Americans who will never know that life begins where the hole in a doughnut ends. But all is forgiven once they arrive in our village.

Like the Goans, they learn to use their loaf.

My day at Rockheart begins with the most cheerful of bugle calls. The boy Anton on a bicycle, handlebars weighed down port and starboard with huge jute bags filled to bursting with a baker's bounty of good and fragrant things. He brings instant cheer to the hearts of the residents of Annavaddo. All of the residents for, Pied Piperlike, he attracts every mongrel, porker and hungry crow in the neighbourhood. Every so often, like a prince dispensing privilege, he tears pieces off a loaf and tosses them nonchalantly behind him, without so much as a glance over his shoulder, driving the animal life to a competitive frenzy in which the pigs (if you will pardon the expression) usually come out top dog.

This is not arrogance on Anton's part; he is absorbed in announcing his arrival. Mounted on the handlebar of his

'Boa Festas!' Food, Feni and Fun

cycle is a tin horn of impressive if bewildering construction. Man-made, it resembles a large bugle in demented mutation and has, in place of a mouthpiece, a huge rubber bulb. By squeezing, pressing, pushing and heaping general physical abuse on the bulb, Anton declares to the vaddo – with a rousing dexterity worthy of the trumpets in the 'William Tell Overture' – that this day's staff of life is, as always, bountiful in its manifold blessings.

He has a point. The breads you see in the picture represent a small fraction of the Goan baker's repertoire. The only constraint to performance is the imagination. There are sweet breads and savoury breads; small, soft paus for consumption with every meal to huge, crusty, celebratory bolos; and speciality breads such as sanas which are eaten with a single dish, in this case sorpotel. My village baker, on order, bakes up for me bread filled with raisins and chopped, seedless dates, a delicious brown bread sweetened with molasses, decorative twists and perfect soup rolls.

If there is a secret to the Goan baker's art, it must surely lie in the use of toddy (the coconut palm's gift to Goan bread) as to so much else, grated coconut and the process of fermentation. Nothing is rushed. Doughs are kneaded by hand, with patience and a slow, rhythmic skill. They are left to ferment between three and eight hours, depending on the composition, before being shaped and baked. In our house at Candolim, bread arrives at the breakfast table no more than half an hour after it leaves the oven, hot enough to melt the white, home-made butter in an instant.

My baker agreed to the inclusion of his sana recipe in this book with good grace. 'Nobody will get it right,' he said cheerfully. However. Soak one kg. of red Goa rice (the unpolished variety; this is very important) in water to cover until soft. Grind the rice on a stone grinder (who said life was easy?). Add, little by little, the grated flesh of two ripe coconuts. Grind away. There is no better aerobic exercise for the upper body. Remove from the grinding stone while still somewhat coarse. Add 400 ml. of toddy, 100 grams sugar and 10 grams salt. Mix well. Allow to ferment for four hours.

Shape into circular, flattish cakes raised slightly at the centre. Steam in small individual bowls.

And do not forget to order the pork sorpotel from the incomparable Gines Viegas at O Coqueiro. You will never get it right.

Last night I dreamt I was in the dock before Judge Terribliano Saldanha for refusing a third helping of bebinca at his daughter's wedding. The judge was in a hanging mood. He passed a severe sentence. 'A week on bread and water,' he said, with a bang of the gavel.

I smiled.

Seven days on Goan bread is a piece of cake.

Everything You Ever Wanted to Know About Feni But Were too Drunk to Ask

I am fortunate in my Goan friends.
The garafaos arrive at a certain time of the year, huge, pear-shaped flagons glazed over with a deep emerald patina, sealed to keep the liquid content as pure and uncontaminated as the morning it was triple-distilled and decanted into each voluptuous garafao. My friend, Steve Miranda, able and honoured President of the Lions Club in Calangute, has sent me two garafaos of caju feni from his own private stock. Brewed on the ancestral estates in North Goa by families who still farm his land and lovingly nurture the plantations of cashew and palm trees, the feni has been distilled in a fashion unchanged for generations. Free of chemicals, fermented as nature intended, in a process which may not be hastened, garnered, drop by exquisite drop in the last distillation, and presented to me each year with a generosity I am never able to repay. Two more garafaos of palm feni arrive the following morning, a gift from Thomas Vaz, scion of Pedro Vincent Vaz & Co., Goa's celebrated clan of bakers and distillers. Wherever good, honestly brewed palm feni is consumed in Goa, more often than not, the

'Boa Festas!' Food, Feni and Fun

282

distinctive pear shape of his bottle encased in plaited straw and bearing the reassuring legend, 'Big Boss Palm Feni' will make its presence cheerfully felt.

A garafao contains six bottles of feni and Esperanca, our diligent housekeeper, decants each bottle with care. Sun-dried orange peel will be introduced into a few of the bottles of caju; the flavours of orange and caju marry wonderfully well. Green chillies slit along their length in six of the bottles of palm feni will impart to Gita's sundowners just the right touch of tongue-tingling tartness. Twenty-four bottles in all. I shall have to call upon every last ounce of character and self-control to let them lie untouched, maturing for the next six months, when I shall be in great good spirits for the rest of the year. Mere words cannot express my gratitude to Steve and Thomas. May their fenis go from strength to strength.

The Department of Agriculture's official definition of feni is many soulless removes from its ebullient metaphysics; 'Feni (the more accurate rendering, as opposed to the Portuguese 'fenim') has achieved the status of a generic term applying to a wide variety of distilled alcoholic liquors derived from extracts of the coconut palm and the cashew fruit.'

A plague on these purveyors of words without spirit. Wherever the heart of Goa beats, there the living essence of the palm and the cashew are celebrated. The cashew fruit has wrought its benign miracle each golden season for three centuries, while the genesis of the glories of the palm is measured not by the passage of time, but held captured now and forever in the sculpted form of a toddy tapper, high above sand and sea, one with the wind and swaying fronds,

'Boa Festas!' Food, Feni and Fun

seeking the heart of the palm for its abundance and blessings.

The qualities of a happy Goan life find the perfect metaphor in the sparkling crystal depths of a bottle of pure feni. Elemental as the sea, the emerald meadows of ripening paddy, the bells of church and temple calling the faithful to prayer, lore and truth, myth and magic enwrap each potent drop in a mystique which warms the heart, clears the mind and may, freely and generously as the spirit moves one, be entertained and embellished. For feni is to the Goan life what the sky is to a bird, a medium of limitless wonder and potential.

Feni is not a generic term. It is a single, specific description from the Konkani root 'fen,' literally 'to froth.' It indicates to the purist (just about all accomplished feni drinkers) that a great-hearted feni, when poured into a glass, should froth a bit, playfully, with just a hint of exuberance, a visual harbinger of the high spirits to come. Clear as vodka, with a slight bouquet in the case of caju, feni may be drunk on the rocks or mixed, as with its Russian cousin, with virtually anything you may care to name.

Source materials derive from two of the most unlikely members of the botanical world, the coconut palm and the cashew fruit. The palm is life and blood to the Goan. Food for the pot; thatch for the home; oil for cooking; tender coconut water for instant refreshment; early morning toddy (the fresh sap at dawn) – no better way to begin the day; and that incomparable gift, feni, all things to all men. The cashew fruit is a mere stripling on the feni scene. Imported by the Portuguese from Brazil three centuries ago, it took to the Goan soil with a zesty fertility. Something of a botanical freak, the cashew seed grows on the exterior of a golden fruit, heart-or apple-shaped. Feni is distilled from both toddy and the juice of the cashew fruit.

So much for description.

Innate virtues which the Goans have known all about for centuries (presumably by a process of relentless osmosis) have now been revealed by the wonders of science. Palm toddy has been found to be rich in sugars, sodium, potassium, iron, manganese, a host of other minerals, proteins, amino acids, Vitamins B-1, B-2, 6, and trace elements. The juice of the cashew is not to be outdone and throws in for good measure generous helpings of Calcium, Phosphorous and Glucose. Small wonder then that feni is good for you.

On the sound theory that you can't have too much of a good thing, the Goans drink heroic quantities of feni. They drink it at births and wakes, solemnly on Maundy Thursday, never on the Friday and joyfully at Easter; they toast the feasts of their saints with it; they celebrate with generous portions when a favourite sow litters; they drink it before, with and often after meals. Workers in the fields pause at the noon break to refresh themselves with a few quick copitos of feni (Glucose ... Vitamin B ... Iron!). They drink it in all ages and conditions; babies are given a few drops dissolved in sugar to ward off the chill; it is rubbed in the joints for gout and rheumatism and generously imbibed by the patient immediately thereafter, recovery being swift and certain. Come to think of it, Goans drink feni whenever they please.

'Boa Festas!' Food, Feni and Fun

As I learned, to my infinite improvement, one fine January morning in the village of Anjuna. Gita and I were to meet a grand-uncle and aunt who had last seen me thirty years earlier, at my First Communion, doubtless toasting my coming into the age of grace with a glass of feni, or two. We were ushered into a parlour by my grand-uncle. My aunt rose to greet us. They might have stepped out of a cameo, or emerged daintily from an old sepia portrait, a perfect still life from a gracious and distant generation. Their marriage bore witness to well over half a century. They could have been twins, sharing a precious and treasured fragility. Their parlour held the scents of perfumed cachets and old, polished mahogany. A brass bird-cage, with a pair of love birds, swung gently in the wind at an open window. The sea murmured and whispered beyond the casuarinas and the palms. Generations of the family, formal in cutaways and hooped skirts, framed in carved rosewood, posed in attitudes of vast seriousness above the grand piano, reminding us of a venerable and solemn past, when 't's were always crossed and no 'i' went undotted. I could hear my own breathing and I felt I had to speak softly and choose my words with care.

My grand-uncle and aunt sat across from us, ramrod straight (as they had been taught as children), the very soul of gentility and autumnal nostalgia. I remember thinking, not for them the cumbersome annoyances of illness and death; they would, with dignity and good breeding, hand in hand, fade away into the gathering dusk. It was half past ten in the morning and my grand-aunt, in impeccable Portuguese, asked us if we would care for some refreshment.

'Yes,' I said, 'a cup of coffee.' Was there a flicker of

amusement in the glance they exchanged? My grand-uncle turned a stern and twinkling eye in my direction. 'We shall drink feni,' he said with a finality that would brook no argument.

The cutglass decanters and glasses were of the finest Belgian crystal. Why two decanters, brimful? I was soon to find out. We drank caju feni and more caju feni. Neighbours, uninvited, warmly greeted, appeared magically as if out of the walls. We were introduced. I was embraced and kissed warmly on both cheeks, a long-lost son of the soil, my Hindu Sindhi wife viewed with curiosity and wonder. A third copito? A fourth? I lost count. My grand-uncle and aunt and the neighbours drank with us, glass for glass, noticeably uninfluenced. The ancestors above the grand piano seemed jollier, less lugubrious, as time went on, positively lovable. The love birds sang. Or did I think they did? The decanters were taken away and refilled. The parlour shimmered with goodwill and bonhomie. Laughter invaded the room. Time did not pass. It cavorted and chuckled and did a little jig and flung the hours about without a care. But good a Goan as I am, the years of alienation from the soil of my fathers began to tell.

I rose to leave. The parlour quivered briefly and (feni never lets you down) refocused. Fragile as ever, my grand-uncle and aunt escorted us to the door. My aunt kissed me on both cheeks. 'Give our love to your parents,' she said. Lavender. Gentle. Nostalgic. She had drunk at least half a bottle of feni. So had my grand-uncle. Not a quaver. Firm-voiced. Erect. Sparkling at two in the afternoon. We said goodbye.

'Boa Festas!' Food, Feni and Fun

Goans drink feni as they please. On festive occasions they please themselves hugely and may even indulge (purists shudder at this) in after dinner derivatives such as Coffee Conserve, double-strength coffee wickedly blended with triple-distilled caju feni. I prefer to stay with pure palm or caju. The standard measure, equivalent to a full two-ounce jigger, is a copito (pronounced kopeeto), a round, full-bodied word, crisply syllabic and never interpreted as it should be, for the copito is a state of mind, an invitation to good fellowship, the equivalent of 'let's have a whale of a time.' It is very bad taste indeed in Goa to take a copito literally. Or offer one as a measure of a drink. For the essence of feni, the true reason for its being, resides first and last in the metaphysics of the belief, felt deeply in Goa, that the breaking of bread and the sharing of a bottle should make brothers of strangers.

As in all happy families brothers may disagree. Individual beliefs are firmly respected even if they differ considerably from your own. You may, of course, know that you are invincibly in the right; still, good manners dictate that you keep your views strictly to yourself. Thus, the Goan from Bardez may drink a feni in Salcette even though he suspects from the bouquet that the new fertilizer complex has, without a shadow of doubt, had a peculiar effect on the soil of that unfortunate district. While the Salcettan will drink at any time, or place, of any feni in Goa, but concede to no man on the virtue of the minerals in the Salcette soil; minerals moreover of a certain quality, which give to Salcette's feni its singular bouquet and body.

It is true that soil, height, moisture, proximity to fresh

or sea water, and many other factors affect the character of a coconut or caju feni. I have an illiterate palate in these matters but many Goans can place the source of a feni from a single sip. Hence you will find a profusion of brands, bewildering to the neophyte eye, labelled with a wanton indulgence in colours, typefaces and illustrations and a lofty disregard for the basic ethics of design. Old Barrel, Red Star, El Nectar (I liked that), Adega da Velha, Real 72, Cocona, Fidalgo, Bandog, Golden Barrel, Black Lion. Fancy takes flight; there is an engaging absence of logic. You take your pick or, if adventurously inclined, work your way through with strong heart and stout liver, finding joy where you will.

All of this is purely academic in the village taverna, an institution as natural to its environment as the feni it serves which, more often than not, comes in a discreet amber bottle, without a label, roughly corked. Approach its contents with care and respect, for this is likely to be genuine, pure and wholesome, distilled by the villagers for generations, happiest and most true when drunk at home.

The village taverna opens at sunset. Visit. Select a seat by a window with view of cottages, gardens and paddy fields. Get to know the magnificent brew. Allow its liquid alchemy to encourage and revive your tired cells. Time is paced by the tolling of angelus bells, a white dog trotting across green fields, making for hearth and home, the conversation of two farmers enquiring about the health and well-being of each other's pigs. Allow the copitos to come as they will. The tavern keeper knows. His disposition, God-given, poured from the happy brown bottle, will lead you gently past sunset and evening star, the flicker of oil lamps in village windows,

'Boa Festas!' Food, Feni and Fun

to quiet introductions and good fellowship as the amber bottle makes the rounds yet again and you are made welcome as guest, friend, boon companion; to laughter and snatches of song as the witching hour approaches; perhaps a plate of prawn, a loaf of bread, the last amber bottle; then home across fields fragrant with dew and the perfume of the delicate white flower which blooms only after dusk, raat ki rani, Queen of the Night. All about you the palms sway beneath a shifting moon, as they have before time began; as they will when a new dawn breaks.

Fare thee well, blithe spirit.

Boa Festas!

'Boa festas!' – happy feast – no two words of greeting gladden the Goan heart more surely or swiftly; second only, if at all, to that other phrase of instant good cheer, 'Have another feni.' It is neither desirable in Goa, nor possible, to have a happy feast without having another feni, and the Goan will have it no other way. If the spirit is willing and the flesh is up to it (and all Goans are awesomely empowered) you may celebrate a festival every other week, except during the weeks of Lent (the longest weeks in the year). Lent is taken very seriously indeed, and so it should be. Swearing off feni, pork and cigarettes is not just good for the soul, it brings back the sparkle in the eye, the spring in the step, the glow to the cheek and the bounce in the liver, preparing one in every way for the fun and games of the rest of the festive year.

The aficionado is well served. Every festival has its own distinct ambience, structure and reason for being. Joaquim and his fishermen friends cordon off three days in the year and a large section of the river on 29 June, the feast of Saint Peter and Paul. Twenty-one boats, lashed together to make three huge floating stages, are anchored mid-stream. River traffic comes to a grateful stop. The drums of the ramponkars boom out an invitation. Hundreds of boats gather like

'Boa Festas!' Food, Feni and Fun

moths to the flame. Thousands of villagers line the riverbanks. The feni flows as generously as the tides, and the festivities – tiatrs, skits, folk dances, heroic banquets – last three days and nights. Nobody sleeps. At the end of one sangor when, in a state of terminal disintegration I swore off festivals for the rest of my life, Joaquim, who was hauling me home, had a single regret, 'Three days too short time for sangor, sah.'

At the other end of the spectrum, there are torchlit ceremonies of exorcism and a celebrated Hindu fire-walking festival which attracts devotees from remote parts of India. Pits thirty feet long and a foot deep are covered with burning coals. The rituals of purification begin fourteen days earlier. The firewalkers rise at first light, meditate, chant, recite from the scriptures and follow the purest of vegetarian diets. On the anointed day, marigold flowers are strewn by the pandits over the molten coals; they burst into incandescent flame no sooner they touch the shimmering waves of heat rising from the pits. The pandits perform an elaborate puja; the chanting of the acolytes rises to a nerve-tingling crescendo; then, barefooted, they take a calm and unhurried stroll across the live coals and emerge smiling and unscathed at the other end. No such hazard attends the sandbar lowering ceremony at the church on Siquerim hill. At the urging of Latin prayer and the sprinkling of holy water, it goes away, obedient as a child, to allow the flotilla of fishing boats to proceed – for the first time in months – to the open sea. The festival of San Joao to welcome the rains offers light-hearted proof that there is reward in risk. The pride of the village males (putting in some dedicated practise for the long wet months ahead)

'Boa Festas!' Food, Feni and Fun

throw sealed bottles of feni into the wells, then dive in, retrieve them and get drunk on the contents. The feni must be paid for by the most recently married among them (who remains, sadly, abstemious), a stern reminder that marital bliss is not without financial obligation.

There are gentler celebrations. The Feast of the Three Kings, the festival of Our Lady of Miracles, the harvest celebration. But these are large affairs with casts of thousands. For my part, I enjoy the village feast days best of all. They occur with engaging regularity; a week doesn't pass without one, a small explosion of collective exuberance, a miniature dress rehearsal for the explosive high spirits of the annual Carnaval, the great pre-Lenten bacchanalia, when a million Goans make merry for the better part of a week.

The transformation of a sleepy village on its feast day is a metamorphosis as enchanting as that of chrysalis to butterfly. The village seems to stretch, yawn, remember this Day of Days, and burst forth in glory and splendid plumage. Young blood and old descend on the Church, attend a High Mass in worshipful silence, ponder on the lessons of the Sermon with particular gravity, receive Communion. Then they pour out, in a boisterous flood, into the village square, the tavernas, the fair ground. Cries of Boa Festas resound to the bursting of fire crackers and the tooting of whistles and horns. They toast each other with vintage feni, port, sparkling wine, cerveza. Children rush about, darting in and out of the cottages like so many magpies, bearing covered dishes of sweets and savouries, for the feast day prompts great feats of culinary accomplishment which must be shown off and shared. The afternoon siesta (which even the

Indian Liberation of Goa failed to disturb) is, on this day, abandoned.

The villagers sing and dance in the streets and at twilight make their way to a tiatr under the stars, where a group performs bold and daring skits on a makeshift stage. Power and Authority – in the persons of the Magistrate, the Landlords, the School Principal, other unnamed but unmistakable village personalities noted for their pomposity – are all fair game. Midnight, and they gather on the beaches about huge bonfires. They serenade the night with mandos and fados, and fugitive guitars call to each other till dawn breaks. The village is quiet, drowsy and peaceful once more, but only till Tuesday week when, Praise the Lord, Arpora, the village next door, celebrates yet another feast day!

*

Festivals are all very well when you are eight years old, but most of the time heaven and hell lay about me in my childhood, while a pantheon of Hindu Gods and Goddesses looked on with serene unconcern. When the church bells of my youth tolled the Angelus at dusk, they carried the faintest echoes of the temple bells of my ancestors. But the devil was no stranger. Fallen angel, sprung alive and malevolent straight from the pages of the Old Testament, he was the evil mastermind behind the tiniest of sins. In the wink of a horny eye, he was known to spirit little boys who played with themselves to the tops of the highest palm trees, there to leave them languishing for days, even weeks on end, catatonic, cross-eyed and drooling. The only solution were tall ladders and exorcism – that shuddering ceremony of torment and rending flight, with a fluttering of musty wings, strange guttural oaths and a terrible stench!

Best to be on the side of the angels and here a Roman Catholic childhood, God-gilded, offered magnificent protection: the solace of commandment, precept and ritual – demanding nothing less than unconditional surrender, promising nothing less than eternal guardianship under an immortal flame – tempered by the flickering illumination of sacred candle, the hypnotic recital of litany and chant, the muted responses to the family rosary at dusk, the bells of the Angelus echoing over twilight spires, the measured revelations of a miracle each Sunday at Mass, the shrouded lamentations of Lent and the joyful, resurrectional Hallelujahs of Easter and Christmas.

Small wonder then that I said good-night to God before I slept and offered grateful prayer to Him in the morning for the blessings of a newly minted day. Before lunch and dinner we gave thanks for that which we were about to receive, Amen. I confessed my sins in the shadows of the Stations of the Cross, guilt and retribution sullen on my young soul as I whispered the words of humility and acceptance, 'Father forgive me, for I have sinned ... ' And when I received Communion the next morning, taking the living host on my tongue, the fluted columns and Gothic arches of St Anne's Church shone with the radiance of redemption; the stained glass triptych bewitched the eye, making many-splendoured glories of the flooding light; there was a triumphant resonance to the very air. Salvation was, by the grace of God, mine again.

But if guilt and redemption were sombre chords (struck

still in a wayward life), the great feast days of the Church offered ebullient crescendos. Easter and Christmas were my favourites, but if you lived in Goa, the Litany of Saints, generously endowed, offered splendid potential for merry-making. I always found Christmas overwhelming. There was so much to do and so little time to do it in. Now Easter came along in a more relaxed manner, a heartening glow at the end of the long, dark tunnel of Lent. If I gave up chocolates, fasted on Fridays, attended a three-day religious 'retreat' barred from all speech, and generally put a brave face on those endless, daunting weeks, the thought of Easter made it all bearable, for the waiting was agreeably leavened by the preparations for Easter Sunday, when the honours were strictly apportioned.

My mother and sisters made the kitchen their inviolate territory. The men of the family – my father and his two sons – were to provide the wherewithal for what would, without the shadow of a doubt, be a memorable Easter lunch. A lifetime's application had prepared my father for this kind of work. Some men are born to fame and fortune; a handful to strife and glory; others to a sticky end; the luckiest, like my father, are born to pursue the simple and ineffable pleasures. He was one of a rare species, life's unquestioning journeyman, who spared no regrets for yesterday or concern for tomorrow, sufficient unto the day the goodness thereof. Now, the finest hour of the year upon him, ably aided and abetted by his sons, he made his presence felt with hawk-eyed authority in the neighbourhood market.

The crabs, destined for immortality, baked in the shell, took three trips in the getting, for he had decided firmly on the plump, black rock crabs, no other. Kingfish after kingfish were poked and prodded, had their gills rudely opened, the interiors keenly examined, the eyes closely inspected for signs of tell-tale cloudiness, before six were selected for the fish curry. An expedition was undertaken at the crack of dawn into darkest Sonapur where a villain of a Goan butcher dispensed the only free range pork in the city, good, honest, bred-to-give-pleasure porker, the only kind truly worthy of a sorpotel. Only chicken which had the run of the countryside were considered eligible for the cafreal; they were selected a fortnight earlier, penned, and put on a fattening diet for the Day. And the prawns for the peri peri had to be the huge, white prawns which bred, scarcely and expensively in the river estuaries, yearning to be lobsters. Anything less was sacrilege.

One would have thought that high seriousness of this order, sustained over weeks would, eventually, allow us to put our feet up. Perish the thought, for this was only food – glorious food to be sure – still ... nosh! Yet to be addressed was the near sacramental question of booze. Everybody drank: the men drank spirits, the ladies palm feni or port or an aperitif, the children wine diluted with soda or water. Here, my father was the sole and final arbiter. A lifetime's critical experience, a spirit of indefatigable enquiry, a curiosity to rival Einstein's, had brought my father in the late autumn of his life to an inescapable conclusion. Not for him the noxious effusions sealed with tin caps, variously described as whisky, rum, gin and vodka – inferior alcohols, distilled from the most dubious of ingredients, brutalized with chemicals, tinted, flavoured, caramelized beyond all hope of salvation. It was caju feni, genuine caju from the old homestead, or nothing.

The family appreciated this fine distinction, for good caju doesn't mess about; it takes you to your destination with a pleasing swiftness. Bottles of the finest ancestral feni, carefully transported from Colvale, where it had matured in the family cellars for well over five years, were now brought forth. Amber bottles, roughly corked, lightly cobwebbed, reverentially dusted off, expansively sampled by my father who became ever more cheerful and self-congratulatory in the tasting, were laid out in a glittering display on the sideboard. The port and aperitifs brought up the rear. A brace or two of bottles of exquisite feni-based liqueur were added to the array. The heady white wine of the monks of Monte de Guirim were put into ice-boxes to cool. My father stepped back and surveyed his handiwork well pleased with himself. 'They won't go thirsty,' he said, patting my head.

To the uninitiated observer, the first question that sprang to mind was, 'Is this a family lunch, or a banquet for a hundred?' Well, yes and yes. Every Easter my parents, as the eldest couple in vigorously extended families, played host to the clan, as colourful and eccentric a collection of Goans as were likely to be found under one roof. Aunts, uncles, cousins twice removed, nieces and nephews – some four dozen strong – would manage, somehow or other, to fit into our modest home, resplendent as peacocks in brand new Easter finery, talking all at once, blessed with growling Goan appetites and, more to the point, with never-say-die Goan livers! (My grandfather once told me that on the eighth day, God said, 'Let there be a liver!' and lo and behold, in faraway Goa, there ploppingly appeared ...) For the women of the house, it was a time of high drama, short tempers and moments of farce. Would the bebinca – monarch of Goan desserts, baked layer upon interminable layer, the recipe for which had been religiously followed – emerge from the oven with delicacy, restraint and the subtlety for which my mother was renowned? At the last minute, the dumb ox of a butcher had delivered lambs' kidneys instead of chicken livers. The devilled starter on toast would never be the same. A generational pox on the man! Would the sorpotel, lovingly prepared three days earlier and now maturing in a huge earthenware pot, live up to its fragrant promise? And if the sanas that went with it were not the fluffiest, lightest, tastiest ever bestowed on an undeserving family, my mother swore she would die the death. Fears happily without foundations, for I had been raised on my mother's cooking and in all of these many Easters I had never been cross with one of her buns.

And on the day, begun with a solemn High Mass, sung by choir and congregation, if there was a distinct lack of penitence in the 'Agnus Deis' and if the 'Kyrie Eleisons' were a trifle impatient and informed with a lilt more buoyant than usual, all was forgiven as the priest ascended the pulpit, turned towards the faithful, and repeated the words of redemption, 'I am the resurrection and the life .. .'

Where will I be next Easter? Why, in Goa, of course. I shall be going home to Rockheart, to celebrate the festival closest to my heart with boon companions, to share the joy of life newly risen; where I shall praise the Lord and pass the feni, and raise a silent toast to those less fortunate, '... a very happy Easter to one and all!'

Epilogue
Alba and Simplicio

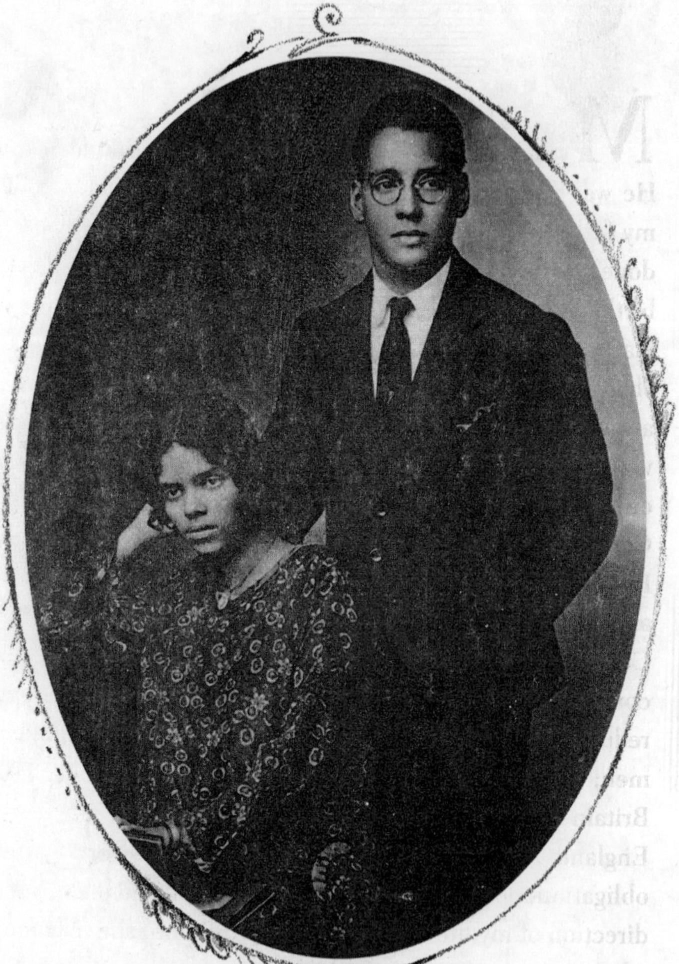

Alba and Simplicio

My mother was eighteen when she married my father. He was twenty-eight. Two years before their golden jubilee my father died and my mother chose to live alone. She has done so for fifteen years and will celebrate her eighty-sixth birthday in September. The years have done her proud. The clarity of purpose is still there; her memory remains as sharply faceted and prismatic as a crystal; and her talents, as always, are eclectic and honed. She takes an active and vigorous interest in the education of her neighbour's children and sits, to good effect, on the Managing Committee of her building's Co-operative Housing Society. Her understanding of current affairs is at once perceptive and hard-nosed. Politicians get short shrift (she exposed Bill Clinton well before the media did); feminism, as far as she is concerned, is so much hoopla, all of the dialectic maybe reduced to one sentence – women are infinitely superior to men; once, when we were discussing the decline and fall of Britain's Conservatives, she said, 'I expected as much when England lost the Ashes.' She has not foresworn parental obligation, nor I a son's prerogatives. When she feels that the direction of my life needs a minor correction, she tells me so; when I am inclined towards a perfect pork sorpotel, I tell her so.

Epilogue

On a recent holiday in Goa I asked her to compile a list of traditional Goan given and last names, the more baroque the better, for use in this book. Within the hour she had put together from memory one hundred and fifty, neatly listed by gender and alphabet. They rung the changes, from such modest offerings as Maria D'Souza and Carlos DaSilva to the delightfully curlicued Zeferino de Garcia Fonseca-Ribiero and Esmeralda Clotides Gozanca-Mascarenhas. No post-graduate research student could have done as well in so short a time. She will never cease to amaze me. That evening, at sunset, we sat up on the balcony and I encouraged her to reminisce about her childhood, not that she needed much urging. Her memory is a repository of lovingly felt experience, held captured in pristine detail and recalled with raconteuring flair and a fine sense of the comical; burnished memories to which this book owes an unrepayable debt. Now she talked about her childhood. At the age of eleven she was sent off to a boarding-school in Panjim, a convent managed by nuns, but was permitted to return home on weekends. My diary makes a rash attempt to record such an occasion.

The problem was keeping her emotions in rein, camouflaged from the penetrating and vigilant eye of Sister Anastasia, who insisted on escorting her from the room she shared with two other girls, along the long, gloomy corridor at a brisk, no-nonsense clip, down the grand balustraded staircase which always made her feel as rapidly diminished as Alice through the Looking Glass, past the enormous iron-studded door of the convent, out to the courtyard where Alex waited for her, perched like an ancient and kindly gnome on the driving seat of the 'match box.' It was possible, by a careful rearrangement of her features, to conceal from Sister Anastasia the overwhelming relief she felt at this temporary respite from the convent's strict regime, particularly the ministrations of Sister Agnes, the refectory supervisor, the innocence of whose name belied the fierceness of her behaviour at lunch and dinner, when she was wont, with muscular zeal, to force boiled cabbage and brinjal down protesting young throats by the simple expedient of holding them open forcibly from behind with one hand and shovelling down enormous spoonfuls of the disgusting legumes with the other, while intoning piously, 'Now, now, come along, this will do you good. One more spoonful. Think of the starving poor.' Relief could be disguised, but it was very much more difficult to conceal the leaping, incandescent joy she felt at the thought of going home. This emotional tug-of-war reached a climax the moment Alex saw her. His grin was sheer delight, and his shout of, 'Albasita' – little Alba – music to her ears.

Her 'Goodbye, Sister Anastasia,' was perhaps a trifle too swift and breathless and revealing, for Sister Anastasia would, invariably, place a firm and restraining hand on her elbow, turn her full circle, fix her with a beady and accusatory eye, allow a few moments of silence to make her presence grimly felt, and say, 'I want every bit of your homework for the weekend done. All of it mind!'

'Yes, Sister Anastasia.'

'And no excuses.'

'No, Sister Anastasia.'

Epilogue

'Pay particular attention to the Portuguese composition.'

'Yes, Sister Anastasia.'

'And don't rush through your sums.'

'No, Sister Anastasia.'

'Say your prayers morning and night.'

'Yes, Sister Anastasia.'

'You will do nothing to make us ashamed of you.'

'No, Sister Anastasia.'

'May the Lord be with you.'

'Yes, Sister Anastasia. Thank you, Sister Anastasia,' – and with an exultant ring to her voice – 'Goodbye, Sister Anastasia!'

The 'match box' on which Alex perched, in a posture between squatting and sitting and, to the untutored eye, in imminent danger of collapse, was owned by the family. It was a venerable, if unstable, contraption, made up of a square wooden frame, wholly enclosed, drawn by a pair of morose bullocks, and supported on four wooden wheels with rusty metal rims. It had tiny windows at either side and an opening in the front which allowed conversation to be addressed to Alex's calloused bare feet, up to but no higher than his knobbly knees; the rest of him and his voice would remain disembodied but comforting entities somewhere above her head for the rest of the four hour journey.

She carried a tin box full of school books – her homework – heavy and cumbersome, held together by metal locks with powerful springs. With the fingers of both hands pressed down on the lid with all the force she could muster, she sprang the locks open and shut with her thumbs, though not without an element of bruising risk. If the box was a necessary penance, her uniform was a purely gratuitous imposition; it was cut with a primness and severity considered minimally appropriate to the moral strictures of the Order of Nuns which had undertaken her Roman Catholic education. Leaden-grey, designed so as to frown at the smallest frivolity, it covered her from throat to wrist to ankle, firmly thwarting even the most slender of eleven-year-old revelations.

The evening before there was a certain waywardness in her responses to the Angelus, and as the blessings of the bells faded upon the twilight, she sat on a rocking chair in a balcony of the convent, rocking with surreptitious care so as not to squeak and draw the unwelcome attention of Sister Priscilla, and watched the sun set across the river. Clean sheets of pale fire ebbed and flowed over the far reaches of the Mandovi where the river embraced the broad estuary and the bay, lapping at tiny crescents of sand on the farther side, foaming and cresting at the rock formations below the lower ramparts of the Fort of Reis Magos etched in black, thundering menace against a sky of molten gold, and moving beyond with the barest of ripples to merge with the endless sweep of the Indian ocean.

As the crow flies, her village lay a few dozen miles across the river, yet it would take her four rock hard hours in the 'match box'; telling her rosary with fervent concentration to make up for the shameful lapse at the Angelus the previous evening; chatting with Alex who had the disconcerting habit of breaking into sudden snatches of excited conversation and, as quickly, relapsing into brooding

Epilogue

silence; restraining a giggle when the bullocks eased themselves without breaking stride to the sound of loud, liquid plops; marvelling, as she never failed to do, at this enchanting journey through a layered past – Hindu, Muslim, Portuguese – held captive, as though in warps of time and revealed at each twist and turn of the winding road, in thrusting minaret and hypnotic temple bell, gardened patio and baroque façade and, around every other corner, in candlelit, white-washed Catholic shrines.

The heights of Altinho where the convent was located, for reasons which owed more to seclusion than to the splendid view, tumbled down precipitously to the river by way of a narrow road which wound down the hill of Dona Paula, in and out of a boisterous cascade of villas and gardens, through the riverside villages of Miramar and Caranzalem where the distant sea caught the last rays of the dying sun and glittered with a thousand points of dancing light behind the black palms. Here were the villas of the powerful gentry, the movers and shakers of Portuguese Goa. Leisurely Iberian in construction, gentled by Mangalore tile and warm laterite brick, they rambled without thought to cost or size over dozens of rooms, gardened indoor patios with marble fountains ever in flow, rustic outhouses and small cottages for the servants, with here and there, a private chapel. Under their sloping roofs (never higher than the highest palms) behind massive teak doors often emblazoned with a Coat of Arms, on floors decorated with Italian glazing, large families gathered en clan for a formal weekend lunch, brown faces with hyphenated names that belied their ancestry, names ending with Saldanha, Fernandes and

Quadros. Conversations were conducted in impeccable Portuguese and the high fashion of that country, wholly inappropriate for the Tropics, was slavishly followed (stiff collars and waistcoats and fob pockets de rigueur for the men, with the starched shirt front and bow tie just so; for the ladies, lace and jewellery at the throat – a gold cross being a favourite affectation discreetly embellished with a precious stone or two – hooped skirts, crinolines and elaborate coiffures held in place with jewelled tortoise-shell combs. An aperitif in the sitting-room, and in they went to lunch, to tables laid with Belgian crystal, china and fine silver, to six courses and more, and to a wine list which was never less than perfectly correct.

She moved with excitement from one small window of the 'match box' to the other, catching a familiar glimpse here, a vignette there, a snatch of conversation, a phrase of song, images of a way of life which was her own and which she loved with a passionate indiscrimination. The cluster of villas descended to a broad promenade, Campal, a sun-dappled, casuarina-fringed boulevard. It ran for a mile along the river and led to the very heart of the capital, Panjim, a dignified congregation of government buildings gathered in self-important conclave about a handsome square, lined with flaming gulmohar. Here, a placid (and, as some cynics would have it, moribund) bureaucracy governed the land with a patronizing and, at times, eccentric diktat.

They came to a halt at the ferry point where the bustle of river traffic paused at a profusion of bars and sidewalk cafés. It was a moment of high adventure when the 'match box' embarked on a distinctly perilous leg of the journey

Epilogue

which never failed to send frissons of excitement, fingerlings of goosebumps, down my mother's spine. With a slow unfolding of protesting body parts and a loud cracking of joints, Alex dismounted, calling on the Litany of Saints, in loud Konkani, to observe his plight, sought succour and strength from his favourite patron, St Christopher, and muttered darkly at the bullocks, 'You give me any trouble, malcreados, and I will hurl you bodily into the river!' He opened the door of the 'match box' and helped my mother down. 'Wait here, Albasita,' he said, 'I have business to attend to.' And with the light of high purpose in his eye, he strode across the wharf to the pier, calling out as he did in a commanding bellow for one so small, 'PEDRO, O PEDRO!'

Pedro, the ferry master, emerged uncertainly from a tin shack on the water's edge which bore the encouraging sign, 'Have a quick one before you leave.' Pedro had taken this injunction to heart. He waved an amber bottle about with what seemed to the little girl dangerous abandon. Were they to put life and limb in the hands of this drunken rogue of a seafarer? He was now engaged in earnest conversation with Alex. The bottle, and loud argument, passed back and forth. They moved, the ferry master a trifle unsteadily, from the country craft which would take them across the river and lay in the water a good foot lower than the edge of the jetty, to the bullocks; back and forth they went, back and forth, heatedly debating what appeared to be engineering issues of the gravest importance.

My mother looked on with the keenest anticipation; the ritual was about to reach its climax. The ferry master held up five fingers; Alex sneered, said something very rude in Konkani and held up two. The ferry master winced, rolled his eyes heavenwards in impassioned entreaty and sought sustenance in the brown bottle which he now drank from in a long, last, gurgling swallow. He raised the bottle, squinted at the remains, and with grudging reluctance let Alex drain the last drop or two. Then he raised three fingers and Alex inclined his head graciously. They disappeared into the tin shack and returned moments later with two long narrow planks. These were laid from the wharf's edge into the country craft. Bitter memories stirred: the bullocks made low bellows in protest, snorted and stamped and tried to walk backwards. To no avail. Pulled along by Alex, pushed with much grunting and groaning from the rear by the ferry master, the reluctant beasts were led, snorting and sliding with the 'match box' in tow, down the planks, to land with a bouncing thump into the country craft. There the bullocks were securely lashed to stanchions at either side of the boat, and given feed bags to keep them quiet.

The blessed serenity of rural Goa lay across the river. The 'match box' swayed along in an immensity of silence, accentuated by the gentle rumble of the wheels, broken from time to time by fitful and entirely gratuitous interruptions by Alex (the merry brown bottle had been employed to splendid effect): spicy bits of news and village gossip, suitably embroidered, offered with theatrical flourish. Isabella, the sow, a hugely loved member of the household, had littered again. 'Mother of God! The number of piglings. Never, in living memory, had there been such a begetting.' The Furtado boy, the rascal, had been caught with his pants

Epilogue

down with that lovely but misguided young girl, Lucia, in the bushes behind the fountain.'

'But what were they doing there, Alex?'

'Never mind, never mind.' A thoughtful pause, 'You don't need to mention it to your mother, Albasita.' A swift, distracting plunge into sorrow and heartbreak. Anton, the ancient churchyard cat, had gone peacefully to his forefathers. The village float was well on its way to a richly deserved first prize at the Carnaval. The church, God be praised, had at long last installed a new organ imported from Lisbon, but it was excessively complicated and Father Vincent was at his wits' end trying to find somebody to play it. Her mother, Donna Martha, had prepared the dessert she loved most, bebinca, and Dottore her father had a gift for her which was a secret ...

His voice laved about her like a kindly benediction. The 'matchbox' made a careful descent to the Saligao valley; then the bullocks, smelling home in the air, broke into a mild trot. Across the fields of rippling paddy, rimmed with the gold of the late afternoon sun, the spires of the Church of Mae de Deus beckoned above the palms. She was going home again, in the true and holy spirit of the words, where the values of kinship and community were held sacred still, where at every home at the end of the Rosary at dusk, the ancient blessings were given, parent to child, grandparent to parent, until the very oldest blessed the youngest by the charismatic laying on of hands, where it was impossible to tell where the village ended and the fields began because the symbiosis between man and nature was whole and complete.

This was the Goa of my mother's childhood, three

Alba and Simplicio

quarters of a century into a golden past, preserved yet in all of the essentials that matter, for I had discovered that in Goa more than any other place in the world I know, the present draws upon all that is good and worthy in the inheritance, so that the future may receive the common legacy shining and alive.

*

I do not ever remember my father reminiscing about his childhood or, indeed, talking about his family and their ancestral past. It was left to my mother and the good Dottore Luiz da Gama Rose, my maternal grandfather, to provide discreetly censored versions of a colourful and, at times, risque paternal history. High passions seemed to have ruled the collective Simoes psyche. There were episodes of financial chicanery of the most ruthless and devious configurations, cause of generational family feuds bitterly unresolved to this day; accounts of arrogant, rough-shod manipulation of peasants and property which seems to come so naturally to unbridled feudal power in faraway places; embarrassing romantic interludes involving clandestine amours, dramatic elopements, incandescent cris-de-coeur and, in one memorable instance, a lustful abduction which resounds over the years; flashpoints of violence and high-handed derring-do which went unremarked and unpunished; phenomenal sloth and meteoric achievement; never, in short, a dull moment.

By the time my father made an appearance, the disorderly Simoes genes had decided to pause for a breather. He was a simple and gentle man in the first meaning of the

Epilogue

words (as his given name, Simplicio, so aptly implied), a stranger to power and pelf of any kind, and serenely unsuccessful by the measures of the time. He was, for example, far more interested in mesmerism than in money, and on the one occasion I can remember when he did talk of the past, it had nothing to do with his family. I trusted my father with a faith that could move mountains, and when he told me the story of Abbe Faria, I believed every word. Which seven-year-old disbelieves his first and best loved friend? My father was immensely proud to have shared a bit of the past with the famous Abbe. Enlightened pastor, medical pioneer, hypnotist who prefigured the work of Mesmer, grand icon of folklore and literature (he was a central character in Alexander Dumas's *The Count of Monte Cristo*), Abbe Faria was a Goan, born in our very own village, Colvale. The purist, however, will have it that he was conceived in Colvale, given birth in his mother's ancestral home in Candolim (as was and still is the custom) and brought back three months later. My father would have none of this nonsense; on my part, coming as I do from Colvale and now resident in Candolim, I am happy to have it both ways. Today a statue of Abbe Faria graces a small green plaza on the bank of the Mandovi alongside the Secretariat. The sculptor has cloaked him in a greatcoat, tall and compelling, arms raised in benediction over a young woman at his feet emerging from a healing trance. He is the most famous son of the village.

My father too, modest heir to Colvale's green hills and verdant plains was a true son of the soil, though he made no claim to fame stronger than his love for the place and its people. Long forgotten legions of his ancestors and mine were born in the grand mansion on the hill; the soaring arches, confessionals and fonts of the Church of St Francis of Assisi gave them a lifetime of holy succour (which, by all accounts, they sorely needed!): baptisms and christenings, confirmations and marriages, endless absolutions and once their time was upon them, and the flame passed on, the final place of rest in the walled cemetery in the family vault which forgave all.

When my mother married and went off to live with my father in Colvale, it was the first time in her young life that the roof over her head would belong to another name. As the only daughter-in-law in the isolated, highland fastness of the Simoes household, she admits to being desperately homesick, no more so than at the hour of dusk when the oil lamps were lit and the Angelus recited to the tolling of the church bells. She was pampered no end to compensate for it, but no amount of loving care seemed to help. She remembers above all a sense of alienness, of being in a time and place frozen in a distant past, far removed from the gentle bustle of Saligao. I recall that I was puzzled by this; how could one Goan village be so different from another?

Thirty years later, on my first visit to Colvale, I began to understand. It is remote and sparsely populated. There is a real apartness about Colvale, a sense when you get there of arrival at a final destination with no possibility of return, of doors closing behind you, of a way of life which is sequestered, turned inwards, brooding, incestuous and exclusive to itself. It is the location, more than anything else, which makes for such a dour first impression. To reach

Epilogue

Colvale, one journeys along a desolate and seemingly endless highland, flat and dry. There are no villages, no people, no flowing water, just scrub and rock and hard red earth. At the end of it all, a plunging descent, broken by ravine and quarry; then, with a suddenness that takes the breath away, my father's village rises out of the hill; thick forest, fecund valley and a tidal river come together in a rich and evocative tapestry of rural Goa. Gardens and orchards merge, one into the other, all but concealing the weathered facades of houses which have stood for centuries. The foliage is so thick and close that you only see the Church of St Francis of Assisi when you are upon it. Built four hundred years earlier on an embankment of the Chapora, it commands the finest prospect of any church in Goa, splendid and immemorial vistas across the river and its shimmering tributaries, to a patchwork of green fields and, beyond, to mist-enshrouded hills.

It was from here that unruly generations of Simoeses were born to make their mark, distinguished or otherwise – it seems now not to matter – in the Portuguese Civil Service, in the far-flung enclaves of the Goan emigre – Brazil, Portugal, East Africa, Canada – and in the village of Colvale by those who chose to stay, with the iron hand of superior caste and privilege and an authority that was a law unto itself.

Occasionally, much to its disgust, but never conceded by so much as a word, the family would produce a maverick. My father, happily for us, was a flourishing example. Cheerful hewer of song and drawer of laughter, he came into young manhood in charmed isolation, accepting with good grace but never entirely seriously, the convictions of the Simoeses. The family despaired of my father for he seemed too casual to care. If he was ever ruthless, uncompromising, relentlessly committed, it was, perhaps, when addressing himself to a perfectly rendered roast suckling pig; when he gave forceful voice, it was in a rousing tenor to the accompaniment of a guitar; and his guardianship of the family's cherished traditions was nowhere in greater evidence than when concerned with the consumption and replenishment of the garafaos of feni in the ancestral cellars.

He enjoyed his birthright hugely, with no trace of guilt or doubt. His life was a celebration of the natural order of things: the miracle of young paddy fields after the first rains, the fellowship of his friends, his sailing boat and the sea, the pleasures of the table, laughter, song, a bottle, children and dogs, and the wonder of green and growing things. He lived by the belief that time past and time future were held within each golden moment, carpe diem, a luminous philosophy which informed his character with a sense of abiding grace.

He left no will – there was nothing to leave – but he gave me a gift of four words in the language. A moveable legacy which I shall bequeath, in turn, to my daughter Radhika. The first is phale from the Konkani and means, literally, tomorrow. This is subterfuge. Phale is an unabashed invitation to the exquisite pleasures of procrastination, and delightfully elastic. It may really mean the day after, the next month, the following year or never. Some months ago I ordered an earthenware vase from a village which specializes in unglazed pottery. Whenever I am in Goa, I visit the village, call upon the potter, and make solicitous enquiries about my

Epilogue

vase. Ignatius smiles gently, says, 'Phale,' and offers me a drink which I never refuse. I seek immediate refuge in phale's crafty sibling, susegade, an old, wise Portuguese word which means they also serve who lie and daydream: take your restful ease while you may, swing in a hammock, observe the playful fronds of the palm trees. Let your thoughts wander as they will. It is a serendipitous universe. Take counsel with the butterflies. Look to the kingfisher. Observe the unknowing brilliance of the gulmohar. See how the eagle makes sport with the wind. Regard again, with grateful thanks, this noble and beneficent palm. Without the fruit, where would one find the true essence of a prawn curry? The fronds offer a fluttering shade and the sap, distilled, gives forth that peerless spirit, feni, a glass of which you now raise to your lips in a silent toast to abandoned resolutions, 'Phale!'

The other words are Portuguese without English equivalents. Alegria is a way of being; the lilting syllables evoke all of Goa's love and laughter, song and happy fellowship. It is the way we are when we are there. Saudade is the way we feel when we are away. It means remembering with melancholy and hope. Melancholy at the passing of a small miracle; hope because we know it will, some day, return ...